House of France

Henri IV ∞ Marguerite de Valois
∞ Marie de Medici

House of Spain

Gaston d'Orléans   Louis XIII ∞ Anne   Philip IV ∞
∞ Mlle.   of Austria   Elizabeth
de Montpensier   of France

La Grande Mademoiselle

Louis XIV ∞ Maria Theresa
∞ Mme. Scarron
(Mme. de Maintenon)

LA PETITE

LA PETITE

The Life of Louise de la Vallière

BY JOAN SANDERS

HOUGHTON MIFFLIN COMPANY BOSTON

The Riverside Press Cambridge

1959

To Raymond

AUTHOR'S PREFACE

F E W serious biographies of Louise de la Vallière have been written, either in French or English — a curious fact, since her story is one of the more moving romances of history. Most available accounts of her love affair with Louis XIV are superficial, either dismissing her as weak and colorless or sentimentalizing her beyond the bounds of possibility. This book is the result of six years' research, mainly in the memoirs of La Vallière's contemporaries, and a growing conviction that she was a person of charm, character, and intelligence, interesting in her own right. I have taken no liberties with any events, scenes, descriptions, or dialogue; everything in this version of the La Vallière adventure is based on published sources.

JOAN SANDERS

CONTENTS

ILLUSTRATIONS

GUIDE TO CHARACTERS

Alençon, Mlle. d'	Youngest sister of the Grande Mademoiselle; girlhood friend of Louise
Anne-Constance de Montalais	Girlhood friend of Louise, later intrigante at Court
Armagnac, Comte d'	Grand Equerry of France, suitor of Madame
Armagnac, Comtesse d'	Friend of Madame, banished because of intrigues
Artigny, Mlle. d'	Maid of honor to Madame, banished temporarily due to scandal, later a follower of Louise and Comtesse du Roure
Bablon	Nickname of Duchesse de Châtillon, later Duchesse de Mecklembourg, friend of Madame
Bellefonds, Gigault, Marquis de	Marshal of France, close friend of Louise
Blois, Marie-Anne, Mlle. de	Daughter of Louise, later Princesse de Conti
Bussy-Rabutin, Comte de	Author of *Histoire Amoureuse des Gauls,* cousin of Mme. de Sévigné
Châtillon, Duchesse de (Bablon)	Friend of Madame, later Duchess of Mecklembourg

Choisy, Mme. de	Influential in Louise's appointment as a maid of honor
Colbert, Jean-Baptiste, Marquis de	Secretary to Fouquet, later Minister of Finance
Condé, Prince de	"Le Grand Condé," famous general, reconciled with Louis XIV at the Peace of the Pyrénées
Conti, Princesse de	Louise's daughter, formerly Mlle. de Blois
Cosnac, Daniel de, Bishop of Valence	Friend of Madame, banished by Monsieur
Fayette, Madeleine, Marquise de	Author of *La Princesse de Montpensier,* confidante of Madame
Feuillet, M.	Canon of Saint-Cloud, Jansenist priest
Fiennes, Mlle. de la	Maid of honor to Madame, mistress of the Chevalier de Lorraine
Gabrielle de la Vallière	Sister-in-law of Louise, formerly Mlle. de la Cotardais
Gaston d'Orléans	Uncle of Louis XIV, father of the Grande Mademoiselle
Gramont, Maréchal de	Father of Armand de Guiche and the Princesse de Monaco, uncle of the Duc de Lauzun
Grande Mademoiselle	Mlle. de Montpensier, heiress, daughter of Gaston d'Orléans
Guiche, Armand, Comte de	Suitor of Louise, later of Madame, brother of the Princesse de Monaco, cousin of the Duc de Lauzun
Hautefeuille, Baronesse de	Formerly Catherine de Saint-Rémi, stepsister of Louise
Heudicourt, Marquise d'	Formerly Bonne de Pons, maid of honor to Maria Theresa
Hillière, Chevalier d'	Captain of Lauzun's guards

Hollis, Lord	English ambassador to France
Kéroualle, Louise de	Maid of honor to Madame, later Duchess of Portsmouth and mistress of Charles II
Lauzun, Duc de	Formerly Marquis de Péguilain, favorite of the King, briefly engaged to the Grande Mademoiselle, cousin of De Guiche
La Vallière, Jean-François, Marquis de	Brother of Louise
La Vallière, Marquise de	Sister-in-law of Louise, formerly Gabrielle de la Cotardais
Le Tellier, Marquis	Minister of State, father of Louvois
Longueville, Duchesse de	Sophisticate, précieuse, later religious penitent
Lorraine, Charles de	Nephew of Duke Charles IV of Lorraine, lover of Marguerite d'Orléans
Lorraine, Charles IV, Duc de	Leader of armed forces against the Crown, governor of Nancy
Lorraine, Chevalier de	Favorite of Monsieur, banished for intrigues
Louvois, Marquis de	Minister of War, son of Le Tellier
Lyonne, Comte de	Minister Secretary of State to Louis XIV
Maintenon, Marquise de	Formerly Mme. Scarron, Louis XIV's second wife
Marguerite d'Orléans	Sister of the Grande Mademoiselle, girlhood friend of Louise
Marie-Charlotte de Raré	Girlhood friend of Louise
Mecklembourg, Duchesse de	Formerly Duchesse de Châtillon, friend of Madame, called Bablon

Monaco, Princesse de	Sister of Armand de Guiche, cousin to Lauzun
Montalais, Anne-Constance, Mlle. de	Maid of honor to Madame, friend of Louise, banished for intrigues
Montausier, Duchesse de	Attendant to Maria Theresa
Montespan, Marquise de	Formerly Athénaïs de Tonnay-Charente, mistress of Louis XIV
Mothe-Houdancourt, Mlle. de	Advanced by the Comtesse de Soissons as a contender for the King's favor
Motte-Argencourt, Mlle.	Maid of honor to Anne of Austria
Motteville, Mme. de	Attendant to Maria Theresa
Navailles, Duchesse de	Lady-in-waiting to Maria Theresa, chaperone of the maids of honor
Olympe Mancini	Later Comtesse de Soissons, superintendent of the Queen's Household
Orléans, Duchesse d' (dowager)	Wife of Gaston d'Orléans, uncle of Louis XIV
Orléans, Marguerite d'	Eldest sister of the Grande Mademoiselle; girlhood friend of Louise
Palatine, Princesse	Friend of Louise
Péguilain, Marquis de	Later Duc de Lauzun, favorite of Louis XIV
Plessis-Bellievre, Mme. du	Friend of Fouquet, approached Louise on his behalf
Pons, Mlle. de	Maid of honor to Maria Theresa, later Marquise d'Heudicourt
Raré, Marie-Charlotte de	Girlhood friend of Louise
Roquelaure, Duc de	Favorite of Louis XIV
Roure, Comtesse du	Formerly Mlle. d'Artigny
Saint-Aignan, Comte de	Later Duc de Saint-Aignan, favorite of the King, organizer of court entertainments

Saint-Chaumont, Mme. de	Governess of Madame's children
Saint-Rémi, Catherine, Mlle. de	Stepsister of Louise, later Baronesse de Hautefeuille
Saint-Rémi, Marquis de	Maître d'hôtel of Gaston d'Orléans, stepfather of Louise
Saint-Rémi, Marquise de	Louise's mother
Scarron, Mme. de	Later Marquise de Maintenon, widow of a poet
Scudéry, Mlle. de	Author of popular novels, friend of Mme. de Sévigné
Sévigné, Mme. de	A leader of the intellectual set, friend of Fouquet, cousin of Bussy-Rabutin
Soissons, Comtesse de	Superintendent of the Queen's Household, enemy of Louise, notorious intrigante, mistress of De Vardes, originally Olympe Mancini
Tonnay-Charente, Mlle. de	Later Marquise de Montespan
Tréville, M. de	Captain of Monsieur's musketeers, friend of Madame
Turenne, M. de	General of the army
Vallot, M.	Physician to Louis XIV
Valois, Mlle. de	Second sister of the Grande Mademoiselle, girlhood friend of Louise
Vardes, Comte de	Favorite of the King, later banished for intrigues
Vermandois, Comte de	Louise's youngest son, Admiral of France, died age sixteen

LA PETITE

THE MAP OF TENDERNESS

THE KING, tall, sullen, very handsome, was twenty-one years old and on his way to the Spanish border to make a political marriage. He was in love with another girl at the time, but prepared to embrace his fate. It was 1659, a nervous year for the matrimonial strategists as well as for Louis the Godgiven. All over the rest of Europe disappointed princesses gave up their hope of Paris, while in Madrid artisans were at work encrusting with jewels the trousseau of the successful Infanta.

The royal retinue followed the bridegroom in carriages strung out for miles along the Loire between autumn-rusted forests and vineyards, escorted by mounted musketeers of the Household, their plumes making color in the wind and their weapons an intermittent glitter against the changing sky.

His Majesty's uncle, Gaston, Duc d'Orléans, lived here with his court, peaceful by necessity but rather bored, out of touch with the real world of war and intrigue. He had betrayed so many old friends to their death in recent years that there was little entertainment left beyond hunting. With genuine heartiness, therefore, he greeted the nephew he had ridden out to meet, and escorted him home for a night's hospitality.

The Duchesse d'Orléans stood with her daughters on the stair of honor, attended by a scanty train of ladies suffering stage fright and wearing old-fashioned gowns. They saw immediately that the King had not been overpraised. Getting out of his carriage he acknowledged their curtsies with his slow, famous bow; and, letting his moody glance slide from a Goujon sculpture on the balustrade to Mlle. d'Orléans, one of his adolescent cousins, he complimented her mother on having produced such a pretty girl. Unfortunately, Marguerite's face had been severely stung by gnats the evening before and was swollen, but the remark was received with as little bridling as possible, and the royal party passed on into the hall.

The praised princess and her six companions stayed behind, peering out from their door at the unloading of the Court. Gentlemen of the Household were attending to their lace, and casually kicking lackeys into action; ladies clacking on high-heeled mules over the cobbles, clutching their muff dogs and followed by pages and maids with boxes, fans, cloaks, stools, headgear. They invaded the castle with their potent perfume and laughter, ridiculing the obsolete furniture and the dowdy clothing of the provincial inhabitants.

Among the loudest critics was Gaston's oldest daughter herself, newly arrived from one of her long sojourns in Paris, Mlle. de Montpensier, the Grande Mademoiselle, first heiress of France, tall as a musketeer, thirty years old, beak-nosed and frank of speech. She was intellectually vague but knew her own importance as a personage, and for this reason had refused to marry several aspiring princes including Charles of England. Such wealth as Mademoiselle had inherited from her mother would bring great power to her husband. Was any man worthy? She thought not.

Gaston was poor by comparison; he placated her while secretly opening little drains into her revenues and providing her with bookkeepers who could be counted on to falsify the record to his advantage.

Father and daughter, having met and embraced with shouts of affection, now went off together, leaving the three plaintive young princesses to await their turn. They were all in awe of their monumental half sister, but whenever she came there was comedy and excitement, news from the vast spangled world outside — a world they themselves would see in time. They were in fact invited to the King's wedding next spring. The door of life once opened to a princess of the blood did not shut again; but the other four, schoolroom friends and lesser nobility, probably doomed to die in the provinces, could only stand around watching, listening, dissolving in wistfulness.

One of these, Louise de la Vallière, was a stepdaughter of the Marquis de Saint-Rémi, first maître d'hôtel of Gaston's household. Shy, fourteen years old, she had stood behind the princesses to escape being noticed — but she had seen the King very well.

This was the man for whom her own father had defended the city of Amboise in the confused and perilous days of the Fronde, the inheritor of her family's ancient loyalty. If the need ever arose, she herself would have to spill her blood for him, even if — and this was the thought most compelling in its pathos — he should never know. All of her name had been bound by the Latin inscription carved on a mantel of their old manor in the Brenne Valley: "To the prince, like an altar fire, love undying."

This was not the first time she had seen Louis XIV. Six years before, at strategic Amboise, she and her brother Jean had stood to watch the royal equipages go by, the black-haired boy beside his mother in a carriage surrounded by guards of His Eminence the Cardinal in their crimson cloaks and blue helmets. They were returning to Paris, carrying the battle back after having been driven out by that strange mixed mob that made up the enemy.

In those days few had known what the issues were or even which side to uphold. Laurent de la Vallière had been one who knew, however, and accordingly the troops he captained had held a small part of the kingdom firm in the King's name. But he died without recognition eighteen months later, leaving his family poor. So his widow had married another marquis of moderate means, and life became pleasant enough, though uneventful.

Louise seldom saw her brother Jean, who was usually away at Tours, but there were other companions — Gaston's daughters, the Mlles. d'Orléans, de Valois, and d'Alençon; her own stepsister, Catherine de Saint-Rémi; Marie-Charlotte de Raré, who was gentle and ladylike; and Anne-Constance de Montalais, who was a devil.

This Montalais was driven and obsessed with curiosity, and having no illusions of her own she had learned early how to use other people's for their control. Louise, through dread of ghosts and the hope of romance, was easily influenced and therefore the chosen friend of Anne-Constance.

Louise herself was thin and still growing out of her gowns. Her mouth was too wide, her breasts too small, and she limped, but in compensation she had sapphire-colored eyes and hair so blond it might have been called silver. Also, though she did not know it yet, her voice was low and memorable. "A voice so sweet that no one who heard it ever forgot it," an enemy was later to say.

A fear of horses, sternly overcome, made her one of the best riders at Blois, to the approval of Gaston, who liked his hunting companions to stay with him all the way. She danced well, her lameness hidden in the dipping patterns of the branle and newly fashionable courante, and could play the guitar and sing.

She lived on glamour as plants live on water and air, taking turns at reading *Astrée* aloud with the other girls and debating the nuances of sensibility to be found in Scudéry's heroes and heroines, relishing their names: Cléonice, Philomide, Cléaque, Aristée. And there was the fascinating study of the Map of Tenderness, that allegorical country with its neighboring villages of Love Notes, Pretty Verse, and Little Cares, the wood of Declarations, the river of Two Sighs winding around Lake Indifference and the somber gulf of Forgetfulness. None of the men at Blois, the girls decided, could be imagined straying in such a chart. True, there was the Marquis de Bragelonne, who loved Louise, but he too was provincial and incoherent.

Anne-Constance de Montalais had a less than courtly experience with a man before she was fifteen, and though the girls' governess, Mme. de Raré, hushed the story up, there was a little scandal.

Gaston, reduced by boredom to taking an interest in these nursery sensations, called Anne-Constance and gave her a lecture on the cultivation of virtue. "Look at Mlle. de la Vallière," he said. "As for her, I'm sure she would have absolutely no part in such an adventure; she is too wise for that." Louise, flattered, tried to be worthy of such a compliment, and her behavior to young Bragelonne from then on puzzled him with its utter spirituality. Nevertheless, he worshiped her and said so in his labored-over letters.

Blois, then, was too far away from Paris for romance to thrive there in its finest form. Yet, perhaps the center of romance was not Paris at all, but Louis XIV himself.

Stories were always arriving on the lips of enthusiastic witnesses. The King's quiet dangerous eye could first disarm opposition, his quick wit follow through and stab it dead. Masked, he could dance with professionals from the theater and be recognized only by his well-shaped legs. Further, he was a powerful athlete and swordsman, and his courtesy was proverbial; it was said he never passed even a scrub maid in the corridors of the Palais-Royal without raising his hat.

And as if these social distinctions were not enough, he was formidably brave, exposing himself to enemy fire in the trenches despite the anguished warnings of his generals. The Grande Mademoiselle owned a full-length portrait by Mignard which showed Louis in field uniform with riding boots covered with powder stains and mud, a simple doublet of yellow velvet, and leather jacket. His face was suntanned, showing a pale scar or two of smallpox and a small mustache. Obviously the King was too good for any available princess — but one must be chosen sooner or later. His cousins at Blois spent many afternoons disposing of his hand. Why shouldn't he marry Marguerite herself — why not? they asked each other, and called her "the little Queen," only half joking.

But now it was too late. The King was on his way to this Spanish match, and Gaston was humiliating his daughters in honor of the occasion by making them perform like gypsies. Mlle. de Valois had to dance, which she did very badly, and then Mlle. d'Alençon was urged to tell some amusing stories. She was unable to open her mouth, of course, but not so the members of the royal party, who were yawning.

The reception had been followed by a supper which brought all the local nobility to the castle, stiff in their perennial best, and Mademoiselle, who was addicted to diary keeping, wrote that night, "As my father's chefs were not in style, magnificent though the repast was Their Majesties ate very little." And, she added unkindly, "all the ladies of Blois, who were very numerous, were

dressed like the dishes of the repast, not in the mode." By now
she was as anxious as the rest of the Court to leave. "The Queen
Mother was in haste to be going, and the King too; I have never
seen the like; it had anything but an obliging air. But I think my
father felt the same on his side and that he was very glad to be rid
of the company."

The Court's progress toward Spain was slow. At Bordeaux on
September 21 the King took time to do something he had been
putting off, writing his personal marriage proposal to the Infanta.

> . . . *I beg you very humbly, Madame, to give your consent,*
> *looking on me as a person who desires very much your friend-*
> *ship and your esteem, and to do me the grace of responding*
> *with your heart. You will always find in me a great inclina-*
> *tion to honor and respect you, and to show in all my actions*
> *that I desire most strongly you may never repent the choice it*
> *has pleased you to make.*

The letter sealed and dispatched by special messenger, Louis
went to bed and thought of his great melancholy and love for
Marie Mancini, who should have been his bride, of whom he had
been cheated by her uncle, the frigid, conniving, political, and
treacherous Cardinal Mazarin. Yet in spite of all this, he was forced
to confess to himself that he had much respect for Mazarin, without whom he would probably have no throne.

At Toulouse they had to wait a full month while details of the
marriage contract were settled and a peace treaty completed. Even
on this happy occasion the ancient enemies France and Spain had
disagreements. Mazarin, fencing for advantage with the crafty
Don Luis de Haro, had two archbishops, four bishops, three marshals, numerous great nobles, and M. de Lyonne, Minister of State,
to help him. Even so, he bested his opponent and was able to slip
a clause into the marriage contract which would give Louis an excuse to fight Spain later if he wished to — as of course he would.
The Infanta, Maria Theresa, was to renounce all pretensions "to

the inheritance of her parents, it being clearly understood that neither she nor her children could succeed to the states of His Catholic Majesty, even in the event of his legitimate successors' becoming extinct" — subject to the full payment of her dowry, however — 500,000 gold crowns. An inoffensive pair of words, that "subject to," but everything hung on them. Mazarin felt sure that Philip IV would grow lax in making the last installments on his daughter's dowry, in which case Louis would be free by the letter of the contract to take whatever he could get of his father-in-law's possessions. Flanders, perhaps — a hen coop ready for raiding, and far from the farmhouse. The Cardinal was content with this little device; the King, his protégé, would see it for himself when the time came.

Meanwhile there were necessarily other matters to be treated at this unprecedented meeting of powers.

Old Charles IV of Lorraine, unchallenged and self-sufficient for years in his principalities, had made the mistake of bearing arms against both Spain and France. Now he felt their united revenge; he lost Nancy entirely and was forbidden to maintain any armed troops. It was more than a blow at his dignity, it was a symbolic breaking of the power of the great French nobles. After this few would dare to challenge Louis openly.

Another victim of his own mistakes, the Prince de Condé sued at this meeting for pardon from the King, whom he had fought during the Fronde. Spain backed his plea and Mazarin gave in after a certain amount of feinting with the legal foils. To restore Condé's old honors would gain France the cities he now held in sovereignty, Rocroi and Câtelet, and several important fortresses. Furthermore, the Prince was a brilliant general, and a thinker, and his allegiance once fastened would hold. Any untried king needed such men around him.

An anxious youth, rather shabby, hung around the council chambers but never succeeded in getting an interview with either the French or Spanish officials. It was Charles II, and what he wanted was help in claiming his rightful inheritance, the throne of England. Now that Cromwell, who had beheaded his father, was dead, the chances seemed to be improving. However, Mazarin kept his door discreetly shut; the English ambassador was in the vicinity too and must not be antagonized. As usual, Charles had to go away disappointed.

Not even his most unworldly and optimistic friend would have guessed that day that within a few weeks — before this same Treaty of the Pyrenees was signed — he would be in London with the crown on his head, recalled by a weeping, cheering populace to triumphal parades and bonfires in the streets. Nor would the Grande Mademoiselle have believed it, whom life never defeated but often unhorsed. She might have been Queen of England if she had known in time. But this was her history; the refusal of Charles was only the most recent in her long record of faux pas.

Through the warm spring the procession of state moved toward Saint-Jean-de-Luz where Philip of Spain was waiting with his daughter. A temporary palace had been built on the Ile des Faisans and connected by bridges to the mainland frontier on each side. These in the form of identical covered galleries led to two salons luxuriously furnished and decorated, each with its connecting smaller chambers and dressing rooms. In the exact center was the grand hall of meeting, lighted on the riverward side and with a straight line dividing the floor. On the Spanish side were Persian carpets wrought on a background of gold and silver — for the French, crimson Genoa velvet — and each side had an armchair and a table with inkstand and clock. Thus quarrels regarding rank and precedent were to be forestalled.

Anne of Austria, the bridegroom's mother, could not keep from crying when she saw King Philip. He was her brother, and they had not met for many years. Running up, she threw her arms around him, but was met with a statuelike coldness and the affronted stares of his whole court. She had forgotten Spanish courtesy; it seemed slovenly time had almost made a Frenchwoman of her. With as much aplomb as possible she retired to her own side of the barriers, a dumpy, somewhat mottled little woman, elegantly dressed. Old acquaintances noticed that her hands at least were still lovely; she carried them around as if they were ornaments, one gloved in Spanish leather, one naked.

The Duc de Créqui made formal presentation of Louis's gift to the bride, a large gold-lined chest holding watches, clocks with chimes, gloves, mirrors, boxes for patches and lozenges, tiny flasks intricately stoppered, scissor cases, knives and toothpicks, miniature paintings to be hung above the bed, crosses, rosaries, rings, bracelets, and brooches. A smaller coffer with a compartment for the crown jewels was packed with pearls and diamond pendant earrings — altogether a surprise any woman should be pleased to open.

The Infanta gave the closed chests to her maid of honor and pocketed the keys. Her restraint was certainly remarkable. "But admirable, charming!" cried Anne of Austria, turning her warmth on this niece so soon to be a daughter-in-law.

The first of the two scheduled wedding ceremonies, held at the church of Fontarabia, was almost ruined because the Bishop of Fréjus was late. Finally he rushed in totally unattended, breathlessly accusing Don Luis de Haro of not having told him the exact time, and passed disheveled to the altar where the other principals were assembled.

Louis had arrived preceded by a group of the Swiss Guard and taken his seat in the tribune upon a dais of gold brocade enclosed by a curtain except on the altar side; next him was Don Luis, and in front the Bishop of Pampeluna with all his clergy in full sacerdotal costume. Benches for the grandees lined one wall, and the almoners had the other.

Philip IV wore a silver-embroidered gray coat and a hat looped up with a large diamond and pendant pearl, and Maria Theresa followed him unattended, the details of her appearance being thoroughly reviewed by the Frenchwomen present, during her progress up the aisle. Her gown was white satin stiff with embroidery and covered with small bows of silver serge, its train carried by a Lady of the Household. The rest of her person was miscellaneous with a quantity of ill-set gems, and she had a mass of false hair. Called on for a "yes" in the course of the ceremony, she turned to face her father and made a low curtsy as if asking his permission. At the end she knelt and kissed his hand, whereupon Philip removed his hat and formally embraced her. The new Queen of France rose, moved to his right hand, and the whole train swept after them from the church with a marvelous rustling and odor of incense.

That evening a deep silence prevailed on the Spanish bank of the river. Prayer, if anything, was in progress. On the opposite side the French sang, feasted, rioted, and drank wine till morning.

The Queen, still not delivered up to her husband, was however allowed a public interview with him next day. This time her hair was mostly her own and decorated with a bouquet of pear-shaped emeralds and brilliants.

Her new countrywomen had searched the language for praising adjectives to apply to Maria Theresa and failed. While not actually ugly, she was a queer little thing, short, with round pale eyes and white lashes, hair thin and blondish, crooked teeth, doubtful waistline. She opened her mouth only to utter gaucheries — and these usually in Spanish — as if she had been brought up in prison. She had. Except for her father and certain priests, no man had ever been permitted to converse with her until now; it was no wonder she was reserved and mechanical. And soon she would be abandoned to a society made of people like the dangerous Duchesse de Longueville, most recently quoted as saying "I don't like innocent pleasures." Anne of Austria thought this child would need to be protected for a time, and so began to educate her gently.

The second ceremony took place a few days later in the church at Saint-Jean-de-Luz, and was a more spirited affair. The bride wore white again, an overmantle of purple velvet dusted with fleur-de-lis, and a crown on her head. A richly carpeted raised platform reached from Anne's quarters to the church entrance, and along this, carrying the bride's train, came the Princesse de Carignan and Gaston's girls, the Mlles. d'Alençon and de Valois, stern with responsibility.

In the evening Her Majesty was dressed for the first time in French style and received the Court while gold and silver tokens commemorating the marriage were being broadcast from her apartment windows into the shouting crowd.

Now her relatives took their solemn leave. Next day all would be back in Spain except five: her confessor, physician, surgeon; Señora Molina, her first waiting woman, and Molina's young nephew. At last it was time for bed. Anne of Austria and all those ladies whose pedigree entitled them to be present, a large congregation, disrobed Maria Theresa, endlessly chatting and working on her ringlets and the buttons and ribbons of her nightgown, and disposing pillows in the great bed hung with sails like a ship of state. A messenger came with a dispatch from the gentlemen in the neighboring chamber — His Majesty was undressed and waiting. Sitting on the *ruelle* fencing the bed platform, the bride went white and said in Spanish, "Quick, quick, the King wants me!"

All the women, withdrawing, exchanged glances of surprise and amusement. Could one believe it? The Queen, that odd little creature, was in love.

Anne stayed behind to see her children tucked in together and give them her benediction, and then the candles were snuffed out one by one.

Anne hoped this marriage would put other women out of her son's mind. The Bourbon blood made its own problems.

Strangely chilled it had been, certainly, in her late husband, Louis XIII. "No naughty thoughts!" he had often warned the courtiers, wagging a finger; and once, affronted by the sight of a lady's bosom too frankly shown, he had first pulled his hatbrim over his eyes, and then as the protest went unnoticed, filled his mouth with wine and shot a stream down the deep décolletage of her gown.

After several years of marriage but no children, His Majesty began to arouse the anxiety of the nobles, who suspected him rightly of not trying. Urged on by the clergy, they began a campaign to rob him of his chastity by praising the delights of love, but Louis refused to listen. He returned prudishly to his hobbies of larding roasts in the kitchen, raising green peas for market, and hawking for sparrows and mice down the desert corridors of the Louvre. Drastic measures were indicated, and were taken.

In January 1619, the King's illegitimate half sister, Mlle. de

Vendôme, was married to the Duc d'Elbeuf. Patriotically overcoming their natural desire for privacy, the couple invited Louis
to the nuptial chamber, and what followed was written down in a
dispatch from the Venetian ambassador to his masters at home.

> *The act was reiterated more than once, to the great applause
> and particular pleasure of His Majesty. Thus it is thought that
> this example has actively concurred to excite the King to do
> the same thing. It is also affirmed that his sister, Mlle. de
> Vendôme, encouraged him thereto, saying to him, "Sire, you
> do the same thing with the Queen, and you will be the better
> for it."*

However, to everybody's disappointment, Louis returned to his own
bedchamber. A few nights later the Duc de Luynes entered the
royal presence, reproached the King with great dignity for his failure to do his duty by France, and ended by picking him up and
carrying him kicking and struggling into the Queen's apartments
and depositing him on her bed. Louis was forced to give in to
public demand, and the Court rejoiced.

Still, lovemaking never became one of his favorite pastimes, and
his son was not conceived until several years later. It happened on
a cold and stormy night when, returning unexpectedly to the
Louvre, the King discovered his bed had been removed to his current lodgings at Versailles and there was no place to sleep except
with his wife.

Nine months later, full of thanksgiving, the Queen had a church
built, Val-de-Grâce, in honor of the seemingly miraculous acquisi-
tion of little Louis the Godgiven. Later there was another boy,
Philippe, but he, though greeted happily enough, was naturally
something of an anticlimax.

Louis XIV was not at all like his father.

As if he had been the sun, opening the tight buds of her personality, Maria Theresa rose from her wedding night smiling,
dreamy, talkative. She told everyone who would listen that she

had always wanted to marry the King of France and no other, that she had fallen in love as a child when she first saw his portrait, and that when she heard the terrible rumor he was engaged to the Princesse de Savoy she had cried out, "It cannot be and it must not be!" to the alarm of all her attendants. These childlike effusions were at first funny and then tiresome to the sophisticated, and a worry to her mother-in-law. Louis was kind to Maria Theresa and publicly pronounced himself well satisfied.

Nonetheless, he left the train as it moved north toward Paris and rode to Brouages to an inn which had once sheltered Marie Mancini, that dark passionate scholar of a girl. He paced the marshy shore "with long sighs" and came back in tears to the little room where she had slept. Would this welling bitterness ever cease? "You are the King — you love me — and yet I go." But he was not the King in actuality, and never would be while Mazarin lived. Soon the battle must be fought. Meanwhile, through weakness, he had let himself fall like a chessman in the political game, and his love was lost forever. He hoped her uncle would soon arrange an expedient marriage for her, far from France.

As soon as the royal party had left Blois in the autumn, Gaston d'Orléans was taken with a lingering sickness. He died early in February, and immediate anarchy erupted in the castle. The servants raced to the death chamber and pillaged everything movable including the Prince's dirty clothes and bedding. The Grande Mademoiselle might have been able to control the situation, but though sent for in haste she had not arrived.

The Duchesse was helpless. She had always devoted to the evasion of duty what time she could spare from religion and the contemplation of her interesting digestion. Custom demanded of widows a forty-day period of seclusion in a chamber hung with black, but the prospect was too dreadful to be faced. Now she recalled, with relief, that in order to retain her family's right to live in the Luxembourg, Gaston's inheritance from his mother, Marie de Médicis, some appearance of residence must be kept up. She would take care of this in person by moving at once to Paris. Packing was started therefore without delay, while her husband's body, stripped and forgotten, began stiffening to an undignified posture in the cold of his sacked and abandoned room.

The Marquis de Saint-Rémi, confirmed in his appointment as Master of the Household, also prepared to leave. His arrangements would take some time; dismantling an establishment the size of Blois was a difficult assignment. Louise and Catherine would of course continue to attend the young princesses as before.

Shocked out of his idyll at this impending separation, Charles de Bragelonne was forced to take action sooner than he had expected to. He went to the Marquise de Saint-Rémi and asked for Louise's hand. Nonsense, the Marquise said, Louise was still too young to marry, and furthermore had no fortune of her own. How did he think they would live, since he too was poor? Unless Louise could manage somehow to get a rich husband, she would probably have to take the veil.

Holding back his tears, Charles told Louise that their plight was bad but not hopeless; he had a plan. His father had left him a little money, and by selling everything he owned he could equip a trading ship and sail for India. Great profits had sometimes been made in this way; it was risky but worth trying. He begged her to refuse all other suitors and wait for him; and overwhelmed at the thought of his devotion and danger, she promised.

But in spite of the tragedy of her situation, Louise was too busy in those last days at Blois to meditate on Charles as he deserved. Later, certainly, when there was more time, realization would touch her with its blighting finger.

The Luxembourg, for all its comfort and magnificence, might have been a convent during that spring and summer for the seven girls caught in the mourning routine of the Duchesse d'Orléans. Back from the royal wedding, the princesses made daily religious pilgrimages with their mother's retinue to the churches of Paris, pressing their faces to the glass of the coach windows en route for glimpses of the world.

No other expeditions were allowed for six months; they grew familiar with and tired of all the surrounding gardens, trim and symmetrical as carpets, fell back on their old childish games of hide-and-seek, wink-musette, and dancing to their own singing, and spent whole afternoons leaning lackadaisically from the windows learning to recognize the arms emblazoned on passing equipages headed for the Palais-Royal and its half-guessed diversions. The lackeys perched with folded arms against the sky were prince-proud, three to a carriage, but it was soon seen, to the watchers' horror and joy, that some economical nobles made a practice of propping up a stuffed lackey between two real ones. This they unanimously condemned.

Luckily Mademoiselle was home for a time, waiting with the rest of society for Their Majesties' triumphal entry. She did what she could to save her sisters and their friends from dying of boredom by holding a few discreet dancing parties and suppers which were brightened by the playing of her privately maintained corps of violinists. At such times her wealth was a great comfort to everyone.

August 25, 1660 — the appointed, the longed-for day. All the inhabitants of Paris were out battling for standing room in the streets to see the Queen of France come home, and to show off their own holiday clothes, beg, cut purses, or hawk things in loud and raucous voices: Dutch biscuits, fans, fruit, medicine, flowers, pictures, rosaries, ribbons, glass trumpets, rosettes, lewd and lauda-tory verses. Shifting and shoving in the heavy heat they took posi-tion against the walls along the narrow route of arrival and show-ered trash on each other from every balcony.

The crowd had been gathering since four in the morning. By five the greatest ladies of the realm were assembled under the tri-umphal arch of the gate Saint-Antoine in full costume, including their hot velvet mantles of ceremony, and the rest of the Court grouped around the dais with its waiting thrones for Anne of Austria and the Queen Mother of England. Here the houses were hidden behind tapestries and the cobblestones spread with fresh flowers and herbs from which the coming wheels would crush out fragrance.

Gaston's two youngest daughters stood behind Anne's throne, and beyond, from a window of the Hôtel de Beauvais, blond and brown heads kept emerging and disappearing — Louise, Catherine, Anne-Constance, and Marie-Charlotte.

The sun rose over the shadowed roofpeaks and ravines of the city, and the day-long procession began. On came successively the household of the Cardinal with his gilded carriages, gentlemen, silver-belled mules; the pages of the Queen's stable bearing her mantle and jewel casket and leading her parade palfrey; the Chancellor on horseback in his long crimson cassock bordered with gold; a white charger with the royal seal on his back in a silver coffer; His Majesty's musketeers like a salute of trumpets in their fine flash of blue velvet cassocks and silver crosses and headed by their popular captain, M. d'Artagnan; a light-horse company in red *justaucorps;* the Grand Prevost of France surrounded by his guards; a flourishing, curvetting cavalcade of gentlemen in multifarious plumes; governors of the King's provinces and their heralds; the Grand Master of Artillery at the head of the Marshals of France, and the Comte d'Harcourt, Grand Equerry, carrying the royal sword in its blue velvet scabbard sewn with gold fleur-de-lis.

Now, at last, the distant swelling roar became an imminent deafening yelling and commotion as the crowd, smitten with love and joy, saw coming Louis XIV, King of France and Navarre — on his right and left the Duc de Bouillon and the Duc de Créqui — behind, the Duc de Tresmes. His mount was a magnificent Spanish bay, its housings glittering with silver thread and its harness crusted with gems.

With that high and becoming mien which makes him so easily discerned among the most accomplished seigneurs of the Court (the Chronicler wrote), he advanced in kingly state, more triumphant than ever by peace and by love, dressed in a habit of silver brocade stitched with pearls and garnished with a quantity of scarlet ribbons and a hat with a flourishing bouquet of plumes, scarlet and white, pinned with diamond insignia.

At the dais, Louis reined in his horse, glanced up, and saluted the women with a graceful gesture and a smile incomparably charming, so that all, including his mother, felt the tears come to their eyes and laughed to hide their emotion.

Among them was the young sister of Charles of England, Henriette d'Angleterre. Now she gazed in excitement up the street toward the next group of riders led by Philippe, her fiancé. He pranced by at the head of his Household, dressed in silver brocade, like his brother Louis, sending her a long proud significant look before the pageant swallowed him in moving color. Then, plunging forward in a new surge of acclaim, came twelve pages of the Queen's chamber and Maria Theresa herself in an open chariot drawn by six Danish grays caparisoned with gold and entirely covered with gold embroidery. Her face was placid amid the clamor of her new subjects and the flashing of the diamonds she wore. After her came the carriage of Mademoiselle, which she was sharing with the Duchesse de Longueville and the Princesse de Bade; another with Marguerite d'Orléans and Mlle. de Nemours; then a dozen more packed with titled ladies, and last, a detachment of the Guard strung out in a two-hour-long parade.

Mme. Scarron, wife of a poor poet, but a respectable young woman who had gained a window sill through connections at Court, wrote the next day, "I do not think it would be possible to see anything so beautiful, and the Queen must have gone to bed last night very content with the husband she has chosen."

So thought Louise, who could scarcely move from the window which had opened on her first sight of the King smiling.

The Luxembourg sank once more into mourning for the Duc d'Orléans, and it seemed to the princesses and their attendants that time moved more slowly than ever. All around them the Court was astir with marvels they could only half imagine.

But early fall brought diversion in the form of a visitor, young Charles of Lorraine, a cousin of the Orléans house. His uncle-guardian was the old warrior recently disarmed at the Peace of the Pyrenees, who, without his army, had nothing to occupy him at home, and was now spending his ebbing strength in the pursuit of nubile Parisiennes.

The boy, though badly dressed and somewhat gauche, was attractive, having long-lashed eyes and an indolent feline manner; and Mademoiselle observed him from all angles, physical and political. She thought of him as a possible candidate for her own hand, ignoring the twelve or thirteen years' difference in their ages, and began to organize expensive suppers and balls for his entertainment.

Unfortunately, he and her sister Marguerite, who at sixteen was becoming a beauty, had already fallen in love — hopelessly, since his uncle would never let him be wasted on such a modest fortune. Still, they were increasingly miserable, and finally Marguerite went to the old prince and knelt to beg for his charity: "I would live with you like the last servant of the Lorraines, if you would let me marry your nephew." Amazed, he said, "You are a fool!"

Not long after this a proposition came by way of ambassador from the Duke of Tuscany, to whom social position meant more than money. Marguerite greeted the delegate with cries of despair and ran for refuge to a cell in the Convent of Charonne. There she was found next morning sniffling and lamenting; she would die rather than marry the Duke of Tuscany. But threats to leave her in the nunnery for good eventually quieted her hysterics and she let herself be brought home. The Duchesse, attacked by gaseous indigestion and feelings of inadequacy, locked herself up in her chamber.

Marguerite began going to the woods every day with her cousin Charles — to hunt, they said — and returning at night with her aspect hard and bright, her coiffure disarranged, and the hooks of her bodice hitched wrong. The philosophical Mademoiselle said, "All were surprised at these promenades"; especially the Tuscan ambassador. He presented his master's proposals nevertheless, and so Marguerite d'Orléans was betrothed and went no more to the woods.

Louise suffered and wondered with her friend, who often came at night to talk in her bedchamber. Life was brutal and strange, to join people in this manner and then tear them apart. Charles de Lorraine, Charles de Bragelonne . . . None escaped, it seemed, except the careless; and the romances one read did not tell everything.

II

OPENING DOORS

D E A T H, the stealer of croupy children, also bundled away Cardinal Mazarin, leaving his famous toys — statues, clocks, cushions, plumes, pomades, diamonds, marionettes, lutes, flutes, fountains, dice, mosaics, tassels, candelabra, decanters, musk-scented gloves, jade and ivory, jasper tables, stables, curio cabinets, library. He would never again move smiling into a salon in his purple velvet skullcap and cloak to announce the winners of a lottery or arrange an execution, nor sit in that armchair at the Palais Mazarin with two little monkeys on his knees, making them dance a parody of Court ladies.

A week earlier his astrologers had seen a comet appear low in the evening sky, trailing flame, and hurried to let him know it was a sure presage of evil. "The comet does me too much honor," said the Prime Minister.

He died more in the style of a philosopher than a Christian, after a long course of bleedings and dosings, his leg plastered with horse dung, his entrails corroded by the purges of M. Vallot, the King's physician.

His left hand let go the purse strings of France; his right fell from the scepter.

Waking that early March morning in an adjoining chamber of the Château de Vincennes, Louis whispered a question to his old nurse who was lying on one of the other two cots: Was the Cardinal dead? Yes, was the answer; and the King got up and began to dress as fast as he could, but quietly not to rouse his mother.

He locked himself up in his study and nobody saw him for the next two hours. Then he came out with an air of calm and sent for his ministers, M. de Brienne, Chancellor Le Tellier, and Super-intendent Fouquet.

What he had to tell them was brief: he had decided that there would never be another Prime Minister of France, nor a churchman admitted to government. "Then," one said, showing some natural surprise at this news, "to whom shall we address ourselves?"

"To me," Louis answered. His foot was set on the path, and he was to be King; therefore, he would rule — make policy, settle dis-putes, transact business, wage war, grant favors and offices, deal out punishment, and answer to no other man.

It was an ambitious plan, one which no recent French monarch had seriously attempted. The ministers bowed respectfully and were amused. Secretly they allowed this pleasure-loving boy a week with his program; his hands would soon tire of holding the reins of that lawless stallion, France. But they had forgotten for the moment how well-earned young Louis's reputation as a horse-man was.

Mazarin's secretary, M. Colbert, had spent a sleepless night and risen before dawn, and now in the King's name he was breaking into all the hiding places of the Cardinal's money. With swift effi-ciency he dug out the millions cached at Vincennes, at the old Louvre, at Courbevoie, and several other country seats, failing only at La Fère. There a fortune in gold hidden in the bastions fell into the hands of Mazarin's heirs, who had sent off a valet moments after the old fox began to die. Louis, suddenly rich, forgave Col-bert this single miscalculation, and their friendship was solidly begun.

The new aide was nothing like the suave and cheerful courtiers His Majesty had favored until now. His manner was brusque and negative, and hollow eyes overhung with wiry black brows made him seem perpetually frowning. Still, he had the subtlety to un-derstand an idea only half expressed and a genius for turning it into successful action. He was, furthermore, incorruptible. These qualities made him within a few weeks not convenient but neces-sary to the King.

Anne of Austria's public mourning was moderate as it should

have been for a government official who had been feared by the nobles and hated by the people, but her private sorrow was deep and complicated. More than mistress and lover, she and Mazarin had been allies in a prolonged war of weapons and moral endurance — an Italian man and a Spanish woman together against the forces pulling France apart. For seventeen years they had fought alone, waiting for Louis to come into his strength. They had prevailed. Now Mazarin was dead, and it was as if lightning had struck an oak. The rooted half might continue to grow leaves for a time, but it was no longer really alive.

In spite of the opportunity a mourning period always brought for dressing up, Prince Philippe, commonly known as Monsieur, was very much annoyed. Now his wedding would be delayed again. And to make matters worse, there was the Duke of Buckingham paying court to his fiancée, Henriette.

Buckingham, full of melodrama, had followed her home from England where she had been on a visit of congratulation to her brother Charles II, and was now playing his role of chivalric lover in public.

It was so unfair; certainly the center of the stage should belong to the bridegroom at such a time. Monsieur sulked, his dark Bourbon eyes gloomy, his rosy mouth drawn down.

Henriette laughed, then appealed to her mother to have Charles recall the Duke. A hint finally brought the required message from the English court, and Buckingham left France with many extravagant vows of perpetual worship and deathless pain.

Monsieur was only partly soothed and became very demanding of his rights, so both Queen Mothers agreed the marriage had better occur at once in spite of the Lenten season and near approach of Passiontide. Between them was an unexpressed satisfaction mixed with amazement at Philippe's interest in his fiancée, since no female had ever roused anything but envy in him before. This new emotion must certainly be encouraged.

Maria Theresa had little concern with either the funeral or the forthcoming wedding. Pregnant, homesick for Spain, she had almost given up trying to learn French pronunciation, and now kept to the seclusion of her own apartments, coming out only when state occasions required it. Play and small talk bewildered, the casualness of French manners shocked her. She had gradually narrowed her day to a few safe activities: morning Mass, embroidery, afternoon promenades, visiting convents, and card playing with her ladies-in-waiting. To their satisfaction she was a poor gambler and always lost large sums of money.

Louis was in some ways an attentive husband, but had abandoned talk since he discovered frivolity alarmed her, and so his visits eventually assumed a pattern and were not long.

The pleasures of dinner were on the whole more dependable. In the Queen's private kitchens Señora Molina presided among the silver cooking utensils tirelessly making clove-scented chocolate, brown soups and gravies, garlic stews with nutmeg and capsicums, and pale thick pastries. "Spanish messes," Mademoiselle called them, all but holding her nose.

Maria Theresa would not try French dishes, but was beset with some curious unease at seeing other people enjoy them. "I know they'll eat everything all up and leave nothing for me," she would say with a quaver of self-pity as the platters went around the table.

This fortnight of arrest brought a few extra hours to the harassed and hardworking playwright Molière. He used them for reworking two or three scenes of *Les Fâcheux* (The Bores), which he hoped to have on the boards by May 1. Though popular at Court, he and his troupe were chronically short of money and time; there were jealous squabbles whenever a nobleman gave Armande or Madeleine Béjart a gown too glorious for the rest onstage, and constant trouble with the apportioning of profits. Some telling performance might gain them the permanent patronage of the King, and enable them to outdistance their rivals of the Théâtre de l'Hôtel de Bourgogne. In honor of the chance presented by Monsieur's wedding, therefore, they must all contrive to be infinitely diverting.

It was the end of March 1661 — more than a year since Louise de la Vallière had arrived in Paris — and still the Luxembourg held her like a cage, though the months of mourning for Gaston were long past. It was time for something to yield, to open. But there was little chance that it would. In spite of her high rank the Duchesse d'Orléans did not attract company nor wish to; she seemed to carry a vacuum with her wherever she went.

There had been talk all winter of her cutting down the size of her household staff after Marguerite's marriage in April and going into semi-retirement. It was a disturbing prospect for the Marquis de Saint-Rémi and his wife, who would in this event be forced to return to the country, to Touraine or the Blaisois. And what would become of the children, Catherine, Jean, and Louise? Their prospects for preferment and marriage would disappear, whereas here in Paris there was always the possibility of a lucky accident. Anne-Constance de Montalais, for instance, had been chosen as a maid of honor for the new Madame, Henriette d'Angleterre, and so was certain to meet all the right people.

Among the ladies who made up the best Society, one of the smart, affected, celebrated Précieuses, was Mme. de Choisy, wife of Gaston d'Orléans's ex-chancellor. She kept her lodgings in the Luxembourg but was seldom home, being occupied all day with running the affairs of important people at Court through intuition, criticism, and little arrangements. She had a son of twelve, a quiet boy much attached to Louise, who often read him stories and invented games as much for her own amusement as his.

The approving eye of Mme. de Choisy fell on these two with their puppets one afternoon, and suddenly she was smitten with a desire to do something nice for the little La Vallière — such an agreeable girl — a complete contrast to Montalais, who was at once brazen and sly. She began considering what she might do, made a few inquiries, and after a day or two was ready to produce her surprise. Louise was to have an interview with Her Highness the Princesse Henriette, and if all went well . . .

Henriette liked Mlle. de la Vallière immediately. She had an intelligent manner, good bearing, and while pretty was not of that formidable beauty which tears female coteries apart with jealousy and makes men misbehave. They were both sixteen, interested in the same things, and had read the same novels, all of which should make for good conversation. The Princesse, therefore, decided on the spot that Louise should enter her service as a maid of honor immediately after the wedding.

Louise's excitement almost made her sick. To be a maid of honor was to hold a key for the unlocking of marvels, something to make Mlle. Scudéry's fanciest romances seem mediocre. To stay always with the King's sister-in-law meant that every palace in France would be her home; to follow the Court in its starry peregrinations would be not a privilege but a duty. There would be music. Light. Life!

The pension was only a hundred livres — hardly enough to buy stockings and collars, her mother reflected shrewdly, but on the other hand this was Louise's chance to make a wealthy marriage. Court life would soon make her forget Bragelonne, and there were plenty of seigneurs in Monsieur's circle rich enough to indulge an inclination for a dowerless wife.

But Louise must remember, she warned, that there were thorns among the roses. For one thing, Madame was not perfect; she had her humors like everyone else. If she should be sleepless, some maid must be up all night reading to her. Or suppose one is all ready for a ball, hair dressed, rendezvous appointed, and Madame becomes piqued with Monsieur — all must stay home together. For another thing, since a maid of honor is appointed only to be diverting, to stimulate gaiety and embellish her mistress's background, she must always be on guard against showing any anger or grief of her own — an accomplishment which always sounds much easier than it is.

Furthermore, the dangers were considerable. The maids of honor were traditionally fair game for all the tricks and blandishments of the Court's cavaliers; beyond the menace to one's virginity was the possibility of becoming involved in some social-political intrigue ruinous to herself and her whole family. The Queen's girls were protected to some extent by Mme. de Navailles, their chaperon, and Anne of Austria's by her own vigilance. But Henriette had appointed no superintendent of her household and perhaps never would. Therefore, the Marquise said, sighing, Louise must be careful, and should above all keep away from Anne-Constance de Montalais, if possible. She attracted trouble as a magnet does pins.

But Louise's mind at this stage of the dissertation was busy with a more serious problem. What on earth was she going to wear?

On March 28 an application was tendered Judge Michel Guillois from Jean-François de la Baume le Blanc, chevalier, Sieur de la Vallière, and the Demoiselle Louise-Françoise, brother and sister free and of age, expressing their "need of some sums of money to put themselves in equipage, the said Sieur de la Vallière to follow His Majesty, and the said Demoiselle de la Baume to be maid of honor to the future Madame."

Jean had expressed his plans perhaps too grandly in this document; he had joined the army, and would be following the King only at a great distance, but this phrasing satisfied his sensitive dignity.

Funds were dispensed in accordance with the request, and Jean and Louise had the experience of seeing each other dressed as a gentleman and lady of fashion, before turning with glances half affectionate, half mocking, to take their separate paths out of childhood.

On Wednesday, March 30, 1661, in the Château of the Palais-Royal, situated in our own parish, was celebrated before Monseigneur Daniel de Cosnac, Bishop and Comte de Valence and de Brie, by our consent and in our presence, the betrothal of the most high and mighty Prince Philippe, son of France, Duc d'Orléans, the King's only brother, of the parish of Saint-Germain-de-l'Auxerrois, and of the most high and mighty Princesse Henriette-Anne of England, only sister of the King of Great Britain, our parishioner. And on the following day, on the 31st of the said month, the marriage of the said lord and lady was solemnized in the Chapel of the said Palace . . . [so said the register of Saint-Eustache].

The King signed it, the bells tolled, the Court gazetteer's prose grew French lilies and English roses in the sunshine of this event, and poets brought forth the results of their secret labors.

La Fontaine retold in verse the story of Henriette's birth in the middle of civil war and anarchy and of her romantic escape in the care of Lady Morton, her mother's faithful Scotch lady-in-waiting. Zephyrs had wafted her, he said, and Loves and Cherubs had followed her to the shores of France where she had become through the years the delight of the Sun King's Court. He praised in immoderate metaphors the beauty, wit, and delicacy that had won her royal lover's heart.

There was some truth in these paeans. Henriette had developed within the past year from a silent, skinny little girl hidden in convent schools and her mother's apartments to a young woman of compelling attraction.

Some said her beauty was classic; others agreed with the Princesse Palatine that Madame had no actual beauty, but so much grace that everything she did became her. Her chestnut hair was cut and curled in such a way as to make other styles obsolete, and she dressed so cleverly that not even Monsieur noticed she had a crooked shoulder until after they were married. One observer said:

> *There is a sweetness and gentleness about her which no one can resist. When she speaks to you, she seems to ask for your heart at once, however trifling are the words that she has to say. Young as she is, her mind is vigorous and cultivated . . . Do not think that I speak as a lover, for if I could make you realize half the charm of her wit and gaiety, you would agree with me.*

Certainly she had the rare talent of making every listener feel something of mysterious and unique importance between them, shared with nobody else. It was dangerous because she herself sensed it, for the moment, genuine.

But though the seed of disaster was there it would not sprout this season. Here was a spring for being enchanted with the world, Philippe, her pretty maids of honor, her own untested power. She was ready to laugh, to understand, to muse, to be loved. Old courtiers saw their youth idealized in her, young ones the mirror of their happy vital present. The unheard music was hers, but others might join the dance.

After the wedding the English Queen Mother retired to her country estate of Colombes and the bride and groom took up residence at the Tuileries with their retinue and staff.

The wedding gifts were laid out, players tuning their instruments, waves of hothouse fragrance pouring through every door, and guests arriving. The little Duchesse d'Orléans became in a day the leader of the fashionable world, followed by the men, imitated by the women, her lightest remarks subject to quotation like the gospel of a new religion.

She laid few duties on her maids of honor, but they had to run fast in their satin shoes even to keep her in sight — the nimble and admired Montalais, La Vallière, D'Artigny, and Barbézière.

On Maundy Thursday they watched her take the Queen's place in the solemn ceremony of washing the feet of the poor in the hall of the Louvre, and April 10 kept them dressing and undressing for the ceremonies and celebrations attendant on Marie Mancini's marriage to Prince Colonna, Constable of the Kingdom of Naples.

Louis's wish was at last realized: Marie was to leave France and cease from troubling his sight. He bore the ordeal of her marriage much better than anybody would have predicted, being by now absolutely absorbed in the company of his sister-in-law.

The wise shook their heads as they noted His Majesty's attendance on Madame and heard their growing stock of private jokes. One of the King's remarks was repeated with raised eyebrows in every gathering. How could he, he had demanded of the air, ever have been fooled into thinking Madame anything but the most attractive woman in the world?

No doubt he was recalling that occasion when it had been suggested he himself might marry Henriette, then eleven. "What, marry the little bones of the Holy Innocents?" he had said with the finality of age seventeen. Inconceivable, that blindness!

In the middle of the month Marguerite d'Orléans was married by proxy to the Duke of Tuscany. She was as lovely but not as virtuous as an angel, Mme. de Choisy said, and gossip predicted a miserable time for her husband.

As soon as these weddings were out of the way the King and Queen departed for their summer residence at Fontainebleau, leaving Philippe and Henriette in Paris to experiment with being a married pair at the head of their own house.

Louise began to see a pattern to her new life. In the afternoon she drove behind Madame's coach to the Cours-la-Reine, those shady avenues beside the Seine where all the fashionable resorted around five o'clock to observe and be seen; back for dinner with Monsieur and a few of his favored companions; then a throwing open of the doors and a brilliant rustling parade of new arrivals for talk and music, dancing and cards. Tablets of amber and jasmine were thrown into flaming censers, and the sideboards were loaded with cakes, fruit, and marzipan, sherbets and rose-flavored lemonade.

Every few nights there would be performances by Molière's troupe in the theater of the Palais-Royal, applauded even by the society of the Hôtel de Rambouillet, the same who had recently stiffened under the satirical whiplash of his *Précieuses* (*Bluestockings*). Madame, who loved Homer and Tacitus, also loved and respected the common M. Molière, it appeared — novel enthusiasm for a lady of quality! Her state of mind began to be widely imitated. Since her marriage Molière had been able to double the price of seats, and now the parterre was always crowded. He began bringing Madame sections of manuscript for reading and comment.

There were also nonprofessional intellectuals to be met in her salon during those long lively evenings — M. de Tréville, gravely handsome, captain of Monsieur's musketeers, said to be the best Greek scholar in France, and surely one of the best conversationalists — Madeleine de la Fayette in her mid-twenties, who had written a book, *La Princesse de Montpensier,* and was the intimate friend of Scudéry and Mme. de Sévigné — the widowed Duchesse de Châtillon, once yearned for by both Charles II and the Grand Condé, and affectionately known as Bablon — the Duchesse de Créqui — Mlle. de Tonnay-Charente, a sophisticate of nineteen who

could twist almost anybody's remark backward and make it bite
him — and gorgeous ivory-and-ebony Mme. de Monaco, married
to a fat, dull prince of the Grimaldi line who was always trying to
get her to come home from Paris.

Monsieur wallowed in the atmosphere provided by these people
like a bee in flowers, proud during those early weeks of the admiration his wife aroused, and conscious too of the good impression he
was creating in his character of adoring husband.

All hoped for the best from Philippe, known as "the prettiest
child in France," forgetting in their optimism his reputation as
Court authority on female underwear, his tendency to appear in
skirts and cosmetics, his insistence on attention from men. "The
miracle of inflaming his heart was not given to any woman," said
Madeleine de la Fayette, who knew him too well to be fooled.

When Louis had been winning his first laurels with the army at
Dunkirk, Philippe had stayed in Calais to play on the beach with
his mother's women and to shop for the gadgets and toys that came
over from England. Coiffed, patched, and plying his embroidery
needle, he was indistinguishable from the ladies.

Even now, at the best of times, he was fond of his rouge pot
and inclined toward superabundant feathers and rosettes, and the
fumes of his perfume announced his arrival some rooms in advance. His good looks were not to be disputed; though small and
slight, he had big dark eyes, white teeth, and regular features between the black waving torrents of his hair.

At one time, to be in style, he had taken a mistress. The for-
tunate girl had received the wages of sin without having to en-
danger her soul or lose any sleep, being called on only to accompany Philippe to parties and confer with him on problems of the
toilette.

Anne of Austria was responsible for this condition. She had
deliberately brought her younger son up as a daughter, distracting
his mind with frivolities. Gaston d'Orléans had spent his life plotting against his brother Louis XIII and the peace of the kingdom,
and Philippe should be prevented at all costs from emulating
Uncle Gaston.

But now Monsieur was enjoying the novelty of being married,

the stir he caused in his own court, and the pleasant awareness of having acquired something Louis wanted. Such combined satisfactions might last as long as a month before discontent reclaimed him, and this was only the second week.

All in a glow he swept his wife and her girls off to their country home, Saint-Cloud, which had been going through a beautification program at the hands of the Court architects Lepante and Girard. Summer was coming; its breath rose out of the cut lawn and the early yellow roses of the gardens unfurled in all directions around the castle; a warm haze of sunlight brought out the shapes of yew hedges and clipped trees, palisades and arbors, grass pyramids and amphitheaters, and lay on the limbs of gods and beasts ranged along the laddered shade of the parterres. This year there were bowers full of the sound of showering and cascading water; fountains, an Italian novelty, installed everywhere, put cool caves in the air and water drops on the leaves.

Louise, walking the terraces with Anne-Constance, looked out across the Seine toward the smoky towers of Paris and wanted nothing more. But their stay this time was to be short.

> *Fontainebleau, Friday*
> *If I wish myself at Saint-Cloud it is not because of its grottoes or the freshness of its foliage. Here we have gardens fair enough to console us, but the company which is there now is so good that I find myself furiously tempted to go there, and if I did not expect to see you here tomorrow, I do not know what I should do, and could not help making a journey to see you. Remember me to all your ladies, and do not forget the affection which I have promised you, and which is, I can assure you, all you could possibly desire, if indeed you wish me to love you very much. Give my best love to my brother.*
> *To my sister.*

Such a note from Louis was not to be resisted, and next day the coaches rolled out onto the road from the avenues of Saint-Cloud, full of masked women in their summer gowns, attended by all the plumed, mustached, sword-armed and epigram-ready cavalry of the household, and escorted by Captain Tréville with most of his musketeers.

In his Renaissance palace at the edge of the forest, windows closed against the seducing soft wandering air, Louis worked hard most of the day.

The problems of being a ruler were perplexing and he needed more help than he was willing yet to request; command was for him still too new a weapon to be wielded otherwise than awkwardly, with both hands. This country lying around him in such apparent calm was as full of agents and conspirators as it had been in the old precarious days of his father's reign. Neither Spain nor Germany, the traditional enemies, could be trusted. It was true that Roussillon, Conflent, and Cerdagne might be counted actual territorial gain, but could they be held? And one must not forget Duke Charles IV, that sour and singleminded old man, back now in his retreat at Nancy, negotiating with the Germans in hope of regaining Lorraine. He was disarmed, but he still had power; once he had led an army to the gates of Paris.

To the north Louis could mark on his map only part of Artois, and what towns he held in the Flanders district were nothing more than outposts. But these things could not be helped for the time being; fifty years of war had worn out the country and he must content himself with building up the army and navy.

If Maria Theresa had known anything she might have been able to advise him regarding the Spanish situation, but her ignorance was so vast as to resemble sanctity. Her father, Philip, was already proving his lack of reconciliation to the Treaty of the Pyrenees by allowing a number of unethical practices to proceed unchecked and without comment — interference with French privateers, the annoyance of businessmen, the stopping of messengers at the border — all small things, but significant.

Louis was painfully conscious of the gaps in his own education. He hid them to some extent by perfecting himself in the arts of conversation and manners, meanwhile surrounding himself with capable scholars and practitioners in all fields and listening carefully to their talk. Such self-education was not easy even for a person of strong will; and Mazarin may have been thinking of this when he told the Maréchal de Gramont, "Ah, M. le Maréchal, you don't know him! He has in him the stuff of four kings and an honest man."

If a vision of that Italian face with its pointed waxed mustache and sardonic eyelids rose sometimes at the conference table, it was not in mockery. There were things he might have told if he had lived longer, but Louis would discover most of them himself, in time.

At twenty-three the King was no egotist; his youth had been too full of privation and trouble for him to have developed illusions of omnipotence. Anne had not been a loving mother in spite of her rejoicing at his birth; this had been a tactical rather than personal consummation for her, meaning that her husband could not legally put her aside.

Louis XIII himself had looked at his offspring as he might some experimental cookery offered on a plate, and then tried to forget all about him. He died five years later, turning away in disgust from the noise of all the fighting at home and abroad, and in four days his son became King.

Before the assembled Parliament, Omer Talon, the red-cloaked Advocate-General, knelt and said, "Sire, the seat occupied by Your Majesty stands in our eyes as a symbol of the throne of the living God. All classes in the Kingdom honor and respect you as a visible divinity." Unconvinced, the new monarch was too overcome with shyness to put on his hat before all the gorgeous people.

To observers his future had looked bleak as January daybreak on a battlefield. France was a broken country with the great nobles fighting for pieces, and years of intrigue and murder were moving like the stages of a disease into that odd paroxysm called the war of the Fronde. Commoners joined aristocrats for scenes of farcical heroics; highborn women wore wisps of straw as a badge and rallied the bourgeoisie; plots exploded within plots, and confused courtiers kept scrambling back and forth over the barricades.

The Grande Mademoiselle, who of old had gone to Louis's nursery to rock him on her knee and call him "little husband," became overstimulated like everyone else. Thinking, maybe, to impress him now with her power and popularity, she mounted to the cannons of the Bastille one luckless day and with her own hands fired on the royal troops. "That shot," someone said, "killed her husband." Though she was soon full of embarrassed excuses, she was later banished to the provinces for several years on account of this girlish trick, and thus lost whatever chance she might have had of becoming Queen of France.

A lifetime of security would never erase Louis's memories of the Fronde — the noise of the mob outside the Palais-Royal; the awful cold of the night when his mother drove with him and Philippe in their nightclothes to Saint-Germain to wait for weeks, hungry and without firewood, until it should be safe to return to Paris.

Even after this crisis was past, life was difficult at Court. There were handsome costumes for parades and state functions, but Mazarin was stingy and ordinarily kept patched doublets on the princes and torn sheets on their beds. The stuffing was always falling out of holes in the coach seats, and even the food was bad; the prospect of a rich omelet was cause for celebration.

The citizens, who preferred vivacious children, thought Philippe the more promising of the brothers, and Anne and Mazarin kept their own company and counsel; so Louis was lonely. He turned again for affection to his old valet, La Porte, who in his early childhood had never failed with the good-night kiss and permission to climb into his own bed when nightmares occurred.

But now in May of 1661 it was time to put aside self-doubt and approach the business of government firmly. He spent his mornings closeted with his ministers and all other available time writing dispatches in his own hand to the foreign ambassadors. Amazement was universal at the King's attention to minutiae and his curiosity about remote affairs.

The French envoy in London was taken aback at his master's request for a list of persons in England noted for all kinds of knowledge, both in the past and present, "such information," Louis added,

"being necessary to the advancement of my glory and service."
M. de Comminges's reply was not very enlightening. He had never
heard of Shakespeare and was only dimly aware of "one named
Miltonius, whose noxious writings have rendered him more infa-
mous than the very assassins of their King."

It was also in Louis's program to enjoy life, and to make this
easy he maintained a miscellaneous horde of masters of music and
the dance, jugglers and comedians, artists, opera singers, and poets
both light and serious.

Lully, once a kitchen scullion, was now "a Florentine gentleman,
superintendent and composer of the King's music," and had under
his command regiments of the world's best players of violins, flutes,
harps, musettes, hautbois, harpsichords, cornets, and trumpets.

The veteran balladeer Benserade was entrusted with verses and
continuity for most of the ballets. At fifty he was still attractive
with his moderately well-groomed red beard and rangy form, able
to throw a roomful of maids of honor into agreeable chaos. He was
a good talker, but given to puns, and likely to fly into a rage at any
criticism of his lines, whether invited or not; the only man of
doubtful birth at Court who could walk with ease among the great
lords. He had an honest passion for the King's glory, and could
produce a few blossoming quatrains for any event of the Household,
no matter how trivial.

And there was Molière, whose troupe appeared on command for
performances wherever the Court went. He held an honorary post
in the royal ménage — that of upholsterer — but a man who could
stick tacks with such effect into personalities had no business wasting his time with furniture. In the past Louis had sometimes taken
him to sleep in his own bedchamber to protect him from the mur-
derous ire of people his actors had satirized too freely.

Around and among these specialists moved the favorites, mostly
men in their twenties, some inclined to sword rattling despite the
edict against dueling, all of them able to make Louis laugh — the
Marquis de Péguilain, the Marquis de Vardes, the Duc de Roquelaure, the Prince de Marsillac, the Comte de Guiche. Older than
the rest, stabler and more able, was that consummate courtier the

Comte de Saint-Aignan. He could turn his hand with equal effect to statesmanship and the organizing of a theatrical extravaganza; he was a realist poet as resourceful on the battlefield as in the salons where noted sensibilities foregathered. Louis prized him; they understood each other well.

Everything, including the weather and the King's mood, was ready for the reception of Madame and her entourage, and before she had been at Fontainebleau a week she held despotic rights over all summer activities.

Now that the King was running after her over the lawns with poems in his hand, ready to laugh and agree whenever she said a word, it was scarcely surprising that she should accept the invitation to capture him. It was more than an invitation, it was a demand. She could hardly be blamed for taking some satisfaction in making him love her too much, this man who had once dismissed her with a few words of juvenile scorn. The whole Court encouraged them, hoping happily for a real scandal. Everyone read with applause the verses they exchanged and began saying in undertones meant for Madame to overhear that it was regrettable she did not hold a higher place at Court.

As soon as Louise, leaning out of her carriage, had seen the steep roofs and castellated chimneys of Fontainebleau rising above a forest rolling away like green clouds, she knew why the King liked this place better than any other in France.

It was an old-fashioned palace, somewhat weathered and unkempt by comparison with the Louvre and the Luxembourg, but indefinably alive as if adventure lay about like griffins in the shade and would presently stretch and get up. The beeches were wild and shaggy and the long grass around the carp pond traveled in silver tosses and arches when the wind blew.

Monsieur's apartments were next the King's in the Pavilion of Princes, entered from the left side of the Cour Ovale, and shared by Madame. The walls of these chambers and closets were decorated with a variety of spirited tableaux, Jupiter eloping with Europe or conversing with Calisto, and Eve offering an apple to Adam.

Upstairs were the tiny rooms of the maids of honor, each with its narrow window where one might stand, too excited to sleep after dancing all night, to feel the river-damp on her skin. Up it came cold as perfume out of the darkness still lying in the deep nets of forest; then, slowly, dawn, with peach-colored clouds teased out like silk floss and the treetops distinguishing themselves into green lace fans.

All day at Fontainebleau different odors met the nose according to the sun's strength and the air's flow — dill and onion from the kitchen gardens, forest-dirt breeding mushrooms, lemon trees in the Garden of Diana, horses in the court where the hunters gathered, ducks roasting, soapsuds drying between the cobbles, and jasmine and rose laurel growing in silver tubs under Madame's windows, replaced every day by Louis's instructions.

Castle and grounds, the whole landscape was haunted by ghosts of a pleasant past, unlike Blois where the iron smell of blood still hung around the stones and terror smiled wanly about the twilight of certain wings, waiting for a dream with a loose latch.

The King and Monsieur had always spent their childhood summers here, playing in the dark wainscoted halls after their afternoon bath in the river, a time already lost and historic. Bony boys they must have been, going down to the river, escorted with formality into the shallows by Queen Anne, half a dozen ladies-in-waiting, and Louis's tutor, the Maréchal de Villeroy, all in gray linen smocks to preserve modesty.

But it was the lovers of other times who owned Fontainebleau, François I and Diane de Poitiers; Henri IV and Gabrielle d'Estrées. Their single and intertwined ciphers were carved everywhere, to last till the walls fell. Diane, Gabrielle . . . They were not to be forgotten even by strangers, so powerful was the memory of their fragility.

The weather was warm as July already, and Henriette with her friends and maids went to bathe in the river every day, driving out by coach and returning on horseback.

"Light" was the word of fashion that year, and Louis riding with his gentlemen to meet them would remember for the rest of his life how light they were in their plumed shady hats, coming down the path in a slant of late sunshine with leaf shadows running like water over lace and bare necks. It seemed they moved in a charmed archaism of summer and youth, and it was easy not only to imagine but to be shepherds, nymphs, and heroes.

Sometimes they would go back to the castle for supper, sometimes ride on to the Hermitage de Franchard for a picnic in the chasm, while Lully's more agile musicians perched overhead rousing the echo with horns and clarions.

After supper the women rode by slow *calèche* around the canal all evening attended by the men on horseback and with windows open to stimulate conversation; other couples walked in the woods listening for nightingales and studying astrology. Said Mme. de la Fayette, herself an experienced stroller, "These promenades lasted until two or three hours after midnight, and had an air more than gallant." The King was Madame's constant companion, "and it seemed to the eyes of all that they had between them that agreement which ordinarily precedes grand passions."

On May 8 the Grande Mademoiselle arrived with her sad little sister in tow, the new Duchess of Tuscany. They were in time to join one of the surprises Louis was always planning for Henriette, a water party featuring gondolas on the Grand Canal, trumpet fanfares, the usual promenade, a performance of the comedy, and finally a *médianoche* with refreshments handed around by Condé and other princes of the blood. By now Louis had ordered the trumpet corps replaced by thirty-six violins; these were more amorous in tone, he said.

Next evening there was a ball, not much enjoyed by Louise, whose friend Marguerite wept on her shoulder over the morrow's prospect of leaving Charles de Lorraine forever and submitting to the probably loathsome embraces of a stranger.

More gondola parties followed the first success, and in the mornings there were hunts in the forest, where Louise, easy in an old skill, let out her rein and galloped conspicuously away.

June brought no pause in the celebrations; concerts and balls alternated with picnics. On the 14th a dance was given by the Duc de Beaufort under the lantern-hung trees of the park; on the 18th came Saint-Aignan's *régal;* the 25th, a festival and torchlight promenade given by the Duc d'Enghien. In the intervals all Benserade's old ballet triumphs were repeated, and a new one was devised for performance on horseback in the serpentine light of flambeaux with the King and Henriette in the main roles.

Philippe had begun by now to complain to his mother that his feelings were never considered, that Henriette got all the attention and glory and had even begun to entice his friends away to her own circle. For example, he never saw the Prince de Marsillac any more, nor the Comte de Guiche. He thought somebody should speak forcefully to Henriette.

Even Maria Theresa had noticed something was wrong; occasionally she would emerge from hiding, peer vacantly around, and go to ask Anne why nobody ever stayed home any more, and where were they all? Sometimes it almost seemed Louis thought other people were more interesting than she was. Anne would blame her mildly for this nascent jealousy and take her for a walk around the court to throw crumbs to pigeons, or lend her a religious treatise to be read aloud by the ladies-in-waiting. But she herself was greatly disturbed. Unthinkable as it was by every tenet of politics and religion that Henriette should become Louis's mistress, one never knew. It might already be so. Those flushed faces and covert glances — those poems — and that running and leaping away into the woods by moonlight! No girl of seventeen could be trusted under such circumstances, and Louis was so headstrong.

She tried to persuade him that the Court should return to Paris and undertake its religious duties, since this was a holy year. He did not seem to hear, so she approached Madame with a tactful hint that all these late hours and damp promenades were injurious to the health. The only answer was an incredulous smile. Now Anne was piqued into taking a sharper tone, and this time succeeded in making the culprit angry.

By this time Henriette could not have stopped if she had wanted to. Power moves by itself. La Fayette was to write later, "Her heart led her to follow after all which did not seem criminal nor entirely contrary to her duty, and which could, moreover, divert her."

On June 27, to bring some interruption to the affair, Anne took Madame and her attendants to visit the Duchesse de Chévreuse in her old castle at Dampierre. His Majesty accompanied them for fourteen leagues, and turned back reluctantly. When they returned, several days later, he greeted Henriette with such exuberance that nobody could doubt his feelings.

Anne wrote immediately to the English Queen Mother at Colombes, informing her of the emergency; and as a result several old retainers including Abbé Montagu and Mme. de Motteville soon closed in with sober faces and words of doom for Madame.

She scoffed, protested, got furious, and cried, but could not escape the evidence that her reputation was in danger. Meanwhile Louis was being courageously addressed to the same effect by his mother's delegates.

In a sardonically clandestine interview, the accused pair discussed ways of solving the problem and finally came to a decision — he should stop coming to see her so often during the day, and instead pretend to have a mildly amorous interest in several other girls. It would be a new game to play and should have the effect of breaking the scandal hunters up into small packs baying in different directions. In this way their own friendship might be cultivated in comparative peace. But who should these girls be? It was not really important. Mlle. de Pons and Mlle. de Chimerault, two of the Queen's maids of honor would do; and there should be one of her own to make three — perhaps Louise de la Vallière? Thus it was agreed.

III

A NYMPH OF DIANA

W H E N Louis was a big though not especially precocious boy of sixteen, Anne of Austria and the Cardinal decided that it was time for his deflowering. He would certainly come to the same conclusion himself before long, and would blunder; therefore his mother prudently forestalled possible publicity and blame by appointing one of her waiting women to the task.

Mme. de Beauvais was neither young nor lovely and had only one eye, but she was a woman of understanding. Open-armed, she waylaid the King on his way from the bath one calm evening at the Palais-Royal, and overcame his fears.

From this encounter Louis kept a lasting sense that women were wonderful, and his behavior to Mme. de Beauvais as long as she lived was marked by particular courtesy and consideration. Anne expressed her own thanks by presenting her servant with a fine house in the Rue Saint-Antoine.

After this the world was not the same to Louis. Almost immediately he began hanging around the quarters of Mazarin's numerous nieces, the Martinozzis and Mancinis, and soon was a close friend of Olympe.

At sixteen she was velvety ripe as an apricot, which caused the King so much enjoyment he failed to notice for a long time that she was plain and had a vicious disposition. But despite the technical seduction of His Majesty, Olympe was never able to make him love her, which prevented the success of all her plans. Even after her marriage to the rich Comte de Soissons she brooded on this failure until the idea of revenge took control of her ambitions.

Having lost Olympe to Hymen, Louis cast his eyes on Mlle. de la Motte-Argencourt, one of his mother's maids of honor. "For the first time," wrote Mme. de Motteville, "he expressed himself as a lover, not very wisely." Anne was surprised at the ardor he showed, and scolded him. Louis, still a submissive and respectful son at the age of nineteen, promised with some sighs and tears to give up the pursuit.

Next year he was back at the Palais Mazarin in the throes of an authentic passion, this time for Marie Mancini. She was small, emotional, sallow of complexion, and a great reader. Her sincere concern for Louis's ignorance brought him belatedly to poetry, fiction, and philosophy, and together they built up a country of fantasy with impregnable walls, its own laws, and a private language. Their love was strong but chaste. The Grande Mademoiselle said, "They were like two lovers in a romance."

At Fontainebleau they wandered holding hands through autumn groves or floated in a boat for hours on the Grand Canal, apparently unconscious of time and the existence of other people.

Their determination to marry was thwarted by her uncle the Cardinal for two good reasons — the Court and country would never tolerate a Queen of the Mazarin blood, and furthermore it would be dangerous to himself to put such power in Marie's hands. She was too strong-minded.

Both Louis and Marie expected and half hoped to die as a result of this decision, but could not challenge it. When she went to Italy to join her husband, Constable Colonna, it was reported that he expressed astonishment on discovering that she was a virgin. But even in his despair Louis had ridden out to meet and inspect a candidate for his hand, Marguerite de Savoy, and had liked her very much. In the course of this visit, however, a more impressive offer came from Spain and was seized by Anne and the Cardinal. They were both encouraged by the evidence Louis gave of being ready for matrimony with almost anybody.

Now, though marriage had kept the King from causing any trouble for about a year, its futility as a permanent measure was being proved. In furtherance of his affair with Madame, according to their plan, he began laying siege to the maids of honor.

Mlle. de Pons had no reputation for spotless virtue and could hardly believe her good luck when His Majesty began to single her out for little attentions. However, her father, the Maréchal d'Albret, heard in Paris of little Bonne's peril and in a panic took to his bed with a spurious malady. She was summoned home, much to her disgust.

Louis suspected he had been the victim of a ruse, and was very angry. The time was not far off when nobody would dare to obstruct his wishes.

Mlle. de Chimerault, next on the list, was a natural flirt and knew how to receive the advances of an important man. She dimpled, retreated, threw up flimsy but complicated defenses, and looked out invitingly. It was the sort of game that could be prolonged indefinitely, and the King knew which plays were his. He made them slowly and put Chimerault herself out of his mind.

La Vallière remained. At not quite seventeen she had a fresh, almost incandescent look, as if her springtime coloring of white, rose, gold, and blue came from her thoughts. Familiarity with Court manners and admiration from several men had by now trained her to disguise her shyness, but the perceptive might still guess it in her soft voice and a certain hesitation at the doors of crowded rooms.

"Tall, shapely, extremely pretty, with a sweet and even temper," Mme. de Montespan would remember her some day. She seemed "fitted for dreamy contemplative lovemaking such as one reads about in idylls and romances."

Critics found only one flaw; her teeth were not beautiful. Otherwise everything pleased, even her little limp; and the poet La Fontaine, seeing her, wrote, "Grace more beautiful than beauty . . ."

"Everyone found her charming. Many young men professed love for her." Among these was a brother of the Princesse de Monaco, Armand de Guiche. He had the dramatic brunette beauty which marked his whole family, accentuated by a haughty manner and impulsive behavior. Besides all this, De Guiche was witty, a famous swordsman in spite of a hand maimed in the wars, and he dressed magnificently.

His energy made him creative, rash, and too exuberant for the taste of older people, who often showed signs of oppression in his company. Mme. de Sévigné, stronger than most, wrote, "I met the Comte de Guiche today . . . He seemed to me very clever, and less supernatural than usual."

He had been brought up as a playmate of the King and Monsieur, and was married young and against his will to a child heiress of the house of Sully. Since then he had all but ignored her existence, though opinion held generally that she was a nice little thing.

His easy success with other women had made him vain and also irresistible; Louise was flattered at Armand's attention and fascinated with his daily letters, which she could not understand because of the style. They were freighted with mythological allusions, knotted with metaphor, bedizened with adjectives, and confused as to direction — in short, beautiful. She answered as well as she could.

Louise had become accustomed now to the sight of the King, but was no more relaxed in his presence than she had been at Blois or on those few occasions when, taken to the Louvre, she had seen him pass at a distance.

Everything he did confirmed her childhood notion of him. Personally elegant, he walked and stood like Charlemagne; his regard was penetrating, and a slightly disdainful quirk of the lips seemed to raise the price of his words.

Now, when he roved around Madame's evening circle, paused before Louise, and spoke directly, to her alone, all poise faltered inside her — faded, almost fainted — and she could manage only murmured replies and "Yes, Sires" to his casual questions.

Louis released her mercifully after a few sentences and strolled away rather pleased. It was not so easy to make a pretty girl tremble like that at one's mere presence.

Her eyes were remarkable. A man less experienced than he might almost think there had been something beyond fright in their look. Thinking it over, he began to see that in this act of the comedy he must move a little carefully. The situation seemed to call for more chivalry than he would have supposed necessary.

What if her sudden pallor and that look had meant more than mere recognition that he was the King?

Next day and every day for more than a week he stopped and spoke to Louise as she sat sewing in Henriette's antechamber, and the other girls withdrew to a distance as etiquette required until he had gone on into the apartment.

The talk was of ordinary things, and Louise was able at last to maintain a precariously bantering tone with him. But day by day below the commonplace exchange there began to occur extraordinary encounters and languors of the unsaid.

Louise was too inexperienced to keep him from knowing her terror and its cause, and he found this more than provocative — wholly compelling to both vanity and imagination. Olympe, Marie, Henriette — they were all three commanding and opinionated. He had never before known such a girl as this one, silently all afire with fierce untouchable submission.

If there was a hunt or ball he found that accident would arrange a meeting and a few words. At the opera he would watch for her to appear in the crowd while pretending interest in something else.

Beside him the Queen sat like a religious effigy under the convoluted architecture of her hair, eating raisins and nuts from an enameled shell in her lap and giving off intermittent shafts of light out of the sleeping splendor of her gems. Unmoved, she munched through the dancing of the entr'actes and the music which was wreaking such intricate havoc on the senses of other listeners.

Louise had never discovered until those midsummer concerts how a song can grow from the singer like a bush of roses from a single brown root, intricate, opulent, thorned with fine small immaculacies of vibrato, leafed left and right in tender varying greens, and unfolding one by one into full-lipped, fire-veined buds and blossoms, to be followed by the faithful copy of a flute's single thread or the striking of a harp into descending perfect surprise.

What sorrow there was in almost all music . . . What did it mourn, in such strait mathematics of sound? And she thought with an ache half dread, half longing, of the hour to come — when, in darkness, a man on horseback would leave Madame's carriage as it drove through the park and the forest, and come silently to escort her own, his ungloved hand resting on the window sill.

Occasionally Anne of Austria gave a party herself. Remembering Mazarin's fondness for lotteries, she had prizes bought and invited Madame one evening to bring her friends and retinue.

All tickets won jewelry and playthings. Louis drew the principal prize, a pair of bracelets set with diamonds. For a moment he sat still, looking around the company, and finally, rising deliberately, made his way across the room and handed them to Louise.

She admired their workmanship, then returned them with a deep curtsy, murmuring that they were indeed extremely beautiful.

"In that case, Mademoiselle, they are in hands too fair to resign them," the King said, bowed, and resumed his seat.

Madame, recovering from her surprise, thanked him for the honor conferred on one of her own suite. The Queen sat surveying the scene with a placid smile.

The house at Versailles, set in pathless woods that dwindled into gnat-breeding, owl-haunted swamps, had never been planned as a pleasure resort for courtiers. It had been built by Louis XIII as a hunting lodge, and was small, drafty, and rustic.

His son was criticized for choosing this unpromising waste as the site of his new palace in preference to the hillsides of sunny Chennevières, or Juvisy, overlooking the Seine. But he never asked for advice.

Followed by those courtiers hardy enough to ride, he toured its fifteen thousand acres pointing out the areas he had selected for gardens, stables, and a great orangery to house potted shrubs. The swamps would have to be drained, part of the forest uprooted, and the ridge on which the ancient castle had stood must be broadened. These Jovian projects were too much for most of the followers to envision as they made their way over fallen logs and spongy bottomland, getting burrs in their lace and starting boars from cover.

In the meantime the hunting continued excellent, and in July a great rout was held for the whole Court. Listeners walking over the damp leaf mold of the forest could hear, far away through the afternoon, a savage tonguing of the unleashed hounds, and then four horns in brilliant unison telling them a stag had broken cover. A quiet broken only by the near sound of birds, or branches creaking in the breeze, meant that the trackers had lost the scent again. Then once more the belling would rise, and the medleyed yelling of the kennelmen behind.

Somewhere the tired stag with raised antlers and bulging eyes was plunging into the water; now the mort was near. *Piqueurs* would be unslinging their horns from the left shoulder, holding them overhead at arms' length, and a clamorous fanfare, "The Queen," would announce to listeners the kill.

Now the kneeling master of the hunt would be offering the King the stag's right front leg while his assistants flailed and disembow-eled the body, blood spattering around them on the littered ground. Then came the ritual cutting of the antlers to signify taking off the dead king's crown, the feeding of choice parts to the frantic hounds, and their slavering descent on the final reward, a mess of flour mixed with blood and poured onto the hide. It would be licked clean, folded by the kennelmen, and brought home later.

Meanwhile at the castle torches were being lit and the supper tables laid to a noise of tuning from Lully's thirty-six violins.

On the last day before the return to Fontainebleau, a picnic was spread under the trees of the park. The atmosphere was sultry; heat lightning shook the horizon, clouds rose giantlike in the west, and a stench of the swamp hung heavy.

Faces glistened in the heat as lemon and violet ices were passed, but before the platters had been cleared away a brisk wind came up, thunder began, and a drop or two of rain fell.

All games were abandoned and the players scattered to find cover, some under the quaking trees, others scuttling off in the direction of the castle, clutching their perishable belongings.

Louise picked up her skirts, which were taffeta and sure to spot, and raced for a thick bay tree some distance away.

It was only when she turned, breathless, to lean against the trunk that she discovered she had not been running alone. The King

LOUISE DE LA VALLIÈRE
from a painting attributed to Mignard
(Marseilles Museum. Photograph from Royal Academy of Arts)

LOUIS XIV AS A YOUNG MAN
from an engraving after a painting by Le Brun
(British Museum)

stood with rainwater running down his face and holding his plumed
hat to protect her from what was plainly a storm.

For more than two hours they talked together while the weather
poured, blew, and cleared. Nobody came near; the park might
have been a virgin continent at whose edge they stood uncertain but
aware. All rank, all reason, had undergone a sudden strange re-
versal. Only in a dream could she have heard that impossible word
from the King — but he said it over and over. He was no longer
the master sure of his way, only an ordinary young man, diffident
and sad, breaking his own profound silences with disorganized solil-
oquies.

"But there I spoke as a happy man," he said at last, "and that I
may never be."

"I don't know what you may be," she answered, "but I know that
if this trouble in me continues I shan't be very happy."

Their return to the castle was noted by many people. "The in-
quietude of love appeared only on his face," one said. "On that of
La Vallière one remarked a great sadness."

After the conversation at Versailles the King's behavior changed
abruptly toward Louise; he never stopped again to speak with her
in the antechamber, and avoided all notice of her in public.

It was a state of affairs which could not continue. Such a passion
must be either fulfilled or murdered outright; it is an incubus hanging on the body and spirit day and night. To give herself up as
Louis begged would be to fall into unspeakable danger — but
wouldn't anything be preferable to such torment of herself and him?
Worst of all was the knowledge that the decision was hers.

At last she asked him to leave her alone, to allow her time to
think. Perhaps without his presence some miracle would happen
to deliver her from this sin so dreaded and longed for, so certain
to ruin her at last. How could it possibly lead to anything but
sorrow?

Louis agreed with perfect courtesy and from then on kept scrupu-
lously away. Sometimes they would catch sight of each other, pass-

ing through a room in opposite directions, and would bow like pleasant enemies.

The miracle did not occur. It was past the middle of July, and the world was full of abortive thunderstorms. Louise thought her insomnia was due to the stifling heat.

Later she thought of giving up her post with Madame and returning to Paris. Now that it was certain the King had forgotten her, how could she stay at Fontainebleau and see him every day? But, on the other hand, how could she live in Paris with the prospect of never seeing him at all? Her thoughts writhed between equally unacceptable alternatives.

Her head ached and she saw in the mirror that her face was pinched, her eyes hollow. How could such a countenance have attracted His Majesty? It was no wonder he was amusing himself elsewhere.

Sometimes she reminded herself that Louis was the King. He was proud as the devil. He would never speak to her again unless she invited it — and that she could never do.

Somehow the week dragged on. Then, just before it ended, a footman came scratching at the door of her room, bringing her a small velvet bag and a note. The bag held a gold watch set with seed pearls and hung on a chain, and a pair of diamond pendant earrings, too valuable to be worn safely by any maid of honor.

The note was short. "Bid me die, or love me. I cannot hide my misery, and the curiosity of my friends drives me mad. They tell me that Madame is not cruel, and that there fortune favors me. The fools! They know not that I love one whose mocking affection is killing me. I implore you in the name of God to relent or to dismiss me forever." She stood in the middle of the empty room and the whole world tolled and swung around her like a bell, like a resurrection — Easter.

Fontainebleau, Versailles, the Palais-Royal, the Louvre, Vincennes, Saint-Germain, and a score of other palaces lay open to the King's disposal; but nowhere in the kingdom was a private place to be had for him and Louise together. Almost demented with joy and frustration he considered what to do, and finally went to Saint-Aignan for advice. The Comte had a little room near the royal

apartments. He gave Louis the key and went away at once to discover urgent business in another part of the palace. So Louise became the King's mistress. She rose out of his arms not like a
phoenix showering sparks of triumph and planning how to invest
her money, as is the usual way with successful courtesans, but as
a bride, so much in love that nothing could protect her.

On July 23 the Court presented for the first time, for its own
entertainment, the Ballet of the Seasons. Planned by Madame and
directed by the Comte de Saint-Aignan, it had for theme the trans-
formation of the pleasant region of Fontainebleau into the lovely
residence of the world's finest court. Dozens of courtiers supported
by a crew of professionals made up the cast, and rehearsals had
been going on since the last week of May.

A stage had been built, gilded, and draped on the lawn at the
edge of the lake, and a hundred and twelve ingenious machines
ensured fast scene changes.

At dusk on the opening night, thousands of torches flared into
scarves of flame and aromatic smoke along all avenues of approach,
and simultaneously the water in the gardens changed to floods of
rainbow-colored light.

The audience thus fittingly prepared to be enchanted settled down
as the overture began, and the curtain rose on the first entry.

"Who leads the Sun through the night?" sang a chorus of shepherds to a group of shepherdesses and fauns. Many familiar knees
were identified among the frills and tinsel.

Mlle. Hilaire, a hired soprano, answered melodiously, as the
Nymph of Fontainebleau. "Woods, nightingales, beautiful ver-
dure," she warbled with practiced gestures and a closing of green
enraptured eyelids, "Charming, delicious place which Nature and
Art have made expressly for the Gods when they are tired of
Heaven."

Before the last chorus subsided, sounds of admiration from the
audience announced the arrival of Henriette as Diana armed with
bow and quiver, wearing a silver crescent on her brow, and attended by ten nymphs who sprang around her singing praises. Their
sylvan green skirts were short and flounced, their hair brushed

loose. Among them were Mlle. de la Motte-Argencourt, once a disturbance to the King, and the Mlles. de Pons and de Chimerault, who now never would be. Louise was the most blond of all, and the best dancer. In the wings the King stood in his costume watching her dance. Had she seen his face she would have missed a step.

Louis was not the only watcher struck that night by the sight of La Vallière in her green dress. His secretary, Loménie de Brienne, an aesthetic if somewhat fat young man, had noticed Louise before on several occasions, and now found himself sensibly pinked by a Cupid's dart. Still another person, much more important, observed her with great interest, Nicolas de Fouquet, Superintendent of Finance, one of the most powerful men in France.

Benserade had prepared verses to be distributed like nosegays to all the principal ladies. To Louise he said:

> *This beauty, recent risen,*
> *In color fresh and clear,*
> *Is springtime with her flowers,*
> *And bodes a pleasant year.*

Such homage was rare for the poet, and he made up for it by including garlic in more than one of the other bouquets. La Mothe-Houdancourt, presenting herself center-stage with a confident smile, fortunately missed the implication that she was more beautiful than bright. Mlle. de Menneville heard gratifying recognition of the Duc de Damville's desire to marry her, but Mlle. de Fouilloux a dubious compliment on the blandness of her attractions.

The smooth-working machines kept pace with Lully's musicians and now presented a spring scene with gardeners working in a gay and desultory manner among the flower beds, overseen by Flora. Whether by coincidence or intent, the poet had put a meaningful quatrain on the lips of one of the gardeners:

> *I see a young plant grow from day to day*
> *Fairer than jasmine, rose, or bergamot;*
> *In tint and perfume she surpasses all —*
> *The loveliest blossom of my garden plot.*

As in nature, summer followed without delay, symbolized by eight harvesters dancing while others rested from their scythes and played a wheat-field concert. The King in a mood of bizarre humor had chosen the role of the Goddess Ceres, and now he danced the travesty with a straight-faced skill that delighted the audience. Monsieur coming afterward was as usual a little anticlimactic, even with the support of De Guiche and several other masters of the technique decked out as vintagers.

Winter was a somber scene in white and gray enlivened by six leaping gallants. Their anticipation, somewhat in contradiction of the main theme, was for a speedy departure to the city. Saint-Aignan followed, leading on seven Masks with a game of Momon, proposing dice to the ladies.

All players were swept together in a spectacular finale which brought Louis back in the dual role of Spring and the Great Lover, kneeling in homage to own Madame the Queen of Love and Beauty. His attendants, Play, Laughter, Joy, and Abundance, brought in their wake the nine Muses, to reside at Fontainebleau, and a train of the seven Liberal Arts, Prosperity, Health, Repose, and Pleasures of various sorts, falling into classic tableaux, smiling, singing, and gesturing as the curtain fell to a lavish concert of all instruments in the orchestra.

IV

THE DARKENING WOOD

THE QUEEN MOTHER, having been freed of any part in affairs of state, was now able to spend all her time worrying about her children. She observed that Louis was evading his religious duties; he had neither confessed nor communicated for a long time.

This meant only one thing, she thought. The worst had happened. Could it be possible that Henriette's condition —? For the first time in her life she could neither speak nor act, afraid that investigation would confirm her suspicions. When a reliable spy brought her the story of La Vallière, therefore, she was filled with conflicting feelings; annoyance at having been fooled, relief, shame at being relieved, and finally doubt as to the best means of defeating the new menace. She went to Henriette's apartments and created a scene, blaming her severely for not having supervised "that girl" more carefully.

Henriette was beside herself with indignation at being thus made accessory to the affair. As if the King's sudden abandonment of her were not enough, she was to accept the blame! She had looked forward to marriage for the freedom it would bring from her own mother's reprimands, and now she was being accused and persecuted by her mother-in-law.

They separated in a most unfriendly manner, and Philippe meanwhile was pouncing up and down the room talking about honor. Through some mental twist he had decided that Louis's passion for a mere servant was a reflection on his own dignity. Out she must go — and Louis would be sorry.

Henriette's typically female reaction was to feel betrayed, not by the King but by La Vallière. Yet she, a great princess, must not take revenge on such a nobody. To do so would raise the girl to the level of a rival, and would be admission at the same time that she cared about Louis. No, only one course was open; for the sake of appearances she must keep Louise in her service, but let her know indirectly what a little fool she was, what a mistake she had made. As for the King, he should detect no difference in her own aspect. Henriette gave him exactly six weeks to tire of his pitifully easy conquest of this little maid of honor. Then, let him try to breach the walls of her own cool friendship again! It would be futile if he were three times King of France and Navarre.

While the mood was on her Anne marched directly to her son and informed him of his duty to God, the State, and public opinion. As a rather weak afterthought she asked whether he had considered his wife's feelings.

Louis listened without much concern to the first exhortations, but promised that he would do his best to prevent Maria Theresa from learning anything about his private life.

This was not exactly what Anne had hoped to hear, but she had to accept it. She could not know how her maternal platitudes blunted on the shield of Mazarin's advice to Louis. Years before, the Cardinal had formulated a set of cynical but useful instructions for compromising between a ruler's duties and desires. No woman's words would ever get under their guard.

Loménie de Brienne was increasingly flirtatious with Louise. He flattered himself that his case was advancing very well; she showed little or no boredom in his company and seemed to listen to almost everything he said.

A new painter had recently arrived from Venice, Le Febvre, French in origin, but with foreign ideas. He painted people as gods and goddesses, or clothed as their patron saints, and had done an interpretation of Madame as Venus accompanied by Cupid, with Adonis hunting in the distance.

Brienne thought that Louise, who looked at once slumbrous and *spirituelle,* should be painted as Madeleine. Enthusiastically suggesting this to her in a sunny corridor one morning, he was interrupted by the approach of the King, and turned to appeal to him as a witness. Wasn't she a perfect type for Madeleine? he demanded, and added, "She has something of Greek statues in her look, which pleases me very much." Louise blushed and His Majesty passed by without answering.

Brienne was not stupid; he sensed something strained in the atmosphere, and later that same evening was made even more uncomfortable at the sight of La Vallière and the King in secluded conversation in a window embrasure. After a moment the King walked away, and Brienne, striving for nonchalance, asked Louise whether she had decided to follow his advice regarding her portrait.

Louis overheard, stopped, and came back. "No," he said firmly, "she's too young to be painted as a penitent. She must be painted as Diana."

Poor Brienne spent a sleepless night. But he had not yet met his ultimate embarrassment. Next morning, going about his secretarial duties, he was beckoned by his master into the adjoining room known as the Cabinet de Théagène et Chariclée. There the King shut and bolted the door, then, turning to his victim, asked politely, "Do you love her, Brienne?"

"Who, Sire? Mlle. de la Vallière?"

"Yes, I'm speaking of her."

A faltered excuse of some sort, and then Loménie lost all sense of relevance and good judgment and announced that he was a married man. Louis did not comment on this peculiar statement, merely leaned forward and fixed him with a look as the tiger does its prey. "Brienne, you love her! What are you lying for?"

"Ah, Sire, she pleases you more than me," Brienne stuttered, cracking completely, "and you love her."

"No matter who it is I love or don't love," said the King coldly, "let her portrait alone, and I'll be pleased."

The interview was over none too soon for Brienne, who sensed the approach of a swoon. Not long afterward Mlle. de la Vallière was painted as Diana, the artist adding for background interest an advancing figure of Acteon.

"And poor Acteon, that was I," Brienne commented ruefully to his memoirs.

It is doubtful that under the circumstances the King's secretary allowed himself the luxury of gossip, but by now the royal folly was common knowledge. In Louis's presence, fear prevented the dropping of a hint or even the lift of an eyebrow; but La Vallière could be freely discussed as she walked holding her head up around the Court, reserved and vulnerable.

She had been prepared for blame from Madame and was receiving instead a sort of disdainful tolerance. Her services were rarely called for. Montalais took over Louise's old duty of reading aloud, though her voice and expression were not so good.

Was she oversensitive, or were the other maids of honor somewhat surreptitious in their friendship, those days? In Madame's presence they scarcely spoke to her.

The Comte de Guiche saw that he must defer to the superior claims of the crown, and so withdrew, but not gracefully. He accused Louise of having deceived him to satisfy her own vanity, and went on to still more cutting insults. She was left shaken, struggling against tears of anger and sadness, aghast at the mirror he had held up. Could she really be so shallow and guilty? So now she had an enemy. But though she did not know it yet, she had another much more dangerous, Olympe de Soissons.

Mazarin had provided well for all his nieces, marrying them carefully and starting little orchards here and there planned to yield plums later. For Olympe he had found the rich and complaisant Comte de Soissons, who would have been no inconvenience if he had not repeatedly made her a mother. Children were, however, only a temporary handicap.

Mazarin had, in addition, got rid of the incumbent Superintendent of the Queen's Household and given the post to Olympe. It carried a good stipend and tremendous advantages; the Superintendent was allowed to live at the Louvre and held absolute power over the social functions of the royal Household. A clever manager could do as she pleased; her critics were few and usually did not remain long at Court.

The bloom which had briefly attracted Louis was gone, and now the Comtesse was only a short Italianate woman with a craving for power. She often consulted the fashionable sorceress La Voisin for beauty prescriptions. If these failed, there were potions and powders to be used on other people. Her hands were her only fine features; she had the habit of laying them at night on little pillows designed to accommodate each finger. During the day she avoided closing them, in order to prevent their skin from wrinkling.

Louis knew she was a typical Mazarin, an *intrigante*. He guessed that she would not like Louise, and therefore devoted some thought to placating her.

The Marquis de Vardes, First Gentleman of the Bedchamber and a Captain of the Swiss Guard, was just the man for the assignment. Big, hard, smooth, he was recently widowed but not inclined to self-pity, since his success with other men's wives was proverbial. And he was discreet; once he had hidden in a cellar for two days to avoid encountering the suspicious Duc de Roquelaure. No dishonor attached to him in this adventure, since it was understood his purpose was to protect the reputation of the Duchesse. In any case, his qualifications for the project Louis had in mind were excellent.

De Vardes looked on the seduction of the Comtesse de Soissons as a challenge to his abilities as a sportsman, accepted it, and went off at once to find her. If any man in France could turn her jealousy away from the King, it was he.

All these cross tides of purpose were forming vortices which would ultimately suck some swimmers down.

De Guiche at the age of twenty could not go long without some adventure in hand, and after leaving Louise went almost at once to sit at Henriette's feet.

Until now he and Madame had found no time to become well acquainted. Under the circumstances, to become acquainted was to become enamored. Both had recently been wounded by perfidious love; both were attractive; and their separate disillusion fused into something more exciting.

Philippe did not like this at all. De Guiche, who had been his boyhood favorite, seemed to be showing his true colors. Like all the rest, he was deserting to Henriette.

But even without Monsieur's pointed accusing finger society would have noticed the extravagance of Armand's behavior. He offered himself to his new idol like a sacrifice, presenting the knife and guiding her hand toward his heart, followed her around in melancholy, and talked wildly to his friends.

Louis was not amused. His own example was not to be imitated by every little courtier. For a few days he suffered the Comte's nonsense, and then sent him an order to leave Fontainebleau.

Everybody was sobered at this sign of the King's displeasure except the Venetian ambassador, who, somewhat lacking in insight, wrote home that the union of the French royal family was growing ever stronger.

Fouquet, the Minister of Finance, was a civilized intellectual, in middle age a little soft as the result of years of self-indulgence, but personally magnetic and genuinely loved by his friends, who were poets, playwrights, and philosophers. His approval of a man meant success; his hospitality was on a princely scale, and some of the best conversationalists in France flashed at each other across his dinner table. His respect for money was justified; so far it had bought everything he wanted.

His inclination was for mature ladies who knew how to create and receive pleasure, who could salt a familiar dish sometimes with humor, and who had no illusions about what might be hoped between men and women. Young girls were dangerous, likely to strip without warning to their naked souls, and, while trying on their jewelry and counting their money, weep and sigh and talk about love.

Yet he had seen the one called La Vallière riding through the forest as if the wind blew only on her, alone in the rattling conversing crowd; watched her surrender to the music at morning mass with a lowering of her long slanting eyelids. There was an interesting reserve about her, decidedly, like a poem that may be read on different levels.

He had learned that she came from a poor family barely within the aristocracy. That was good; it would make the most simple approach the most persuasive. He asked his friend Mme. du Plessis-Bellièvre to deliver a message.

Tactlessly, this lady chose to present Fouquet's compliments at a time when there were other people near Louise, and her response was overheard by the straining ears of Mlle. de Menneville.

Like something hot wrapped in a napkin, the story was hurried to the Queen Mother and shared with Madame and the Comtesse de Soissons, who happened to be in attendance. Picked up in crumbs by Mlle. de Fouilloux, it was given to another lady, La Loy, who happened to be a spy in Fouquet's pay.

As a result he knew within an hour what had happened to his invitation.

In her own chamber, stabbing the inkwell with outraged quill, Mme. du Plessis-Bellièvre was meanwhile writing him a note.

> *I can't move, from anger, when I think what that little La Vallière did to me. To capture her good will, I assured her of the greatness of her beauty, and then let her know that you were anxious to make sure she should lose nothing, and that you had twenty thousand pistoles for her. She became quite militant against me, saying that two hundred thousand pistoles would not be capable of making her make such a faux pas. And she repeated it with so much fierceness, even though I did everything I could to smooth things over before separating from her, so that I'm afraid she will say something to the King . . . Don't you think it would be apropos to forestall her by telling him that she asked you for money, and you refused? This would render all her statements suspect . . .*

But Fouquet was a gentleman by nature and long practice, and furthermore saw that such a course could lead only to disaster.

In any case, the gossip had already reached Louis.

No sign of warning appeared to the Finance Minister that evening, no presaging comet bloody in the serene violet of the sky over Vaux, no family specter lifting an empty sleeve on the staircase; no black dog of ill omen came with clicking claws to confront him with its red smile where he stood thinking in the middle of the torchlit corridor — perhaps because it was already too late.

The climax of the summer festivals came on August 17 with Fouquet's party at Vaux-le-Vicomte. His builders and landscape architects had been busy for several years turning the castle secluded in woods near Melun into the most magnificent residence in France, and now their accomplishments were to be shown the King and the whole Court.

All became wordless with amazement on entering the park that morning. Powerful fountains sent their jets and cataracts into the sunlight, throwing off opalescent spray. Such luxurious fountains were a novelty Louis himself was not yet able to afford. To achieve them, Fouquet explained with rueful good humor, he had been forced to buy and raze three villages and divert their water supply from five leagues away into his reservoirs of Italian marble.

Reflected in its surrounding water the kingly castle looked out over descending balustraded terraces onto perfect gardens; far-off Olympian statues made gestures of obeisance toward the strolling company.

"I shall never again, sir, invite you to visit me," Louis said coldly. "You would find yourself inconvenienced." But he let himself be escorted through the rest of the grounds and constructions to see staircases and columns, rare birds and plants, bas-reliefs, vases, and paintings.

One of these in Fouquet's private cabinet made him pause; it portrayed a naked nymph, blond and slender. Beneath it was a line borrowed from La Fontaine, "Grace more beautiful than beauty." And the face? One could not be sure who had been the model, but there was a striking, if coincidental, resemblance to La Vallière. The King had no doubt whatever that Fouquet had been struck by it.

Ominously silent, he went on through the large octagonal salon

with its high vaulted ceiling and mosaic floor like a carpet of
arabesques, birds, butterflies, flowers, and fruit, and through the
smaller buildings behind the castle. These were decorated in the
same fashion and housed baths, a theater, a paume ground, swings,
a chapel, and billiard rooms, and were furnished with new things
of the utmost richness. No roulette table nor sedan chair showed
so much as a scratch in its lacquer.

Later the King stood with his gentlemen in his appointed bedchamber while their host called attention to the view from the
window. A cloud mass passing under the sun cast a moving pastel
bloom on the tapestry of lawns and flower beds, the serene reflecting pools, the leaping fountains, and the forest beyond.

"What a shame," Louis said, "that such a fine landscape should
be marred by a blighted space." All heads turned in the direction
indicated. There was indeed a whitish spot among the trees. Fouquet said nothing, but left the royal presence as soon as possible
and hurried to his household offices as if on business.

During this time the ladies had been in the grand salon wandering among the little gilded stalls where trinkets were being distributed, notebooks and pocket mirrors, gloves, knives and scissors,
purses, fans, sweetmeats, pastilles, and perfumes.

For the first of the evening entertainments a theater had been
built under a canopy of pines among the orange groves and fountains. Molière's *Les Fâcheux* (*The Bores*) had been commissioned.

As a play it was slight, being made of loosely connected scenes
which parodied familiar personalities at Court, a device which from
time to time caused islands of offended silence in the general hilar-
ity of the audience; but the interludes raised the performance to the
level of a spectacle. At one moment twenty water jets shot colored
light into the darkness; at another, long-haired naiads rose out of
the rocks, and a shell slowly opened to reveal the shapely reclining
actress Madeleine Béjart. It was said Molière wished to marry her
younger sister, Armande, but that she found the patronage of noblemen financially more profitable.

Louis took the playwright aside and praised him for the performance. "But," he said, "there's an original you haven't copied yet."

Molière smiled, bowed, and drifted unobtrusively within eaves-dropping distance of the Marquis de Saucourt, who was in the proc-ess of numbing a listener with one of his hunting stories. A new Bore was about to be immortalized in the drama.

Madame, in whose honor the fête was said to be given, was not well, and watched the festivities from a litter. Her health was un-dependable at best, and now her symptoms, freely discussed by the courtiers, seemed to indicate pregnancy.

All observers saw that His Majesty danced often that night with Mlle. de la Vallière. Though their talk was circumspect, no more than polite, they could not meet without noticeably charging the atmosphere, and in intervals of separation their glances kept search-ing and catching.

Toward morning, during an intermission of the orchestra, the King took his partner's hand and led her out of the salon. They strolled through rooms lit by hanging crystal mountains of chande-liers, over Persian carpets, between groups of courtiers pausing in conversation and pretending not to spy. They came to a fireplace carved with Fouquet's armorial bearings and stopped. Two others joined them, respectfully behind, Colbert and the poet Pélisson, Fouquet's secretary, who had spoken the prologue of the evening's play.

A symbolic squirrel climbed a tree above the motto *"Quo non ascendam?"*

"What does it mean?" Louise asked.

Smoothly Colbert answered, "It means, Mademoiselle, 'To what height may I not attain?' " He paused, then added, "It is under-stood by those who know the boldness of the squirrel — or that of his master."

Louis bit his lip and looked sharply at Colbert as if to speak, but changed his mind.

Pélisson, going red, spoke to the King but with his eye fixed on Colbert. "Your Majesty has probably not remarked that in every instance the squirrel is pursued by an adder." With this he bowed and went away.

Ever since his arrival at Vaux the King had been angry. Now

he was near losing control. "Get me D'Artagnan," he said. He would have the squirrel Fouquet arrested at once, and dig out his stolen hoard. Colbert, calm as usual, remarked that it would be exceedingly impolitic to arrest their host in his own house, and urged Louis to give the matter a little more time and thought. Reluctantly the King let himself be put off for the moment. But his patience would not last much longer; evidence turned up in May had convinced him that Fouquet's fortune came from the theft and misuse of government funds, and the reckoning was therefore years overdue.

Embezzlement alone, being an offense with the dignity of a certain tradition behind it, might be treated with some leniency. But Fouquet had put himself beyond the reach of mercy by two other absolutely unforgivable crimes; he had outdone his sovereign in splendor and flaunted his arrogant motto as if to advertise the fact; and he had tried to buy the royal mistress. He was doomed.

When the King rose next morning at the hour of levee, to be dressed by his concourse of favored nobles, his attention was called to the window and the view he had criticized on arriving the day before. Harmonious foliage covered the landscape; the clearing was gone.

It was explained that M. Fouquet had called out his workmen and they had been busy all night transplanting trees to correct the vista to His Majesty's taste.

"Such extravagance is criminal," Louis said shortly, and turned to the selection of a cravat pin from the presented tray.

Four uneventful days passed after the fête at Vaux. To the courtiers Fontainebleau seemed, by comparison with the glory they had left, antiquated and poorly furnished, and they greeted M. Fouquet with new respect as he went to and from the ministerial chambers.

Then the King ordered the Court to prepare for a journey to Nantes. It was important to his health, he said, to get away from business, and this would be a fine opportunity to show the city to the Queen.

The Ministers went on ahead of the royal party, making sport of the excursion. Fouquet and his friend Hughes de Lyonne embarked, joking, in a barge with eight rowers, and Colbert pushed off in the next.

It was a breezy exhilarating day, and the two boats shot down the river in a race, oars lifting and cutting clean as swords. The Marquis de Vardes watched them go and said with a strange smile, "One of those two is going to suffer shipwreck at Nantes."

Next day the King followed by post with several friends, including his new favorite, Péguilain, a terrible little marquis whose enemies said, though not in his presence, that he looked like a skinned cat. His sarcasm was so scathing, his behavior so tricky and savage, that nobody at Court dared provoke him. Louis enjoyed his company greatly, as a rule. But on this trip the King was preoccupied and unresponsive. Immediately on arrival at Nantes he sent Brienne to ask whether Chancellor Le Tellier had arrived, and to inquire regarding the health of M. Fouquet.

Brienne found the Minister of Finance in bed with a slight fever but not seriously sick. The window curtains were drawn, a fire burned in the grate in spite of the summer weather outside, and Fouquet, drinking burnt brandy and asses' milk for his ills, received the secretary inside the *ruelle* of his bed.

"What news from Court?"

Brienne hesitated. "It is said that you are about to be arrested."

Fouquet looked up in surprise but finished his drink. "My dear young friend, you are wrong."

"I wish I could think so."

"Oh, you are. Someone is to be arrested, it's true, but it will be M. Colbert."

"Colbert?" Brienne asked in amazement.

"Yes. I myself have had charge of the orders that will take him to the Château of Angers, and it was Pélisson who paid the workmen entrusted to place the prison beyond all chance of assault."

Brienne left, mystified. But in the course of the day the King's manner convinced him that gossip was right, and that it was the Minister of Finance who sat between the teeth of the trap he had helped to weld. Louis referred to him several times merely as "Fouquet," omitting the courtesy "Monsieur," and sent word by another messenger that he wished to see him early next morning before the hunt.

Obediently at six o'clock Fouquet arrived at the castle, well groomed and perfumed to attend his master, and they conferred uneventfully on business matters for half an hour.

Returning afterward through the gallery, Fouquet and his valet were met by a friend, M. de la Feuillade, who, shaken and furtive, took his arm and whispered, "Orders are out against you. I can say no more — but my coach is in the courtyard. Take it and escape. God help you."

Running together, he and the valet found the promised coach, sprang in and yanked the curtains shut, and went careening away without having encountered any pursuers.

But, at a corner in the town where the main street meets an alley, another carriage was waiting. From behind it, four musketeers stepped forward and blocked the street. Now a man well known to Fouquet for his courage and good manners came forward, bowed, and apologized for the inconvenience he was about to occasion.

"Good morning, M. d'Artagnan," the Minister said with a rather bleak smile, and returned the bow. Then he changed coaches for the long ride to the escape-proof prison of Angers.

Behind, in the early morning crowd of curious citizens, Fouquet's valet stood horrified and helpless, then turned and ran back toward the castle. He laid hands on one of the private relays always kept ready for an emergency, and left for Paris at a gallop. He was a strong young man and rode so well that Fouquet's friends there were thrown into a state of grief and shock a full twelve hours before the King's courier came to deliver news of the arrest to Anne of Austria.

In that short time before the officials reached Vaux to place seals on all the Minister's property, remove his wife and children to Limoges, and collect evidence of his guilt, his distraught friends wavered and disagreed about their proper course of action. Mme. du Plessis-Bellièvre made the fatal mistake of not burning Fouquet's private papers, of which there was a huge mass, since he had made a practice of saving every communication that reached his hands. These letters and records brought to Fontainebleau a few days later proved extremely interesting to Louis.

The knowledge that they were in his possession caused terror and embarrassment to sweep the entire Court, and like the symptoms of a contagious disease, paleness and sweating came on any courtier singled out for more than momentary scrutiny by the King. The revelations of the papers left few great names unsmirched. But Louis was too well pleased with his material gains to waste much time in hunting down the only moderately begrimed. He had not guessed that Fouquet was so rich; each day brought new confiscations, large and small.

Thousands of blossoming orange trees were removed from Vaux and taken to Versailles. It was justice; in the end Versailles would make Vaux look like a gardener's cottage.

Some changes were made in the staff. Colbert was appointed Minister of Finance, and Michel le Tellier obtained for his eldest son, the Marquis de Louvois, survivorship of the office of Secretary of State. Progress was being made toward a competent and loyal cabinet, grateful to the King, convinced of his greatness. He foresaw a time when the government could be used like a machine to work whatever he wished.

The rising sun gathered strength, blazing toward midmorning.

When the King left for Nantes, Fontainebleau seemed to settle into melancholy. It had been officially announced that Madame was to have a child. She lay in bed most of the day while Anne-Constance de Montalais, who was determinedly becoming her confidante, read to her out of Montaigne's *Essays*.

Louise, seldom called to wait on her mistress, walked alone in the gardens which were beginning to show an autumn beige among the greenery, or stayed in her steep little room turning her thoughts over. These were by now worn smooth, and had, like coins, only two faces.

Every night Anne-Constance, full of energy and importance,

came in to apprise her of new developments in the De Guiche affair. It seemed Monsieur was causing all sorts of trouble, though he knew Madame had returned Armand's letters unopened. He was sulky, pestered her nearly to madness over trifles, and had quarreled with the Princesse de Monaco. The poor girl had never encouraged her brother's pretensions, as both she and Henriette insisted, but now her feelings were so hurt by Monsieur's insults that she was packing her boxes and going home to her husband.

Anne of Austria would have taken advantage of the Court's absence to get rid of Louise, had it not been for a growing fear of her son, who was proving himself with every act the complete monarch. A year earlier she would not have hesitated to order this maid of honor or any other off to a convent; but now she dared no more than to freeze "that girl" with an occasional glare and ostracize from her own circle anybody suspected of speaking to her.

Montalais enjoyed the situation. It surrounded Louise with an atmosphere of intrigue, made her need friendship and sympathy, created secrets. Her only annoyance was that Louise refused to tell any details of her intimacy with His Majesty. This was hardly a fair exchange of confidence, since Anne-Constance was perfectly frank in discussing her own lover, Malicorne. Still, she knew Louise had nobody else to talk to, and with patience one might learn all.

The maid of honor D'Artigny had lost, it seemed, both maidenhood and honor. Her mother arrived suddenly and removed her from Court without any reasonable explanation. As usual Montalais knew more about the matter than anyone else; she found a letter written by D'Artigny to the father of her expected child, and took it to Henriette.

Madame's nerves were frayed already; she had enough difficulties of her own without having to endure the vagaries of the maids, and sent a brusque note to D'Artigny in her retreat to let her know she was banished for good. D'Artigny appealed to the only person likely to give her any sympathy — La Vallière.

Louise, herself seriously out of favor, could do nothing but put the matter before the King as soon as he returned. Whether he commanded or persuaded Madame to leniency was never made public, but as a result of their talk D'Artigny was saved. She was not to return until some months later, pale, subdued, and apparently devoted to Louise. But between her and the traitor Montalais there could be only war.

After Nantes, there were no more balls and ballets. Spontaneous gaiety was gone; Madame was sick and sad, De Guiche banished, Mme. de Monaco gone. And Louis had shown himself tyrannical, unmoved by the poetic pleas of Fouquet's friends. He was not, after all, Amadis the perfect knight; and now he knew all his courtiers better than he had at the beginning of the year. Such a June could never come again in this reign.

Maria Theresa on the verge of motherhood never appeared in public except to accompany her mother-in-law on religious visits around the neighborhood. Dressed in stately black as if for mourning, they went from one devotion to another.

Anne's thwarted wish for revenge on Louise changed direction and became an obsessive determination to protect Maria Theresa. To ensure her permanent ignorance, all attendants must be chosen for maturity, discretion, and absolute fidelity. Luckily the Queen had no natural curiosity, or the project would have been impossible. A conspiracy of silence must surround her, filtering out all careless talk.

Still Louis did not confess or communicate. Every day after his eight hours of work were finished he went hunting, and Louise went with him, followed by a small group of familiars put in his confidence.

"The King was too much in love," De Choisy said, "to make of it an impenetrable mystery."

V

EXILE

L O U I S E'S F R E E D O M was illusory. Ignored or not by her mistress, she remained a servant, subject to command. In mid-September Madame decided she would feel better in her own house with her mother close at hand, and accordingly, Monsieur's household began preparations for the departure to Saint-Cloud. It was a crisis for the King, who could not bear to let Louise go, yet could not keep her without in effect announcing her status, something he was still too bound by respect for his mother and convention to do.

Louise herself had, furthermore, an unconquerable dread of publicity. To be suspected of being the King's mistress was inevitable, but to set up her own household and appear boldly in character was beyond her nerve. When he rashly offered to acknowledge her and put an end to the secrecy and inconvenience she fell into a panic of refusal. He accused her of being ashamed of him, but realized there was no real choice to be made. While Louise remained in Henriette's service she was protected to some extent from the malicious plotting of little enemies. At Court she would be friendless. Some women might flourish among the challenges of such a situation, but not Louise, too gentle to hit back, too truthful to suspect a liar.

After she left, the King endured his loneliness for a time with stoicism. Then he rose early one morning after a sleepless night, mounted his horse, and left at a gallop for Vincennes, followed by only the sketchiest equipage. Since Vincennes was not his real goal, his inspection of the work there was swift and perfunctory.

From Vincennes he rode equally hard to Paris, stopped to look without interest at the constructions going up in the court of the Tuileries, and was once more on the road to Saint-Cloud.

Philippe was surprised and not especially pleased at this unheralded visit from his brother, but invited him to stay for supper. Having accomplished his purpose — half an hour's conversation with Louise — and almost killed his men with the rigorous journey, Louis rode back to Fontainebleau that same evening. He had covered more than forty leagues since dawn.

The end of summer brought a series of violent storms that destroyed the crops all over France, and news from the provinces predicted famine for the coming winter — a threat too widespread and imminent to be met adequately by the government, though the council met for long sessions of consideration.

The Fouquet affair, too, was still causing scattered trouble; there were warnings and alarms, sudden inexplicable departures from Court, tales of extortion and blackmail, and occasional arrests. Mme. de Sévigné had begun to mobilize the ex-minister's old friends in his defense, though nobody knew yet when the trial would take place.

Madame did not find the peace of mind she had hoped for in seclusion, and now beginning to feel better physically, decided to rejoin the Court for the rest of the autumn season. Her friends assured her that such exile as she was presently imposing on herself would be very bad for her unborn son; it might give him hermitlike tendencies. Nobody mentioned that De Guiche had returned from banishment, but she knew.

It was an October to belie all recent storms, and Louise meeting her lover again went to the forest to ride under the yellowing leaves, over the bronze and copper drifts that seemed to give off with their bitter perfume gusts of dusty light.

Their solitude was a luxury to be tasted to the last minute, remembered, and anticipated again with profound joy, an experience so moving as almost to stop words, in spite of all there was to say.

It was happiness distilled and given meaning as air may be by a single drop of death, by the knowledge that it was limited.

Would it be different, Louise wondered, if like ordinary people she and Louis were free to see each other often, even to marry? The mind could not gather in such a thought. Yes, she would be religious in this no matter what the conditions of their birth and encounter might have been. Love was not what she had always supposed — a certain common complaint — it was herself.

M. d'Estrades, the French ambassador in London, went out in his carriage on September 30 to meet the Swedish ambassador on the occasion of his official entry to the city. His arrival coincided with that of the Spanish representative, the Baron de Vateville, a fact which instantly caused belligerence and put all questions of the Scandinavian welcome in the background.

Driving ahead, D'Estrades was blocked by De Vateville's servants, and in a temper he ordered his driver to proceed at all costs; it was a matter not of personal honor alone but of patriotism. At once the servants were on each other with fists, staves, and swords; some fell and were hurt by the trampling of the excited English crowd. De Vateville had the larger retinue and also gained the favor of the French-hating mob, and in a few minutes D'Estrades' forces were wounded or dispersed and his carriage horses killed and left lying in the traces.

All this was described without any understatement in a letter to Louis and received the next week at Fontainebleau, just as the company was settling down to a peaceful game of omber in Monsieur's firelit salon.

The King took the dispatches and withdrew to a nearby writing table to look them over. In an instant he was up again, hitting the top so hard that the inkwell rattled, and striding to wave the papers at Saint-Aignan and Le Tellier.

"Here's news for you, gentlemen. Our ambassador in London has been publicly insulted by the Spanish envoy." He went on as they read. "What do you think of this, gentlemen? Should I wait to answer this insult from my father-in-law till my mustache is as long as his? No doubt he thinks we're still under Mazarin's thumb."

"I beg, Sire, that you consider the matter and do nothing in haste," Le Tellier put in.

"M. le Tellier, let my ambassador in Madrid leave the city immediately and let the Spanish ambassador here leave Paris within twenty-four hours." Halfway down the room he wheeled and came back. "The conferences in Flanders are at an end, of course. And it should be made perfectly clear to Spain that unless the superiority of the French crown is made known, publicly, she may hold herself prepared for war."

Hesitating as if to remonstrate, Le Tellier instead gave in, bowed, and left the room. Now Louis turned to his wife and, pointing a finger, forbade her to hold any further communication with Madrid.

The Queen's Spanish temper did not often express itself, but she had been brought up to regard her father as next to God, and this was a threat to her deepest allegiance. She rose now, though with a flooding blush, faced the King, and to the astonishment of all witnesses, declared herself firmly on the Spanish side. Louis was taken aback, but stared her down. Then he moved away to the other end of the salon and took up the subject of his conversation with the ladies where it had been broken by the messenger's interruption.

This quarrel with Maria Theresa, as Louis chose to regard it, lasted for several weeks. He welcomed it as a chance to escape her company completely and spend all his free time with Louise.

The Queen was wretched; having rediscovered pride, like an old doll, she hugged it to herself and wept.

Philip IV, duly threatened with a reopening of the war, called the Baron de Vateville home from London, and it was understood he had charged his ambassador in Paris to make formal apology. Louis was grimly jubilant at the news. It proved dramatically that Spain was afraid of France. He would put the knowledge to good use.

On November 1 all the royal physicians and a great many sightseers gathered to watch the Queen in labor. It was evident that she would have a hard time. Louis, who had risen at five to confess and communicate, sat at her bedside "sensibly penetrated with grief" as priests, astrologers, and all the nobility entitled by rank to be present crowded close over the *ruelle* and passed continually back and forth from the chamber to the chapel.

Frightened by her pains, Maria Theresa bawled, "I don't want a baby! I want to die!" and threw herself from side to side so that her limbs had to be secured by the ladies-in-waiting.

Toward the end she quieted, and the priests moved a step forward thinking she was on the verge of death. But it was only exhaustion; at noon she suddenly gave birth to a boy.

The child was immediately bundled up and laid in his father's arms, and stepping outside into the Cour Ovale, Louis raised him high with pride and tenderness before the crowd. Wild cheering burst forth, and spectators shed tears and beat each other on the back in an orgy of emotion, a spectacle which was later commented on a little acidly by the Spanish ambassador. The French had loved Louis before; now that he had fathered a dauphin, they worshiped him.

Louise saw from an upstairs window the King's great laugh of triumph, and stood back behind the curtain. This was a day in which she could have no share. It would never be in her power to give Louis anything a fraction so valuable as what he held.

From Fontainebleau, where fireworks scribbled the night sky and fountains spurted wine for three days, rejoicing spread out into all provinces of the kingdom.

Queen Henrietta of England was invited to stand as godmother to the Dauphin, and named him Louis Toussaint because of his birth on All Saints' Day. He was sure to have a pious and lucky life.

Two weeks later, Philippe and his followers returned to set up winter housekeeping in the Tuileries.

Madame in her litter was surreptitiously reading a packet of letters from the Comte de Guiche which Montalais had dropped into her lap at departure. The dissipations of summer followed by her long illness had ruined Henriette's beauty, always dependent on color and sparkle. She was skeletally thin and constantly convulsed with coughing.

Most of her time was spent in bed, but occasionally on a good afternoon she would take advantage of the sunshine and drive, well bundled in shawls, to the Cours-la-Reine, wanly cheered by the conversation of her English friend, Frances Stewart, and the faithful Madeleine de la Fayette. The maids of honor in their black velvet masks and scented gloves followed in another carriage.

Through the elms the late November light was the yellow of old parchment etched with a black tracery of twigs to which a few leaves still clung. Only when one of the royal family drove through was there any confusion of traffic in the Cours, which could hold a hundred carriages easily. At these times etiquette demanded the stopping of all other vehicles and low bows at the window.

Sometimes, feeling strong enough, Madame would prolong the ride through the city to the river baths at Saint-Bernard's gate where a few eccentrics still waded in spite of the lateness of the season, or to the vast gardens of the Arsenal, abandoned and autumnal now with storm-broken fronds from the old trees planted by Henri IV. And once they turned toward the north end of the Pont-Neuf to see the vulgar but fascinating sights at the Samaritaine where, on the hour, a Jack-o'-the-clock struck his sonorous gong, four lions rolled their eyes, and all the time an organ was playing hymn tunes while angels and the Magi circled around it plucking at harps and blowing trumpets.

In the meantime the King and Queen were at Notre Dame de Chartres on a pilgrimage of thanksgiving for her safe delivery.

Anne of Austria was beginning to speak confidently of her son's return to religion, and the rumors which are always running around palaces, tireless as mice, said His Majesty had sworn at the altar to give up youthful follies and rededicate his life to duty.

The rumors were not true. Louis, returning to Paris after an absence of fifteen days, deposited his wife at the Louvre and hurried to the Tuileries to Louise. He never would leave her again, he said. Such separations were too terrible a torture.

By this time Henriette was seriously sick with her wasting disease and not able to leave her bed.

Anxious letters of inquiry began arriving from Charles II regarding his beloved Minette, and all of society came to visit, play cards, eat refreshments at the patient's bedside, and confirm what they had heard about her shocking alteration. Louis came too, every day, with gay talk and brotherly advice, but his visits were never long; he said he feared tiring her. She did not reply with justified sarcasm that these scruples did not extend to her maids of honor. Everyone knew he would be with Louise for the rest of the afternoon.

"All doors remained open," said Mme. de la Fayette, "but one was as far from entering as if they had been barred with brass." The King's privacy was inviolate.

Since the birth of her son the Queen had been brooding on the little she knew of Louis's life in the outside world beyond her bedroom. Gradually she began to understand that she was the victim of a conspiracy. Everybody was trying to prevent her from guessing he was interested in another woman. Didn't he go to the Tuileries every afternoon? She wept and went into a decline, all her energy gathered into a tight little knot of hatred for her suspected rival, Henriette. Angrily she struck aside her mother-in-law's assurances that she was misled. Louis acted like a man in love — that was the final testimony. A blind woman could have guessed.

Louis could have fooled her back into complacency, but not without interrupting his visits to Louise, and this was not to be considered. He continued as before, nagged by his mother, reproached by Maria Theresa's silent tears, and resented by Henriette, who was thus belatedly in trouble with the Queen. Her natural reaction was to treat Louise with freezing coldness and subject her to a variety of small public humiliations.

Anne-Constance de Montalais, the accomplished *intrigante,* was safe now in Madame's favor. She had made herself indispensable to the Comte de Guiche as a spy and carrier of messages, and being more intelligent than Monsieur was able not only to foil his investigations but to turn them into comedy.

Madame, helpless in bed, could not combat the force of Montalais's personality, the appeal of her insinuations, the comfort of her many pleasant skills. When De Guiche had learned of Madame's danger he had given way to an outburst of grief that startled his friends and sent several of them hurrying to the patient with first-hand accounts. Montalais made good use of the anecdote there-after; it could be applied as subtle flattery at the right moment, or to draw a tear, or merely as a reminder of the debt to Cupid. She would tend the weak plant of this love affair until it became a jungle.

The King, from long experience, knew Montalais's type — the girl who, denied a leading role in Court life, must gain self-importance by stirring up trouble among the great. He forbade Louise to associate with her, but obedience was impossible. In public she complied, "but Montalais passed entire nights with her and was often there during the day."

The girl D'Artigny sometimes joined them. Like Anne-Constance she was intelligent but unimportant, and therefore avid for vicarious adventure. These two would have hated each other even if it had not been for Montalais's earlier treachery; they were too much alike to be friends.

Wanting to see Louise gorgeously dressed, Louis was not to be prevented from sending her presents. Pressed, however, he had to give in to her argument that any display would be likely to end in a crisis, perhaps with her being discharged from Madame's service. He satisfied himself to some extent with sending his equerry to inquire each evening what colors Louise would wear on the morrow, and matching them in his own costume. It was a secret homage, pointless but comforting to the participants.

Only at night with the door locked would Louise try on her diamond pendants, looking a little sidelong in the mirror — diamonds made her more beautiful than she was.

Spain's readiness to yield in the Affaire d'Estrades had surprised Louis, as the sudden toppling of a stout opponent surprises a wrestler who has not yet used his full force. If the old worst enemy was so weak, why should France fear any others? It was hard for Louis to withhold his power; he would not wait much longer to challenge and overcome.

Ships of all nations were accustomed to yield a salute to British men-of-war; this seemed to Louis in his changed mood an unnecessary ceremony, and he had Madame notify her brother Charles that France would no longer continue this out-of-date practice. Charles responded vigorously.

Whithall
23 Decem., 1661

I receaved yours of the 27th so late this night, and the post being ready to goe, that I have only time to tell you that I extremely wonder at that which you writ to me of, for certainly never any ships refused to strike their pavilion when they met any ships belonging to the Crowne of England. This is a right so well known, and never disputed by any kinge before, that, if I should have it questioned now, I must conclude it to be a querelle d'Allemand . . .

Louis was annoyed by Charles's attitude, but had no wish to provoke a war with his cousin over such a minor matter. He was too much occupied, anyway, with trouble at home that winter to seek it afield. Severe cold following the bad harvest, high taxes, and the exorbitant cost of foreign grain had sunk the people in disease and near-starvation.

Sickened and conscience-stricken at the sights he saw in the frozen filth of the city, he began work on his long-planned financial reform. By spring he would be ready to grant a four million reduction in taxes; meanwhile he did what he could for the immediate needs of the poor at his gates. The halls of the Louvre were turned into a storehouse of foreign grain and sold at cheap rates to the Paris citizens, and thousands of loaves of bread were given away every day at the doors of the Tuileries, some by the hands of the two queens themselves.

The Princesse de Conti sold her jewels and gave the proceeds to the hospitals; other noble ladies moved by her example devised their own charities.

That Christmas brought something new in the way of universal edification. The great princess, Mme. de Longueville, famous for her cleverness, beauty, and scandalous exploits of gallantry, made a general confession of her faults — "stirring the dung heap of these crimes" — and retired forever from the world into a life of religious contemplation.

Some blamed her, others were filled with a sort of curious envy. What could it mean, Louise wondered, to throw away the colorful various virile world with such an unhesitating gesture? She kept the phenomenon for her imagination to work on, trying to understand.

Henriette wrote to Charles early in the new year:

> *I would not lose this opportunity of writing to you by Mrs. Stewart, who is taking over her daughter to become one of the Queen, your wife's, future maids. If this were not the reason for her departure, I should be very unwilling to let her go, for she is the prettiest girl in the world, and one of the best fitted of any I know to adorn a court . . .*

Thus Madame sent her excitable brother one of the deep sorrows of his life. This prettiest girl in the world was a prude who would not hesitate to reject his love, before many months were past, and ruin his pride.

In the meantime his marriage with the Infanta of Portugal, Catherine of Braganza, was being concluded, and she would arrive at Whitehall early the next spring. It was an occasion for national celebration.

In Paris the winter social season continued brilliant as always. Madame lay on her couch day after day receiving guests and watching performances of plays and ballets, starting a new fashion with loops of yellow satin ribbon in her hair to match her sophisticated négligée, playing rhyming games with the season's wits, and receiving homage. She was fully entertained.

At the Tuileries on January 5 the King gave a dinner for the traditional Feast of Kings, honoring his mother and Maria Theresa.

That same month Corneille's *La Toison d'Or* (*The Golden Fleece*) had its first performance, and Monsieur gave the most elaborate ball of the winter.

Here Louise met her old friends again, the Mlles. de Valois and d'Alençon. There was a great deal to talk about, and almost as much to hold back. Memories of the childish adventures at Blois flooded back; the escape of one silly reminiscence started others, and then laughter from all of them. Perhaps it was a sense of that momentary disloyalty that made Louise buy a surprise for Louis soon after. It was much more expensive than she could afford, a coat trimmed with fur and accompanied by a note.

The answer came promptly back: "Yes, my darling! You are indeed in a position to make me presents. I accept them with great joy at your hands, for it is the possession of your heart which causes me to regard all others with pleasure. Be a little impatient to see me dressed in the coat which you have given me." He wore it for fifteen days in succession.

Early in February the Court gathered at the Tuileries to see a long-planned spectacle, the ballet *Hercules Amoureux* (*Amorous Hercules*). It was a performance which would have fully satisfied the old connoisseur Mazarin, who had commissioned it three years earlier, sending to Rome, Turin, Florence, and Venice for the right music and hiring the famous engineer Gaspare Vigorani to lift scenic effects into the supernatural.

A complete opera was included in the six-hour event, but for the audience even this was eclipsed by the décor of the new theater itself, the results of Vigorani's machines, and the thrill of seeing the King and Queen dance together in the second entry.

Little beyond an air of dignity was required of Maria Theresa in her role of the House of Austria, and this she achieved to admiration. Louis danced also in most of the other entries, appearing as the Sun in a magnificent golden wig, the masterpiece of Mme. Touzé. He had excused Louise from the cast with reluctance, reminding her that the time must come when she would have to face the curiosity of the Court openly, and he hoped gloriously. She should soon begin to prepare herself for her destined place in society.

LOUISE DE LA VALLIÈRE AND HER CHILDREN,
ANNE-MARIE AND LOUIS
from a painting by Mignard
(Versailles. Bulloz photograph)

LOUIS XIV
from a painting by Le Brun
(Douai Museum. Bulloz photograph)

Benserade's verses brought smiles from the knowing, as usual. For the ladies' man De Guiche, appropriately cast as the Hour of Silence, he had a warning.

In the community of belles
One cannot always be
The Hour of Recreation —
To preserve their good will,
You shall be the Hour of Silence.

Monsieur, as Hymen, was complimented. Most of the evening's praise was heaped on Athénaïs de Tonnay-Charente, one of Madame's circle, who at twenty-one was beginning to be described as the most fascinating woman in France. She had two sisters who might have disputed the title with her, but the more beautiful of these was in a convent, the other away from Court. All three were likewise distinguished for their mental sharpness. Wit was a traditional attribute of their ancient family, the Mortémarts.

So it was with some justification that Athénaïs felt herself designed by nature to become the King's mate. But her burning charms were focused on Louis without noticeable effect during the rehearsals and consummation of *Hercules Amoureux.* His thoughts were elsewhere.

Louise-Marguerite de Guiche, Armand's wife, got only a rather snide quatrain from the librettist. Why, he asked, had this young woman had no babies? It was an idle question; everyone knew the answer — her husband had rarely been to visit her since their marriage five years before. She was now twenty, and, it was said, still in love with him.

Hercules Amoureux was altogether too brilliant a success to be abandoned after only one performance, so it was revived at frequent intervals during the rest of the winter and spring. The Queen had to give up her part on account of pregnancy; there was the constant danger that, never very sure-footed, she might fall down.

Madame was by now well enough to step into such a comparatively sedentary role, and did so with the style which had once made an admirer remark, "She has wit even in her toes."

At midwinter Molière married his ingénue, Armande Béjart of the angel face and sullen disposition. All their friends thought this an unpromising match but did not try to dissuade the adoring bridegroom. Armande was nineteen years old, he forty. Madame attended the wedding at their parish church of Saint-Germain de l'Auxerrois, and was lavish of gifts and good wishes.

There was the season's usual mischief and brawling among the hot young nobles with nothing to defend but their veering honor. Louis's edict against dueling was, he knew, generally disregarded, and it was time for an example.

Two of Monsieur's favorites provided it. At the Palais-Royal the Prince de Chalais and the Marquis de Noirmoutier whipped out their swords in the course of an argument, and somehow one of them killed a brother of the powerful Duc de Beauvilliers. Cooled at the thought of probable penalties, they fled immediately to England and took refuge with King Charles.

Monsieur complained of Louis's hardheartedness at refusing forgiveness and even tried to enlist his brother-in-law's help in getting his friends home again. Charles good-naturedly sent an envoy on their behalf to Louis, who was then at Calais inspecting frontier fortifications, but the King spoke so strongly to Monsieur that even he was quelled, and the envoy went back to England without having introduced the subject.

Chalais subsequently died in exile; Noirmoutier was allowed to return to France but not to Court, and was therefore as good as dead to himself, his friends, and Athénaïs de Tonnay-Charente, whom he loved.

Louis was becoming intolerant of restraint of any sort, now that he had discovered how to command with a look, overcome opposition with a mere word. But he was still defeated by the problem of Louise. He loathed the furtive inconvenience of having to make love to her in sitting rooms, in full dress. It savored somehow of footmen and chambermaids. He told her to pretend illness and stay in her own bedroom, and so was able to visit her there for a few days. It was flagrant, but more worthy of his dignity than the antechamber encounters. Thus a new phase of the affair began. Shutting herself away saved Louise direct attention, but at the same time made her situation obvious to the world.

The King's ardor amounted to obsession, preventing rest, and a bust sculptured at this period by Bernini shows the face of a young Don Juan worn out by unslaked passion, muscles drawn tight, cheeks hollow, nostrils distended. This partly frustrated force carried over into everything he did, made him work his servants as relentlessly as himself and drive his body to perfection in difficult feats of athletics.

Anne, concerned about his health, lectured him continually. Lent with its abstinences would not check him this year, but he listened with respect to the voice of a new preacher in the royal chapel.

The Abbé Bossuet had an eye penetrating as God's, and his blame for the vices of the great cut sharply through the metaphorical adornments of fashionable sermonizing. Not even Louis was left out of the examples — a fact he approved of, on the whole.

The Court, always ready to fall under the spell of a good preacher, packed the chapel for the Lenten sermons. Bossuet's poetic language and organlike voice gave every listener the impression that his own conscience was being fondled by its sensual power. Mme. de Sévigné was transported by him, as were older and more austere ladies. With Bossuet they found new charm in charity, felt in the long-unexercised limbs of virtue a stirring of life.

But he was to have his greatest influence on two ladies of widely different situation — Madame, and Louise de la Vallière. To Henriette he would bring a clear lens for correcting the world's distortions — to Louise, surgical instruments for the soul.

But the time was still far away.

VI

CLARICE

IT WAS INEVITABLE that the King should learn of De Guiche's continued pursuit of Madame. What evidence he had was too slight to justify an arrest or even an accusation, but the rumors sent him directly to Louise with a command that she tell what she knew about this scandal. She knew everything, including the fact that Montalais kept De Guiche's letters in a casket in her bedroom. And she had been present when that old gypsy woman hobbled into Madame's presence, addressed her in a weirdly cracked yet somehow familiar voice, and held her palm too long while gazing into her eyes. Henriette had laughed with quite unnatural vivacity.

But all this was none of Louise's business — nor the King's, she thought — and his insistence hardened her stubborn refusal to answer any questions. He left in an extremely bad humor.

Alone, she struggled with the impulse to run after him and surrender. She was beginning to know Louis's nature, his decisions final as the turning of keys in locks, his sensitive self-regard; and it was more than possible that her disobedience had offended him so much he would never come back.

They had, however, foreseen this emergency in their earliest days together at Fontainebleau, and Louis had made a proposal. Suppose, he said, that the impossible were to occur — a misunderstanding, fancied neglect, even hard words — neither one must lie down to sleep without first writing a message aimed at reconciliation. In this way they could prevent any small difficulty from becoming serious.

Would he remember? She had to believe it. Her panic allayed somewhat by the recollection, she sat down at once and scribbled a few lines, folded and sealed the paper, and left it on the table to wait for the coming of his messenger. She guessed he would try to punish her by delaying his own note until late, and therefore decided sensibly to go to sleep. But no messenger came. Lying in a paralysis of insomnia, Louise heard every hour of the night strike on the palace clocks, and knew at last without any doubt that she was lost.

It was dawn, February 24. She got up and dressed and put on her black cloak and hood without any clear notion of where she was going, knowing only that she could not live out the coming day at the Tuileries. Her mother was still at the Luxembourg, but there had been no communication between them since her lapse from religion and chastity. There never could be a refuge there. She turned down a back staircase and out into the courtyard, then moved on along the Seine in the gray snow-light of early morning. It was very cold.

At the little village of Chaillot there was a small impoverished order of the Sisters of Sainte-Marie, devoted to the rescue of souls in extremity, but since it was a weekday in Lent all the nuns were in their cells, deep in retreat. It was some time before a Sister responded to the knocking on the door. Through the grill she noted the supplicant's distraught manner and Court gown, and told her grudgingly that she might sit in the parlor for a while, but could not be received in the cloister. Louise went into the glacial parlor and fell to the floor, frozen, exhausted, half mad with anguish. Nobody came near her for three or four hours.

That morning at the Louvre the King was receiving in special audience the Spanish ambassador, Don Christoval de Gaviria.

Suddenly the conversation slowed, and then stopped; His Majesty was noticeably disquieted by a slight disturbance among the courtiers. The Marquis de Sourdis, entering quietly, had spoken a few low words in Saint-Aignan's ear. "What! La Vallière!" the Comte exclaimed.

"What is it, gentlemen? Tell me!" Louis said.

"La Vallière is in religion at Chaillot."

Don Christoval de Gaviria never heard the point His Majesty had been about to make in summation of their talk. He was dismissed unceremoniously, and the King strode out calling for a horse to be saddled. He did not appear at the sermon following the audience, a fact much whispered about, and Maria Theresa was querulous and upset.

Anne of Austria, on her way to the chapel, had seen her son sprinting out the door booted and spurred, a gray hat pulled low over his nose. She remarked that he hardly seemed master of himself.

"Ah, but I will be master of those who outrage my feelings!" he flung back, and sprang into the saddle.

His suspicion of Anne's complicity in the event was justified. She had recently forced his old inamorata La Motte-Argencourt into a nun's habit — it was her way of dealing with disobedient girls.

Followed by a single officer of the Guard, Louis rode furiously all the way to Chaillot, and announced himself at the gate of the convent in a loud voice. The Sisters made haste to open, and admitted him to the parlor where Louise lay waiting to die, worn out by sobs which began again when he picked her up.

Louis had resolved to treat her with the severity such nonsense deserved, but the sight of her face overcame him, and suddenly he, too, wept, saying, "You appear to think but little of those who love you, Mademoiselle." After regaining control they talked for a long time both in the parlor and on the way home in a carriage procured by the officer of the Guard, wrapped like drowning people in each other's arms.

In spite of his emotion at retrieving Louise, and in spite of her avowal of everything she had hidden from him the day before, he could not, as King, pardon her completely for her defiance. As a lover, he was wounded that she had been able to keep secrets from him, and felt her love must be less strong than he had thought. This grievance might pass, but the day's ordeals were not yet over.

Monsieur, in an orgy of righteousness, had proclaimed to everybody who would listen that his wife was well rid of "that girl," and now met the returning couple at the door, barring their way. He was astonished at Louis's conduct, he said, and his roof should shelter La Vallière no longer.

Dismayed, the King left Louise locked in her room and mounted to Henriette's apartments by a back stair. There he lurked in the doorway until she noticed him and let him enter her little private cabinet. He kept his face turned aside to prevent her seeing that he had been weeping. Nothing could have hurt her more than this last indisputable proof of his feeling for another woman, and she listened coldly to his requests.

The refusal broke out with surprising bitterness. How, she asked, could Louis expect her to go on sheltering a girl who had done nothing but cause trouble from the beginning and who was now the center of a grave scandal? Besides, Philippe had said the culprit must go, and she could not overrule him.

Louis descended to pleading. La Vallière had nowhere else to go. Certainly he could not take her home to the Louvre. And if she were left alone, her enemies would soon find ingenious ways of making her life intolerable. Henriette shrugged her shoulders, implying that he should have thought of all this earlier.

Now he began to be angry. For a moment she had made him forget who he was. Did she think it was for her to make decisions in this or any other family matter? Pointing a finger, he reminded her that she had no right to assume an air of superior virtue. Her flirtation with the Comte de Guiche — if such a euphemism might be used — was no secret. A tactical error for Louis. Henriette was not a woman to be intimidated and blackmailed, and they stood on opposite sides of the room deadlocked and hating each other.

"For my friendship, then," Louis said at last.

She gave in with a humorless little laugh. "All right. Let her stay — I can't refuse if you command it. But from this day on I claim no duties of her. She is yours, not mine."

It was the cutting of Louise's last tie to anonymity.

On the following Sunday, Bossuet raised his leonine head before the chapel congregation and condemned "false gallantry and delicate passion." There was some uneasy shifting on embroidered prayer cushions, but no straying of attention.

Skillful as a stalker, the Abbé moved through a cover of verbal arabesques toward his prey. Would he dare to address the King directly? He did, crying in a great voice, "Return to the counsels of conscience! It is there that the divine word must make its saving ravages, in breaking all idols, in casting from the altar the adored mortal creature."

Nobody in the congregation had the audacity to raise his eyes toward Louis in the tribune. Maria Theresa went on smiling throughout Mass with her habitual vague beatitude.

Then, at the end of March, Louise was singled out for her own sermon.

Humiliated, pilloried before the world, she was at the same time strangely struck by Bossuet's evocation of the Madeleine image.

"The heart of Madeleine is broken, her face covered with shame, her spirit profoundly attentive to her intimate view of her state and the reflection of her perils. The immense pain which presses her makes her run to the physician; the shame which accompanies it makes her throw herself at his feet with submission; the knowledge of her danger makes her leave his hands only with fear, and she is no less occupied with the means of not falling again than with the joy of having been so happily, so mercifully, relieved."

Louise was not yet Madeleine in spite of this oratory, and for her pain there was no relief outside her seducer's mortal arms. But the message was clear. In such lives as hers, sacred and profane passion must battle until one or the other dies; there can be no truce, no compromise.

Many at Court disapproved of the King's choice. The position of royal mistress should, they felt, be held by someone politically sensible, having irons of her own in the fire and consequently willing to barter influence for consideration — preferably an extravagant woman who through debt would fall into their hands — someone, in short, who could be managed and controlled to the benefit of a large number of people. Mlle. de la Vallière was hopeless; she dressed like a schoolgirl, had no apparent interest in money or power, and was too much in love with the King to use him.

The Comtesse de Soissons and the Marquis de Vardes, tired of waiting for the royal fancy to stray elsewhere, decided to get rid of the obstruction, or rather, to let the Queen get rid of her. A hearty uproar caused by an insulted queen has sent more than one girl home to the farm for good. With Louise gone, the place would be open for a substitute — if not Olympe herself, at least her candidate.

As Superintendent of the Queen's Household the Comtesse was able to procure an empty envelope which had recently held a letter from Madrid; and helped by De Guiche, who had some knowledge of Spanish, she and De Vardes composed an anonymous letter.

> *To the Queen — The King is involved in an affair of which only Your Majesty is ignorant; Mlle. de la Vallière is the object of his love and attachment. This word is given you by faithful servants. It is for you to decide whether you can love your husband in the arms of another, or if you wish to correct a thing the duration of which cannot be to your glory.*

This message was entrusted to a servant on his way out of the country, given to one of Maria Theresa's maids of honor, and handed in turn to Doña Molina. She was apprehensive of bad news from Spain. Perhaps Philip IV, who had been sick, was now dead or dying. She hesitated, then opened the envelope and read. There was only one prudent thing to do: Molina hurried with the piece of villainy to the Queen Mother, who advised her to present it to Louis on his return later that day from Versailles. Louis read the letter with dark rage mounting into his face. He would not have believed anybody in the kingdom could be hardy enough to attempt such interference with his intimate affairs. He demanded brusquely for the third time whether the Queen had seen it, and Molina repeated, "No, Sire."

De Vardes, standing by in an attitude of studied nonchalance,

was ready with an opinion as to the criminal's identity. Overcoming his evident scruples, he said that one could not ignore the fact that Mme. de Navailles, the Queen's lady-in-waiting, was a prudish female. He hinted delicately, also, that the Grande Mademoiselle had a "spirit continually agitated."

Considering the ease with which she could have obtained the Spanish envelope, Louis was inclined to let his suspicion hang around the Duchesse de Navailles. But there was no proof. He would watch her most carefully from here on.

At the end of March Madame was delivered of a weak and premature daughter. The King and Queen were at her bedside before six in the morning, but Philippe received them gloomily, disappointed that the child was not a boy.

Henriette was even more stricken, weeping for hours and refusing to look at the baby presented by her anxious mother. "Throw her into the river!" she wailed. But the news was celebrated in England by Charles and those old family friends she had so captivated on her visit to London two years before. "We are very much surprised," Lady Derby wrote, "at the news you have sent of Madame's accouchement. She is young enough to have many sons and daughters if she goes on as she has begun."

Henriette's recovery was rapid. Color came back to her face and something of her characteristic gaiety, and by the end of the month she was back in society. At Saint-Eustache she appeared with the infant Marie-Louise to offer the traditional *pains bénits,* looking to indulgent spectators like a child with a doll.

Armand de Guiche was exiled again, this time under cover of a military appointment. It would be a long time before he learned to what particular cause he owed his unwelcome promotion to the rank of commander of the royal troops before Nancy.

De Vardes had two good reasons for having brought this about. De Guiche, who had been a party to the Spanish letter fiasco, was a menace to the security of the other conspirators; and furthermore, De Vardes was beginning to think seriously about Madame. She was physically desirable and politically powerful — superior in both

respects to Olympe de Soissons. The attaining of such a woman's boudoir would confer great prestige on any man in France.

But first the removal of De Guiche was necessary. The Marquis, therefore, went to Armand's father, the old Maréchal de Gramont, hinting of his son's danger and the advisability of getting him out of Paris till the royal rancor was cooled.

The Maréchal buttoned his coat with trembling fingers, got his hat and sword on with De Vardes's help, and hurried to Louis to petition a military post for his son. It was generously granted. Madame, sorrowing, agreed to see Armand once more before he left Paris. Up the back stair he came, smuggled from corner to corner by Anne-Constance de Montalais, and gained Henriette's cabinet. They had scarcely had time to clasp hands before Monsieur was sighted approaching down the corridor. With a seasoned soldier's presence of mind, Armand met the crisis by climbing into the chimney.

Philippe frittered around the room inspecting his chin for pimples in this mirror and that, lolled on the couches, riffled through books and put them down, and finally selected a Spanish orange and began peeling it. As he approached the fireplace to throw the remnants away, Anne-Constance pounced on him, crying out, "My prince, don't throw that peeling away! It's the part I like." He graciously gave it to her and she ate it bravely. Madame, who had been on the point of pretending a faint, recovered her composure, and in a few moments managed to decoy Philippe into the next room while De Guiche made his escape.

The show's heroine was indubitably Anne-Constance, but she had little time to enjoy her triumph. D'Artigny, having waited only long enough to be sure it was all over, was scuttling away to the Louvre to see Anne of Austria. Here was a chance to settle a score with Montalais, at last.

Anne had been waiting a long time to catch Henriette in such an act of infidelity, and immediately sent one of her women, Mme. de la Basinière, to put Philippe in possession of the truth.

Monsieur, too, gave commands, and as a result Anne-Constance learned within an hour from Mme. du Plessis that her services were no longer needed, and she must leave. She was not informed of her destination, and no friends were at the gate to see her off.

No doubt, as the high walls of the English convent rose into view, she congratulated herself with having had the presence of mind to bring along a full casket of De Guiche's letters to Henriette. Most of these were still unread — scarcely a surprising fact, since he had been in the habit of writing four times a day. However, they could be described as compromising, and might be useful for bargaining in case this nunnery, like Fouquet's prison, turned out to be escape-proof.

Perhaps, if Montalais had used this advantage wisely, she might have succeeded in getting her sentence commuted to a mere period of banishment from Court. But she could no more resist the lure of intrigue than a cat can the caged bird. A month or two later she wrote Louise two letters, instructing her how to conduct her love affair.

Louis's anger flared. He sat down and penned a brief note to the Sisters at Fontevrault, advising them that they would soon have custody of a girl in sore need of religion. She was to be permitted no indulgences and no correspondence.

Many a reluctant novice, once received at Fontevrault, has dropped from the records of history. Montalais was to be no exception to the rule.

The King's reconciliation with Louise was imperfect; he still felt hurt by her brief disloyalty, and was, besides, neurotically jealous.

Earlier in the year he had even lowered himself to question Montalais, who let him know by innuendo that Louise's old sweetheart, Bragelonne, was handsome, manly, and that she had promised to wait for him a hundred years, if necessary.

This was bitter medicine for Louis. Doubts tormented him. How far could Louise, who had betrayed this country boy so readily, be trusted with his own incomparably more important heart? Was she after all so rare a creature as he had supposed? Were pride and shyness real proof that she was different from those others around Court who offered themselves in a curtsy like cakes for sale? In these moods Louis was sarcastic, silent, and hard to placate, although in the attempt Louise promised to give up speaking and corresponding with all her old friends who had known Charles.

Sternly faithful to the letter of the Lenten observances by reason of his private infractions, the King read the office of the Holy Ghost, and on Good Friday washed the feet of twelve paupers, dried and kissed them; and each time he received Communion, laid hands on the sick. Louise at her window watched him among the yellow-faced ragged crowd in the courtyard, moving with his superb and individual ease, around his neck the great collar of the Order of the Holy Ghost, and a heavy black mantle picked out with tongues of flame hanging from his shoulders.

"May God heal you. The King touches you."

The ancient prayer was for her, too. But how should God heal one touched by this king, a soul steeped eagerly in sin, given daily, enraptured, to the Enemy? Compared to such joy, sin was nothing.

Being so much alone since her divorce from the routine of Madame's household, Louise devised ways of prolonging her shopping, invented errands, and became a sightseer around Paris.

The Palais-Royal was a little city in itself, endlessly interesting; and so were the covered corridors of the Palais de Justice with their open shops where bareheaded girls tied up packages with string. Children and dogs ran in and out, stirring up the dirt between stalls, and in the spring sunlight chambermaids and musketeers met and kissed behind pillars.

Through the dust and confusion, booksellers' voices rasped out available titles, and all down the arcades hopeful venders yelled at the strolling crowd, holding out looped lengths of lace, shirt collars, Polish knives, pin boxes, scissors, fine felt hats for wet weather, and jerkins made of English leather.

All around police headquarters, archers and attorneys' clerks lounged, waiting for a crime to occur; and farther on in the Cimetière des Innocents, letter writers sat on the sunwarmed tombstones scribbling messages at the commission of hard-pressed housemaids.

Down in Les Halles, the fish-market district, the mongering voices took on an inhuman shrill ferocity, suggesting to the stranger that his bones would be stripped as a herring's are by gulls, should he dare to leave the carriage. Yet these belonged to the same sentimental, hero-worshiping women who loved the big blond Duc de Beaufort. It was said he could outcurse them. Certainly he frequented the place for amusement and to replenish his stock of jokes.

Out in the broader streets under the striking of the hour from near and distant clock towers rattled the barrows of hawkers crying timeworn tunes, and black-robed, round-toqued doctors on their mules rode toward their dying patients. Sometimes a Court gallant cleft the grimy crowd in his wide feather garden of a hat, swinging his sword, planting his staff, knees tossing forward their surf of lace and ribbons.

There were parts of the city not to be lingered in — the Place de la Grève where half-naked women were flogged and branded — little alleys and cul-de-sacs dark with stench where pigs and children waded in the garbage and slaughterhouse blood reddened the middle ditch draining sluggishly toward the Seine.

Elsewhere, however, there were small pleasant courts with benches and tulips; great plantations such as the Jardin des Simples with its orient spicy herbs; and Roman ruins bearing their housetop-high hanging gardens — brick arches crowned with roses and boxwood, striding away into the breezy distance.

And now, on short rides in the Cours-la-Reine, Louise received and acknowledged bows or was cut like a great lady.

At Louis's insistence she had begun to dress more elaborately. But to appear in such company with the King's jewels in her ears and his favor on her face was not as safe a pastime as it seemed, that spring of 1662.

May 21 was an important day at both the French and English Courts.

In Paris at the chapel of the Palais-Royal, Monsieur's daughter was christened. She was expected to live in spite of her premature birth, a hope which occasioned thanksgiving from her now fond parents.

The same afternoon brought a tournament in the great square of the Tuileries. It was patterned on the old chivalric games, with every gentleman able to ride contesting for the ring while trumpets and cymbals made a barbaric blare. This was only a forecast, however, of the real jousting to come in a few days.

At Portsmouth King Charles was married to the Infanta of Portugal a day after she landed. The bridegroom described himself as agreeably impressed with Catherine of Braganza, but her suite almost drove him to desertion.

"Portingall ladies," Lord Chesterfield called them. There were more than a hundred of these strange anachronisms with their huge foretops, monstrous fardingales or guardinfantas, such as had not been seen in civilized countries for more than a generation, and bizarre notions of propriety. They refused to go outdoors for fear of being seen by men, and refused to go to bed until oaths had been taken that no males had previously slept there. None knew when maternity might overtake her out of some unaired mattress.

In spite of these idiotic women and their almost as numerous priests, Charles was for some months quite taken up with his wife. Her very ignorance amused him. But Lady Castlemaine, returning forthright and amoral, eventually ousted this amateur rival for His Majesty's attention, and before long had made the easygoing man arrange for her official presentation to the Queen.

Charles, who had written sympathetic letters to Minette regarding the problem of La Vallière, now fell noticeably silent on the whole subject of mistresses. Life at Whitehall was returning to normal.

The Venetian ambassador in Paris wrote home admiringly, "The King of France is so vigorous and so strong that before and after every ball he goes to exercise with the lance and Game of Heads." In addition, Louis tumbled and took dancing lessons every day from his master, Beauchamp. He was getting ready to excel in the forthcoming tournament. It was presented early in June. Ostensibly the festival was in Maria Theresa's honor, but she alone was deceived.

The Court poets had inked their pens in praise of someone called by mysterious unanimous consent Clarice — Light — the chosen of the Sun God. In the vast quadrangle between the Louvre and Tuileries, always afterward to be known as the Carrousel because of that day, seats had been raised for five thousand spectators. The queens and princesses, backed by their ladies, sat under a canopy of cloth of gold and purple velvet and had charge of awarding prizes to the victors. Preceded by cymbals and trumpets came mounted pages in gold-embroidered tunics and squires on foot in Roman costume; behind them His Majesty's equerries, De Brenonville and De Vantelet, one carrying the royal golden lance and the other a shield struck with the symbol of a blazing sun.

Louis himself was, that morning, glory made visible. Riding at the head of a Roman squadron, he wore silver and gold brocade sown over with diamonds, epaulettes held by diamond clips, and a belt covered with a hundred and twenty diamond roses wound three times around his magnificent cuirasse. His face, like that of a young Caesar, looked out beneath a silver helmet ornamented with gold leaves and crested with flame-colored plumes. He wore ankle boots of gilded leather and carried a long golden javelin at rest, and at his side hung a gem-encrusted glaive.

His mount, a tall *isabelle,* carried plumes on its metallic thread-embroidered harness and threw off diamond fire from all sides. "This fierce courser," wrote the chronicler of the *Court Gazette,* "merits the name of Bucephalus the more, since he carried a prince who has effaced the glory of Alexander."

Behind the King came the Duc de Navailles and the Messieurs de Vivonne and de Saint-Aignan, also brilliantly costumed, followed by four ensigns of the Body Guard and twenty pages of the King's Household. Stopping before the queens in a quiet stirred only by the silken slipping of forked flags in the warm air, all riders on a given signal made their mounts rear in salute. Other contingents entered the square with the same pomp — Monsieur, stiff as a candied fig in the casings of a Persian conqueror — the Prince de Condé leading a Turkish force — the Duc d'Enghien as an Indian prince — and finally the Duc de Guise imaginatively begemmed as King of the Americans. Now, in feudal style, heralds raised a flourish of trumpets from the lists' four corners, proclaiming the opening of the games.

The first trial was that of the Course of Heads, an English pastime rarely seen before in France. The contestants galloped in turn along the barriers, aiming successively with lance, javelin, and sword at a series of loathsome heads — Turks, Negroes, and Medusas ranged at varying heights along the course. It was as much a trial of horsemanship as of skill in handling weapons.

The King rode first, with smooth power mowing off all sixteen heads like clover, somewhat to the discouragement of his followers. But he lost points in the next event, and the day's declared winner was the Marquis de Bellefonds, a quiet young man, one of the Court's intellectuals. His reward from Maria Theresa was a gold box set with diamonds.

Next day was given to the classic ring courses such as Henri IV had loved to practice. Each cavalier ran three times, and most did well in spite of the blinding glare of the sun on the targets.

The King carried off a ring on his first stroke, only to be beaten by the demonically accurate Comte de Sault. Louise, seated at a distance from the royal dais, watched the contest with complex emotions.

The whisperers called her Clarice, dropping half compliments when this could be managed out of hearing of the queens and Madame. They were the climbers, insecure at Court, anxious to share the light of this rising star but afraid of being themselves revealed by it. And there were others, once friends, who now seemed never to see her at all. But first and last there was Louis the man, more beautiful than any king had ever been before, with a god's power in his arm and a glance for her among the thousands, just before he entered the lists. She had seen the other women watching him too. They were ready as ripe fruit, bending as he passed. When would he unthinkingly put out his hand?

VII

KING'S FAVOR

"I HAVE directed Comte de Brienne to write you in detail about the antique medals and rings that you sent on by Héron. As for the painted silk bedspread forwarded by the same messenger, I am very pleased with it."

Louis wrote often in this vein to his agents who, like M. l'Abbé Elpidio Benedetti, were collecting rare objects for him abroad. His taste for antiques, paintings, and tapestries was developing. They filled him with ideas, and he planned aloud to Colbert, walking up and down and making sweeping gestures with his arms.

The Romans had built palaces to house their treasures and to impress neighboring barbarians. He could surpass the Romans because he had superior advantages — engines of all kinds, compasses, gunpowder, clocks, telescopes. He would end by making France a refuge for scientists and inventors, himself their sympathetic protector. And for the encouragement of art he would organize academies and workshops. These porcelains and bronzes from the ancient world were fine enough, but only modern artists could express the genius of a modern king.

Versailles was of course the main project, but Paris must not be neglected.

The Louvre was in need of extensive renovation. It was crowded, dark, and almost uninhabitable, surrounded by stagnant moats, obstructed by ruins, outbuildings, and various unsightly remaining towers of the old palace. A noisome little street ran along beside it toward the Seine. This should be replaced by a stately corridor, perhaps with colonnades. But the view should be preserved from Louis's own bedchamber. Small as it was, gloomy and musty, it overlooked the river with its buildings — picturesque from a distance — and the wharves piled with goods from every province in the kingdom and every country in the world. There would be more.

Later there must be included in a new wing a Palace of the Nations, with rooms for Italy, Spain, Germany, Turkey, Persia, Mongolia, China — all designed and embellished in appropriate fashion, so that the visiting foreigner would feel at home. But more than architecture was needed. The whole structure of the Kingdom of France was sagging.

Mazarin had never had an efficient army, for example. It was still feudal — a heavy machine, perhaps, but rusted, unmaneuverable. The men were an underfed, uncontrolled, lousy rabble held precariously together by the prestige of generals, living by loot and extortion. Occasional discipline took the form of wholesale hangings alternating with long periods of total license. The officer was an investor who bought a company or regiment, and the subsequent grant of commission was not the King's business but that of two military overlords, the Colonel-General of Cavalry and the Colonel-General of Infantry. The King was at best a principal shareholder. His was the casting vote, true enough, but his control was far from absolute.

Louis felt deeply that the whole system was wrong, but nobody could reform it alone. What he needed was a Hercules, some tireless loyal genius to tear the army apart and remake it. But he would not have his man for another four years. Louvois in 1662 was only twenty, and not quite ready.

The future smelled of gunpowder; already Louis had signed a treaty with the Dutch, pledging his help in case of war. This step was a prudent one for a man planning a large enterprise of his own — the conquest of Flanders.

Now that the weather was good again and the roads passable, the Court were off by coach and horseback to the summer palaces.

In July the King gave a stag hunt at Versailles, where Louise rode at his side, wearing like Madame's other girls a gray hat and plumes. It was the last time she and Louis met for many weeks. The English Queen Mother was soon to return to England, and Madame's court spent most of the summer with her at Colombes and at Saint-Cloud. Packed like baggage from there to Beauvais, where Madame weepingly parted from her mother, Louise and the others were then taken to Chantilly to spend a few days as guests of the Grand Condé.

The old hero of Rocroi found great amusement in Henriette's precocious conversation; he was a friend of artists and scholars, and enjoyed showing the famous treasures of his house to company.

To Louise it was a vacation in purgatory. The King and Court were at Saint-Germain; and every few days someone there addressed to her in a carefully disguised hand a letter describing the progress of His Majesty's new love affair. "She had inconceivable jealousy and despair," wrote La Fayette.

The Queen had a maid of honor named Mlle. de la Mothe-Houdancourt, "pretty enough to bring a grand passion to life." Dressed like a doll in rose silk and coached by Olympe de Soissons, this girl had been angling for the King's attention all spring. Her coquetry, at first tremulous, improved quickly owing to natural talent, the Comtesse's instructions, and the prospect of many shiny prizes hung — perhaps — within reach.

With La Vallière so long away, Louis became bored and lustful. Obviously this little maid of honor was playing something, first inviting and then resisting. She had another suitor, too — Philibert de Gramont. "If love makes conditions equal, it is not between rivals." Louis exiled Philibert to England. The pursuit as usual involved the exchange of many letters. Anne-Lucie's were very inflammatory; it should have been easy for Louis to prevail, but somehow it was not. One evening, having insomnia, he climbed onto the roof, slid around chimneys, descended into rain gutters, and reached a place opposite the chambers of the Queen's attendants, called his tormentor to the window, and offered to come over. She held him off, mindful of Soissons's instructions, but conversed with him sweetly for some time.

Next day there was excitement in that wing of the palace. Several people had seen a shadowy figure climbing over the roof late at night, though nobody had been robbed. The Duchesse de Navailles gave orders that all windows on the exposed side should be blocked with iron grilles. This was accomplished without delay. The grilles were heavy, requiring no fewer than forty of the Swiss Guard to mount them in place, and were much wondered at by people passing below in the courtyard, especially Louis.

The Duchesse may have suspected the true identity of the prowler. She took her duennaship seriously, and had noticed the King's gallantry toward Anne-Lucie a few days before. "Like a Christian and an honest woman," wrote Mme. de Motteville, "she dared to address to the King her respectful remonstrances," conjuring him "to seek elsewhere than in the Household of the Queen the object of his pleasures and inclinations, which he appeared already to have chosen in the person of Mlle. de la Vallière." The King found this speech in extremely poor taste and answered so rudely that she hurried off in consternation to Paris to ask her confessor for advice. He told her to stand firm for virtue.

Anne of Austria, also consulted, gave the same counsel. Louis encountered the two women in discussion, and going to Navailles, "held out his hand, and with an air gentle and pleasant, asked her to make peace." This was done, Mme. de Motteville reports, "like a great prince who wishes to vanquish himself and triumph over his own weaknesses." But the weaknesses prevailed. That afternoon he was again seen chasing Anne-Lucie through the gardens. He was getting tired of coquetry, and wanted to know her terms. They were given without hesitation: the dismissal of La Vallière. Louis was silenced. Next day he sent her a pair of earrings, but no message.

His mother had been occupying herself meanwhile to some effect. She was alarmed at Louis's interest in this sneaky girl. If he must have a mistress — and by now it seemed clear that he must — surely the little La Vallière with her good manners and reserve was preferable. Years of plotting against plots had made her sensitive to undertones and the colors of details. She felt somehow that there was more to this affair than a mere flirtation.

In a short time her most efficient spy had news to report. The letters from Anne-Lucie to Louis were not her own; they had been copied from a sheaf in the possession of one of Soissons's secretaries. Further, the spy had been able to copy this collection entire. Triumphantly Anne delivered the evidence to her son and left it to speak for itself. That afternoon Louis received his usual note, made up of half promises and sly incitements, and ending with a demand for the exile of La Vallière. He could have quoted it word for word.

Thus fell the ambitions of La Mothe-Houdancourt and her sponsor, at least for the time being.

Louise came back to Saint-Germain with Monsieur and Madame in August, just after her eighteenth birthday. No longer crushed and crying, grown up in the space of a few weeks, she listened to the King's confession and then told him that she did not dare to love him any longer. He had never seen her angry before; it made her formidably lovely. He suffered humiliation, shame, incredulity at the memory of his own behavior, and wild grief at Louise's refusal to forgive. Besieging her at every turn for a week or so, he finally lost all pride and fell to hold her around the knees and weep. She could not be proof against this.

Louis liked Saint-Germain because it was near the forest. He could look from his balcony across midsummer lawns and flower beds and an expanse of wilderness to the distant towers of Saint-Denis, where so many of his restless ancestors lay resting at last.

The rooms here were high and airy, with floors of multicolored marble in patterned mosaics, ceiling and walls covered with mirrors so that in solitude one was always confronted by splendid silent strangers, and everywhere fell the sound of water from silver fountains and the screeching of cockatoos in their baroque aviaries.

Anne was concerned that summer about Louis's health and sent M. Vallot to examine him. Determined to discover something wrong, the learned man described His Majesty's symptoms as "a dull heaviness in the head, some signs of vertigo, heart trouble, weakness, and prostration."

His advice to the patient was to go hunting less often and to sleep more. Louis agreed with his usual politeness, and took, philosophically, the prescribed dose: peonies and red roses mixed with pearls dissolved in spirits of vitriol. But it is doubtful that he rested more after this.

He was increasingly absorbed in his planting and landscaping projects at Versailles, and seized every chance to inspect the workmen's progress. Only a few close friends were allowed to accompany him and Louise on these expeditions — De Vardes, Saint-Aignan, Brienne, Roquelaure, and the fantastical Péguilain, full of songs and crackpot oratory.

An idea came to Louis during one of the trips; he would have these attendants dress henceforth in blue moiré doublets like his own, ornamented with the same silver facings — in fact, in uniform. In case of need this would provide him with the convenient alibi of having been confused with a courtier. Louis seldom forgot completely that he was a married man. But at Versailles there was no need for caution. He and Louise on horseback could easily outdistance the others, and the terrain was full of hiding places. They were very happy. At summer's end they stayed a week, the King consulting with gardeners and architects, Louise sitting for her portrait by Nocret. They rode home on the eighth day. Not far from Saint-Germain her nervous horse shied at a blowing weed, reared, and threw her. She was badly jarred but no bones were broken. Louis, in a severe state of shock, had her carried to her lodgings in the Château Neuf and put her to bed himself, shouting meanwhile for his physicians.

It was decided in consultation to bleed the patient. A basin was brought, and a rather frightened surgeon stepped forward, knelt, and took Louise's heel in his hand. The King, whispering in his ear, unnerved him; he began sweating and missed his aim twice. Louise paled, jerked her foot on the third thrust, and broke the lancet. The King gave the surgeon such a violent kick on the rump that he was knocked across the room. Then, kneeling and holding the foot himself, he watched grimly while a second surgeon dug out a fragment of the broken lancet and finished the bleeding.

At the beginning of autumn Monsieur and Madame were off again to Saint-Cloud. The parting was both sad and anxious for

Louis, who, still humbly aware of his recent folly, needed his mistress close at hand as a sort of touchstone for his emotions. To comfort and reassure each other they wrote constantly and under all manner of conditions.

Louis sent her a verse scribbled on a two of diamonds during a card game. She answered promptly on a two of hearts, amusing the Précieuses to whom he subsequently showed it.

> *To improve poetic arts*
> *One should choose a two of hearts.*
> *Diamonds, it would appear,*
> *Speak of Jupiter and fear.*
> *But when heart and heart unite*
> *It can only mean delight.*

The French ambassador at Rome had been poorly chosen, it seemed. Haughty, insolent, and bellicose, the Duc de Créqui had antagonized the whole city within a few weeks after his arrival.

On August 20 he got into a scuffle which was to have international complications. After a certain exchange of insults with the Pope's Corsican Guard, the Duc's rough servants drew their swords and sprang to the attack. At this, the entire corps (encouraged, it was later said, by Don Mario Chigi, brother of Alexander VII himself) surrounded Créqui's house and fired on the Duchesse as she alighted from her carriage. A page was killed and several attendants wounded. The Duc and his entourage left Rome at once, threatening revenge on the Pope and all his relatives.

Louis heard the news at supper. This time, having learned from the Spanish incident how to handle such affairs, he controlled his temper. Italy too should be brought to her knees in apology. He gave orders for the organization of an Italian expeditionary force and waited for the rumors of this to do their work.

Rome was thrown into panic. Messages came and went for some time before Louis consented to relent. There were, naturally, certain terms. The Pope must disband his Guard, raise a pyramid in Rome bearing a full account of the crime and its expiation, surrender

Avignon to the crown of France, and send his nephew, Cardinal Chigi, to Paris to read a full public apology. The Pope squirmed and considered and looked for loopholes. In Paris the citizenry went wild with enthusiasm. Up with the mailed fist!

While he waited for Rome to concede, Louis turned to other political matters. There were, for example, formalities incident to the erection of fourteen new duchies. Among others, Saint-Aignan was to be elevated to the peerage and should henceforth be known as the Duc de Saint-Aignan, as he deserved. But such things were incidental to Louis's main business. For some months he had been negotiating with England and now saw success for one of his main efforts, the cession of the port of Dunkirk.

Charles could scarcely afford the unpopularity this would win him with the English, but he needed money. Bussy-Rabutin wrote, "The King of England has turned into a shopkeeper. He has sold us Dunkirk, and I hope we shall buy London tomorrow!" But the sting of such attacks was forgotten by Charles with the arrival of the first installment of his price, five thousand French livres, poured golden into the coffers of the Tower of London. That fall he appointed Madame his special ambassador to Louis. Henceforth she should serve as mediator and adviser to the two kings in all matters touching their alliance. Perhaps never before had such a grave assignment fallen into the lap of a girl eighteen years old.

Maria Theresa gave birth to a daughter in mid-November. Couriers left in all directions to apprise the courts of Europe of the happy event, and from all courts ambassadors were dispatched with felicitations. But Anne-Elizabeth was a thin, hollow-eyed rabbit of an infant for whom the physicians held little hope. They bled her judiciously and she went dwindling along for six weeks before dying. Her end was a great relief to the Court, whose holiday celebrations had been curtailed for several days. It was the first time Louis had suffered the death of one of his own. His outburst of grief surprised everyone, since there had been a growing feeling among his friends that the King was a little hardhearted. He went at once to Saint-Cloud, to Louise. Even while she held his head in her arms, herself too moved for triumph, her blood praised the moment with inexpressible gratitude. Only she could comfort him in his loss and helplessness.

Sometimes the Queen could disconcert her attendants with a remark which in anyone else might be called knowing. On a winter night she lay abed early, face turned toward the half-open door of her chamber, and saw somebody pass in the corridor with a light, lame step.

"That girl," she said, "in the diamond earrings. She's the one the King loves."

Mme. de Motteville, aghast at this unnatural perspicacity, answered rather flusteredly that husbands often, without ceasing to love their wives, pretend to court another merely for the sake of fashion. Maria Theresa did not reply, but closed her eyes with an expression almost of contempt.

Perhaps her women had thought her ignorance could go on forever, because for two years she had remained unsure of the exact object of Louis's love. But she was Spanish, like the best fortunetellers, and royal, with the inherent or cultivated pride which sometimes makes queens behave as they should. She never considered espionage or inquisitions. Suspicious she was, of everyone, and full of dark little imaginings, but never vindictive. Her women pitied, occasionally came close to admiring her.

Molière had a new play, *L'Ecole des Femmes* (*School for Wives*), the funniest he had ever produced. Wiping his eyes after a scene of Brécourt's, the King said, "That man would make a stone laugh."

The author himself played Arnolphe, guardian of the ingénue. He seldom appeared in anything but comedies these days, having bowed to public opinion that he had no talent for tragedy. A great tragic actor must rant, and Molière's interpretation of the classic roles was too tame for most audiences. His bride Armande, however, was heartrending in scenes of murder and suicide.

Stage effects were gradually improving. Recently there had been criticism from the sophisticated when, in response to the cry, "To me, soldiers!" a sheet was jerked down to reveal a crude painting of soldiers crossing a bridge. Now some of the simpler tricks used in staging the royal ballets were beginning to be copied. Molière could not afford to be outdone by the theater of the Hôtel de Bourgogne.

Legitimate stage, however, could not compete that season with the scenes of Court life itself. On January 8 came the Ballet of the Arts, composed by the matchless team of Lully and Benserade. Madame and Saint-Aignan had arranged the entrées and collaborated on designing costumes. The opening scene was dominated by Louis as a shepherd romantically arrayed to feed his flock by the streams of Arcady. His peace was soon broken by the appearance of Henriette and four young attending shepherdesses in flowery hats and a profusion of ribbons: these were Louise, Athénaïs de Tonnay-Charente, and the Mlles. de Saint-Simon and de Sévigné. The quintet appeared again in the finale, dressed this time as Pallas Athene and Amazons in classic draperies and helmets, carrying spears and shields.

In later years, remembering this group, their fresh faces still untouched by disillusion, Mme. de Sévigné would write nostalgically, "Ah, what shepherdesses and what Amazons! Madame, whom the centuries will never replace . . ."

The verses written for Louise were long and laudatory, consistent with her recognized standing at Court.

> *She has in her beautiful eyes a sweet languor . . .*
> *And I do not think that in all the village*
> *He will find a heart better placed than hers.*

> *The agreeable La Vallière . . .*
> *Dances with an air*
> *More divine than human . . .*

Veiled in rural metaphors, the King's exploits were catalogued. But flattery was never more inspired by truth. In eighteen months this young man, who saw incarnate in himself the honor of France, had subdued Spain, regained Dunkirk, re-established order in the national finances, begun to reform the military organization, and united his own people.

Colbert, himself an indefatigable worker, marveled no less than Benserade at Louis's ability to leave his council chambers at the end of a hard day fresh, serene, and ready for pleasure. The Grande Mademoiselle, no weakling, complained of being made faint with exhaustion during the rehearsals of *Hercules,* driven on by her perfectionist cousin, who seemed able to dance all night. But she was not present for this winter's performance, or any of the festivals presented in honor of the visiting Crown Prince of Denmark. She was out of favor again. A marriage had been arranged for her with the King of Portugal. He was diseased, dirty, and insane, it was said — slobbered when he ate, and enjoyed shooting at strangers with a musket out of his palace windows. Mademoiselle had refused this strategically sound alliance, and so was banished by Louis for the third or fourth time in their association. Cross and melancholy, she retired to Saint-Fargeau, one of her spider-ridden castles in the country, to wait for a gesture of charity from Court.

Near the end of January, Athénaïs de Tonnay-Charente was married to the Marquis de Montespan. In her bridal gown, among the candles of the *médianoche,* she seemed easily the most beautiful woman in the world, not only to her husband but the Court's most jaded connoisseurs.

The Marquis was a pleasant young man, though reportedly jealous, disliked Court life, and was impatiently waiting for a chance to carry his bride away. All popular sympathy was on Athénaïs's side. She was only twenty-two — too young for such living burial.

Another lady menaced with the hideous prospect of leaving Paris was the Duchesse de Châtillon, Henriette's dear friend Bablon, soon to marry the Duke of Mecklembourg. She had carefully stipulated in the marriage contract, however, that she must have leave to visit in France as much as she chose. It was doubtful that Germany would hold her long.

The Carnival season glittered away in balls, comedies, lotteries, operas, games, and chamber music; and there was the annual fair of Saint-Germain, held from the beginning of February till the last week of Lent. During this time it was the fashionable rendezvous for courtiers, who drove to the place, a market area near the old church, in hired coaches with servants in gray livery, the better to preserve the illusion of being incognito. There were games of skill to be tried, fortunetelling by gypsies and astrologers, Indian jugglers and strolling musicians.

In the first wild-breathed nights of false spring, dark cloaks whipped out glimpses of damask skirts; feathers and earrings swung, eye-whites turned in the devilish slits of black vizards, and smoking torches tarnished the dark down all the nine streets of bazaar temptations — perfumes and mirrors, fans cunningly painted with cupids and chimney sweeps, candle snuffers, little wooden combs, dainty silver brushes for cleaning the teeth, bronze spittoons, ivory crosses, Persian carpets, sponge boxes, cameo brooches and strings of coral, Venetian brocades, perfume sprays with ebony handles inlaid with silver, tapestries, slippers with carved high heels, embossed and gilded leather, sandalwood caskets, sea shells, glass green as a mermaid's eye, candy, peacock feathers, laquered cabinets from Coromandel. Then late at night the lovers would go home carrying their armfuls of toys, up the familiar back stair, to that chamber and the single pillow they could find without any light except what the moonwhite clouds spilled through the window.

On the last day of Carnival, Philippe and Henriette gave a masked ball. Maria Theresa had publicly asked Louis to escort her, and he refused, making some vague excuse. Humiliated, by now half able to read the expressions of her husband's companions, she retired. Anne of Austria was outraged and grieved, and promised her daughter-in-law that she herself would take her to this ball, since His Majesty was otherwise occupied.

Accordingly the royal ladies dressed unobtrusively in black taffeta cloaks and veils and went to lose themselves in the masked crowd shifting up and down the stairs, in and out of the mirrored salon daylight-bright with candles.

The King was unmistakable, and his partner's disguise failed to hide a strand of silver-blond hair. Her voice, too, was famous — perhaps because it was so quiet.

The queens did not stay very long.

A few nights later Louis returned to his own chambers at four hours after midnight and found Maria Theresa and her heavy-eyed attendant, Mme. de Chevreuse, in dressing gowns beside the embered fire.

"And why, Madame, are you not in bed?"

"I am waiting for you."

"You have the appearance of one who waits often."

"It's true," she said, her voice thin. "You are never pleased with me any more, only with my enemies."

The King stood watching her with distaste. "Well, Madame, and who has been telling you this?" He went across the room and said, with his hand on the doorknob, "Go to bed, without so many foolish excuses."

The Queen jumped up suddenly, ran to him, and huddled down on her knees.

"What do you want?"

"I want to tell you — I want to tell you I will always love you."

"And I," he said distantly, "can assure you that you will always be well treated. But if you want to please me, don't listen any more to Mme. de Soissons or Mme. de Navailles."

There was nothing more to say than there had been at first. She would never dare to wait up for Louis again.

The cause of Maria Theresa's trouble still lived like a serving maid in her little room at the Tuileries, under constraints to which a servant would have refused to submit. Except for some jewels and dresses, she had nothing to prove the King's favor, and was widely criticized for her unworldly behavior. Another girl, given her opportunities, would have a house of her own by now, and some safe investments for old age. "Proud and delicate, for the love that she gave she asked only love." And, despite all the gossips' predictions, she continued to receive it. Louis, jealously observant, was disturbed to see her smile at a passing cadet during a military review one afternoon.

"Who was that young man?" he asked severely. After searching her recollection, mystified as to what he meant, Louise answered that she had seen her brother Jean, and laughed, much amused.

At the time, Louis was organizing with particular care the military household of his son, and now it seemed to him that the Marquis de la Vallière was a deserving person. He awarded him the command of a new company, the Light Horse of the Dauphin, "magnificently recruited, equipped, and mounted," having on their standard three leaping dolphins in an agitated sea. Honorary captain, the King; honorary lieutenant, the Dauphin, not yet two years old.

In addition, the new commander, dazed by the speed of his promotion, received a pension of four thousand livres. He subsequently acquitted himself quite well of his duties, it is reported, considering that he was only twenty-two, had just been through his first campaign, and had a company made up of veterans. If any of these muttered, it was not within earshot of the King.

VIII

A HOUSE OF HER OWN

A L L D U R I N G Lent the ladies of the Court had followed the
two queens on their devotional rounds from Val-de-Grâce to Chaillot and on pilgrimages to the Dominican shrine on Mount Valérien,
enduring it all in expectation of a renewal of fêtes at Easter. Then
Anne, who had not been well for a long time, fell seriously ill, as
if death had shrunk her overnight with a single speculative touch.
Pain began its horrifying first invasions; she lay with her lips tight
and sweat wilting the starched white lace of the caps Mme. de
Navailles had to change so often. Her physicians recognized the
malady and had very little hope, but prepared decoctions of potable
gold, syrup of roses, senna, and powdered rhinoceros horn. They
waited to let blood until the first and last quarters of the moon,
when the humors would be at the center of her body, and ordered
frequent burning of aromatic preparations as a safeguard against
contagion.

Long before, visiting a Paris hospital, Anne had seen a woman in
the last stages of such a corroding cancer of the breast, and struck
by a sickening fear she had gone away and prayed, "God, God, any
other scourge than this." Now she lay for more than a month in
her dark airless chamber, apparently dying. Louis came to sit beside her for hours at a time, gratifying the eyes of the ladies-in-
waiting with this tableau of penitent son. Sometimes Anne would
turn her head on the pillow and speak to him. With bowed head
he promised everything she asked. He would reform his life, return, as she and Bossuet prayed, to the way of God, and foreswear

his criminal allegiance to earthly love. Almost without prompting he vowed that he would make a pilgrimage to Chartres in gratitude, if his mother should recover.

After this, slowly and miraculously, Anne began to show some improvement, as a boat caught in the current may hesitate and then swing back toward shore. Prayers of thanksgiving were offered in all the churches of Paris, and Louis duly made his pilgrimage to Chartres.

This duty done, he rode home as fast as possible to Louise. If anybody had heard him foreswear her, it was not himself speaking, but pain; and now the pain was gone. God, as another monarch, should understand that arrangements would be made. He would lose nothing by closing His eyes to a few minor deviations from the rule. But discipline from this fellow sovereign was to fall on Louis like a sword, as he himself was accustomed to deal it.

At Versailles, at two on the morning of May 28, he was up, perfectly well, talking philosophy with Saint-Aignan. At seven he was taken with vomiting and violent pains in the head. The Court was roused, and informed that His Majesty had the measles — a serious disease for a man his age. For a day and night he got steadily worse. His temperature crept up. The medical men stood by but could do little. Next morning the Court dressed in black for mourning, and there were undertones of panic. Word went out through Paris that the King was dying, and flew to alarm officials in the provinces. For three days the end seemed imminent. During lucid intervals Louis considered the prospect of death calculatingly and spoke of certain settlements he wished made. Most important was the Dauphin's safety; he must be put into the hands of the loyal Prince de Conti. And, privately, he gave Saint-Aignan strict orders to keep Louise away; her health must not be risked, especially now that she was going to have a child. In delirium he muttered disconnectedly about her.

At the Tuileries, restless in her own chamber or walking the half-lit corridors, she waited for messengers bringing news from Versailles, as if vigilance could hold off bad news, or her own tight nerve threads tether the King to life.

On the fourth day there was some quiet congratulating, much churchgoing, and among the opportunists who had foreseen a change in government, hasty and secret revision of plans.

"I am still shaking with fright," wrote the minister Lyonne, to England. "On Friday His Majesty's life was in danger, up till twelve o'clock. On Saturday afternoon, he was at work with his secretaries as usual."

One of Louis's first items of business was arranging for the marriage of Jean-François, Marquis de la Vallière. He could not afford delay, realizing now that if he died, Louise would have been left defenseless among her enemies. He would provide a refuge for her by providing a household for her brother.

There was an orphan heiress available, Gabrielle de la Cotardais, owner of several properties in Bretagne and an income of forty thousand livres — a girl whose name had been placed in Mazarin's own notebook with an eye to some future combination. Accordingly, the marriage contract was signed within a few days by Louis, Maria Theresa, Anne of Austria, Philippe, Henriette, the Prince de Condé, the Duc d'Enghien, and finally by a small fat hand tracing a majestic unformed L and D. It was that of the Dauphin, eighteen months old, who thus tendered evidence of his satisfaction with the good service of his Light Horse company's officer.

Sixty of the noblest gentlemen and ladies in the realm witnessed the signing, and the wedding two days later at the Church of the Assumption called out the season's largest crowd, proving by the magnificence of their dress a prevailing feeling that the royal mistress was a power to be courted. The bride was in awe of her gay, somewhat flamboyant husband. She was a pleasant-tempered girl with large brown eyes and curly hair like that of a spaniel hanging over her plump shoulders. During the next few years she would prove herself an affectionate friend to Louise.

Anne of Austria, still not strong enough to travel, kept the Court in Paris almost all summer. To allay the boredom, Louis, Philippe, and Henriette went often to Versailles, and the usual rash of summer fads broke out — swinging, hide-and-seek, blind man's buff.

Louise, whose gowns were beginning to be too tight, suffered from the heat and so preferred boating parties to everything else.

Madame had received a present from Charles recently, a pleasure barge painted blue, with blue velvet cushions and hangings embroidered in gold. "The whole most royal and gallant in appearance . . . a fitting present," the gazetteer rhapsodized, "from the King of the Sea to his fair sister." In this Henriette and her women rowed up and down the Seine to the music of guitars and lutes in the lazy afternoons, observed from the distant banks by poets in search of new inspiration. In the resultant rhymes this craft became, repeatedly, a Magic Bark wafted by Loves and Zephyrs to its haven.

There was much speculation regarding Madame's feeling for the Comte de Guiche. It was well known that she had promised never to see his face again, and had commissioned Louis himself to get her letters back, but she always became silent when anybody mentioned his name, and looked very strange once or twice at the sight of a dark head in the crowd. Her maids of honor said authoritatively that her thoughts were often with the army in Lorraine. But at home there were various contestants for the place he was supposed to hold in her heart. The young Prince de Marsillac, desperately in love, had made such a fool of himself that his father, the cynical Duc de la Rochefoucauld, had sent him off to a more cooling climate.

M. d'Armagnac, as Grand Equerry of France, should have behaved with more dignity, but persisted in dropping little notes in Madame's pocket until the Archbishop of Sens came to her rescue with a well-timed "Tut!" in the lusting one's direction. She was also loved, with respect and in varying degrees, by most of the men of letters around Court, to whom she seemed Athena. Molière had dedicated *L'Ecole des Femmes* to her in one of history's floweriest epistles, and this devotion was copied, not insincerely, by his friends Boileau and La Fontaine, and by Racine.

"Racine," said Mme. de Sévigné, "will never go very far." Madame, being of a different opinion, made him read his works to an audience of selected friends, and shed tears over the sorrows of *Andromaque*.

De Vardes alone, too subtle to be called persevering, was dangerous. He pursued his plan as much for love of the game as for the prize. "De Vardes! Always De Vardes! He is the gospel according to the day." His ease at making epigrams, his knack for turning awkward situations to his own advantage, his reputation — all these were useful. His approach to Henriette was carefully unromantic; he visited her on days when her spirits were low, and made her laugh, and never left without having dropped some infinitely subtle hint that his great friend De Guiche was a thorough villain. The next step was to decoy Monsieur's attention away from himself by drawing delicate attention to the idiocy of Marsillac and others. Monsieur reacted like a weathervane. De Vardes made a joke which involved taking Madame's hand, and gazed into her eyes. She thought he was her best friend.

Toward the end of August, Louis saw that he must join his troops at the siege of Marsal in order to deal final defeat to the Duc de Lorraine.

Louise's pregnancy would soon be impossible to hide. He was heavyhearted at the thought of leaving her, and had formed and thrown away several plans to insure her protection during his absence. He had been turning with increasing confidence the past year to the solid Colbert for help in government matters, and now recruited him as La Vallière's guardian. There was a further advantage in the fact that Mme. Colbert came from Louise's part of the country, and had borne seven children of her own. Sensible and kind, she could be counted on to reassure a girl trapped for the first time by procreation's timeworn trick.

Immediately on Louis's departure the Colberts began to make inquiries and arrangements. There was a certain house overlooking the gardens of the Palais-Royal, small but pleasant enough, which had belonged to a bankrupt gallant named Brion. His hope for a rich marriage had gone down with Fouquet — that sinking which took with it so many smaller floating fortunes. Brion had disposed of all his own consequent difficulties by dying. His house, therefore, was bought and filled with luxurious new furniture, including four complete sets of tapestry to be changed according to the season.

Soon afterward a girl moved in and began stocking the chests of the household with fine linen of all sorts. Mlle. du Plessis had been chosen by the Colberts not only for her efficiency but for an admirable ability to keep her mouth shut.

At last, on a clear day of autumn, everything was ready for Louise to come home. How smoothly the big brass key turned in the oiled lock. It was her key to all rest and tranquillity of mind. She thought she would never tire of walking upstairs and down to catch off guard the gleam of crystal and brass, pausing to hear the comfortable talk of the clocks. Candlesticks, cushions, books, cups, soap — all were hers — a minor miracle.

The King was away two months. His letters, anxious and tender, were never addressed directly to Louise, but to Colbert. "I send you these letters for the queens, and then, you know, this which has no address for the person I mentioned in parting."

Marsal fell, and Paris celebrated the triumph before the end of October. There seemed no reason why the French armies should not conquer other cities just as easily.

De Guiche, whose theatrical courage had made him the hero of his men in the field and the Court at home, had been fully reconciled with the King, and they parted as good friends. It is doubtful that Louis knew about Madame's portrait in a little case next Armand's heart; but under the circumstances he judged it best to keep the hero away from Paris for a while longer, and therefore granted him the requested leave to go and fight Russians in Poland.

Tears came to Henriette's eyes when Armand's exploits were recounted. "I believe I care more for him than I knew, before." The tone and look told De Vardes more than any protestations could that he would never live to seduce this girl. He might compete with a human rival, but not with such a glamorous legend as De Guiche had become. Never a man to acknowledge failure chivalrously, he changed his purpose but kept up the old techniques. He still paid court to Madame, read plays with her, ran errands, and considered how to destroy her. This was already half done. Gossip in certain quarters had her his mistress; he could arrange for its spread to other quarters.

If Olympe was jealous of De Vardes she overcame it for the sake of practical aims. They trusted each other with secrets, but only because their separate scheming overlapped and interlocked. There could be no question of betrayal.

Soissons, still intent on removing La Vallière, had not been stopped by the La Mothe-Houdancourt fiasco. There were other, more clever, girls at Court. And if they failed, there was always the risky but effective expedient of witchcraft.

Even the Queen had visited the elegantly furnished rooms of sorceress La Voisin for a reading of the cards, and aging belles continually sought her out for potions and cosmetics. Most of these had no suspicion about the gloomy garden of Villeneuve-sur-Gravois, where nameless babies lay buried, the house where toads were boiled alive, or the little chapel where an ex-priest held unorthodox services. But Olympe knew. There were many ways of accomplishing the necessary.

To celebrate the glory of Marsal, Louis held a military review soon after his return. A thousand beauties assembled to be seen and honored; ten thousand cavaliers and foot soldiers deployed before Their Majesties and fired discharges. Through gunpowder smoke and a raging of trumpets reared the plumes of the great war horses, and at night the battle-hard young nobles ran through fountains and loops of flame, lancing for prizes in a Carrousel of Fire. This was a reborn France, a new world blazing. There was a noise of chariots in the sky. Louis laughed, his teeth white in the blasts of infernal light, and raised his sword.

The echoes of all this came only faintly to Louise through the walls of the Palais Brion. She no longer went out except in her coach, after dark, and received her few visitors as fashionable ladies did, in bed, formally coiffed, with her best jewels on, her figure camouflaged by pillows. All day her little lapdogs ran over the satin landscape of her bedcover while she practiced the guitar or accomplished prodigies of needlework. At night Louis came in to bring her the day's news and rest beside her, watching the fire, moonlight on the frost of the gardens outside; to feel with careful hand on her side the mysterious slow struggling of his royal child.

Colbert's arrangements were almost complete.

For the care of the infant [*he writes*], *with the secrecy the King had ordained, I secured one Beauchamp and his wife, old servants of my family, who lived in the Rue aux Ours, on the corner of the street which turns behind Saint-Leu–Saint-Gilles, having told them, for discretion, that one of my brothers having made an infant with a girl of quality, to save his honor I have been obliged to take care of the child and confide it to them, which charge they accepted with joy.*

Finally, the indispensable services of an accoucheur, Boucher. In letters incident to this business Louise is called only "the person," Boucher "the man." Whatever hands would be there at the last hour to brace hers, they would not be Louis's. The demands of secrecy must keep him in the council room or at the theater. In due time Colbert would take his master the news, good or bad.

On December 18 Louise felt her first premonitory pains. The King stood meditating at the head of her bed. His calendar for the day, including a hunt to Saint-Germain, was set; to countermand the order would certainly rouse suspicion. Therefore, he kissed her and left, commanding Boucher to take care.

At three-thirty on the following morning, December 19 — four days after the full moon, as Colbert noted with astrological concern — a note from Boucher was delivered His Majesty. "We have a boy, very strong. The mother and child are well, thank God. I await orders."

All moved according to schedule. Promptly at six in the morning, Mme. Colbert carried something swathed in shawls across the gardens of the Palais-Royal to a dark carriage waiting in the square before the Hôtel Bouillon. The newborn was to be given little rest on his first day, begun so early, carried on the current of his father's orders from house to house and finally to the church of Saint-Leu. There he was named — Charles, son of M. de Lincourt and the lady Elisabeth de Beux; his godparents, Colbert's old servants, Beauchamp and his wife Clémence Pré. Louise was not permitted a glimpse of her son again for many days.

But in spite of precautions, the Court's attention turned immediately toward the Palais Brion. Tales sprang up everywhere. The most dramatic and therefore most commonly credited told how a messenger had been sent to Boucher at midnight and had bandaged his eyes before leading him to a masked lady on the point of delivery. After the birth he had been blindfolded again and led away with the same precaution. And there was no denying that Mlle. de la Vallière had stopped receiving visitors for four days before the date in question and had not resumed her audiences in the bedchamber until four days later. It was time for her to face the gossip and save appearances, if possible. On Christmas Eve she rose and went to Midnight Mass in the chapel of the Quinze-Vingts. The curious found her "very pale . . . very changed," in the candlelight. "Nobody could doubt that she had borne a child, which it is said has been given into the care of Mme. de Choisy."

Throughout the ceremony, Louise looked at the image of the Virgin, child in arms. Her own were empty. She could smile in her enemies' faces as deceitfully as any other sinner, but she could not pray.

"Respect for the Queen," says De Sourches, "prevented ladies of quality from visiting or receiving the mistress of the King."

Madame's maid of honor had held a reserved place in every important affair — not so the favorite, hidden away in her own house. Nymph of Fontainebleau she might be, the poets' Clarice, dancer of surpassing style; but no role was given her in the great winter ballet *Amours Déguisés* (*Loves Disguised*), in which most of her old friends appeared as nymphs of Flora.

Benserade had outdone himself with verses for this occasion; and as usual the lewd were pleased with his references to the sexually capable Marquis de Saucourt:

> *. . . A reputation solidly sustained*
> *Precedes my coming . . .*

Athénaïs de Montespan excited the chroniclers with her luscious appearance as a marine goddess; but she was not at the moment in

favor with the King, having been foolish enough to fall into one
of De Vardes's snares.

The Court now spoke freely of the Marquis as Madame's lover;
only she and the rest of the royal family were ignorant of his
boasts. Soon he would be ready to shoot her down like a bird in
a tree. Meanwhile he dallied along, starting up baseless rumors of
other sorts, and causing trouble among her women.

Bablon, now Mme. de Mecklembourg, back in Paris after an
amusingly short honeymoon with her German husband, had inno-
cently served De Vardes's purpose. Very quickly he had Mme. de
Montespan and Mme. d'Armagnac (once his own mistress) jealous
of Bablon and plotting to banish her. Together they stirred up
Philippe's frivolous ire, and he forbade Henriette to receive her
old playmate any more. Incensed at this parody of the heavy husband, she appealed to Louis. Philippe in turn appealed to his
mother, who still looked coldly on her daughter-in-law, and at last
Charles II, Bablon's friend, became concerned and wrote letters of
condolence to his sister in her trials.

The whole flimsy structure of absurdities was ready now for the
architect to kick over. He had, however, grown bored and gone off
to other projects; so the situation finally fell of itself, piece by piece,
leaving as the only genuine wreckage Athénaïs's credit with the
King. He was still too fond of Henriette to countenance those who
plotted against her. So, although Athénaïs tried to charm His Majesty, he continued to ignore her. From Louis XIV such ignoring
was enough to wither most plants from the root up, but Mme. de
Montespan was an exceedingly hardy rose.

Often, those winter days, Louis took a party of male friends
to the little Palais Brion to admire Louise in her fireside gown of
mulberry red, and to play his favorite game of *brelan* in the room
overlooking the leafless garden.

Mlle. d'Artigny was Louise's only friend. She was good enough
company, and less malicious, it seemed, since the banishment of
Anne-Constance de Montalais. Louis, ordinarily so discerning a
judge of people, was too grateful for D'Artigny's friendliness to
Louise to worry about her reputation. He was pleasant to her and
hinted more than once that her future would be considered. He

felt increasing resentment of the world's coolness toward Louise, and would have enjoyed settling the matter with a few arrests and beheadings. But the guilt was universal.

The Comtesse de Soissons had produced without much hope a new contender for the King's attention. One morning she saw Louise pass this girl, the daughter of a parliamentary advocate, without any greeting, and remarked sourly to Mme. de Ventadour, "I have always known La Vallière was lame, but I didn't suppose she was blind." This, repeated to the King, brought him in a rage to confer with Louise. "Speak, Mademoiselle, and tell me what you wish to do to those who insult you. I do not think it will be impossible to satisfy you." Being human, she must have been strongly tempted to let Louis send this implacable enemy away from Paris and all the machinery of her mischief. But Louise was becoming wise — perhaps a little disillusioned now — and could hardly suppose Olympe's place would be vacant long. The King's mistress must always be schemed against by someone. It is a law of nature. Let her stay, she said.

Louis's feelings were not to be soothed by such reasonable considerations as hers. A blow at Louise reached himself. Without his command, palaces could not rise, ships sail, nor armies conquer — yet he must accept insults from small-minded women. On the way out he met Saint-Aignan, made him get into his coach, and they rode for a time in silence. Then, dismounting at his own door, Louis said, "Well, because I love a woman, is that any reason for all France to hate her? But I will not content myself with complaints. Go presently to Mme. de Soissons and tell her I command her not to enter the Louvre again." Disturbed, the Duc asked whether His Majesty had considered the consequences, and reminded him tactfully of his former friendship with this woman. Louis denied that there ever had been any. What, then, of respect for her family, especially for the memory of her uncle, the great Mazarin?

"You do not know me, Saint-Aignan, if you think that consideration for the person I love is not paramount to the good will of a family. There is not one little gentleman in my Court who does not make his mistress respected by his friends — and a king can't effect this. Oh, but I will effect it, and I'll begin with Mme. de Soissons."

Saint-Aignan still persisted, reminding him of La Vallière's own interests. "The Queen would be glad to have such an opportunity for removing her, on the grounds she causes only trouble."

"True," Louis said, his face changing. "The Queen would be enraged, and people would only offend, insult, and mistreat her." He suddenly burst into tears.

Louise learned of this conversation later from Saint-Aignan, and went immediately to her writing desk. The words scribbled off the pen in her strong, uneven hand. He must not be troubled, she wrote — nothing of this mattered at all — nothing but his love.

While it was hers she was too strong to be overcome by any enemy in the world.

Louis liked scholars and artists and they liked him. That year Racine was given a fine pension and made his first formal Court appearance. He was to become the most successful of a new literary generation on easy terms with the nobility. "A very handsome man," the King praised him to Louise, and she hid a small smile. It was said that this Racine bore a striking resemblance to His Majesty. He was a member of the group which met habitually in Boileau's lodgings or the convivial Mouton Blanc, where Molière and he would join in teasing the gentle, absent-minded La Fontaine, "le bonhomme," to his friends. Punishment for any broken rule of the club was to read a verse of Chapelain's poetry — or in near-criminal offenses, a whole page. This was ungrateful of Racine, since it was Chapelain who had got him a handsome gratuity for his poem on the occasion of the King's marriage, and made him noticed.

Molière as always produced more manuscript than anybody else. That autumn he had brought out his *Impromptu de Versailles,* a self-defense in the form of a satirical drama, very funny to all but his targets. Now came *Le Mariage Forcé (The Forced Marriage),* acted at the Louvre, and the King danced as an Egyptian in the entr'acte ballet. Already the author was at work on a new play to be performed in May for a great fête which had begun its evolution in His Majesty's mind.

That winter Henriette stood as godmother to Molière's firstborn son, Louis, named for his godfather the King. No actor-playwright in France had ever before received such an honor.

In March the Grande Mademoiselle was permitted to return from exile, a little grayheaded, her gowns somewhat out of style, her disposition crotchety. Her insistence on the rights of rank was remarkable even in a Court where people schemed about and fought over little else. She was quite a bore.

Lord Hollis, the English ambassador, wrote in a dispatch:

> *The Court removes hence very suddenly to Saint-Germain and after to Fontainebleau for all the summer that the building of the Louvre may be followed. I think Madame's keeping her bed put it off for some days, which is to be yet for five days longer, by reason of a fall she had, Tuesday night at the Louvre, by her foot catching in a ribbon which hung down at her masking gown, and that, very heavy with jewels, might have made the fall very dangerous against the silver grate upon which she was coming, if a gentleman (M. Clérembault, I think) had not stayed her. But, God be thanked, she hath not the least hurt, only the trouble of always lying, and not putting her foot to the ground for nine days.*

Madame was pregnant again and therefore caused extra worry on both sides of the Channel. As soon as she was up again, she and Philippe took the Queen Mother with them and set off in the Magic Bark for Saint-Cloud. Toward the end of May they rejoined the Court at Fontainebleau, and were struck by the King's open homage to La Vallière. Suddenly she was the acknowledged queen of all the *fêtes galantes*. For her fireworks made looping double L's in the sky and violins played across the water at midnight. The stag was brought down by torchlight in her name, and the versifiers exhausted all rhymes for La Vallière.

The greatest king in the world loves me
For three years constantly,
In spite of wife and mother's care —
I am La Vallière, I am La Vallière.

So went the words of a popular song.

The King had abandoned hypocritical discretion. If he could not destroy Louise's enemies, at least he could make them bow. He had begun by dedicating to her a seven-day celebration early in May — the scene, Versailles, now in its new splendor ready to be shown the world. Only the landscape had been beautified. He was not yet certain he wanted the castle itself changed, it was so charming with its pink and white brick and steep blue-gray roofs. To contemplate their destruction, to let them be engulfed, gave him unexpected qualms of reluctance. Le Nôtre had been able to persuade him only with the greatest difficulty to cut out masses of timber planted by his father, and Mansard, hot with eagerness to begin on the reconstruction, was forced to contain himself.

Louis would see what effect his innovations had on people before appropriating any more money to Versailles. And, on this same occasion, he could honor his favorite by presenting her, in a sense, this gift — the first tangible result of his creative vision.

Here was the abode of the sorceress Alcine, the story began, holding prisoned by her amorous enchantments the paladin Roger and his chevaliers. In eight days an army of carpenters and decorators had raised stages, amphitheaters, and porticoes, all elaborately decorated. Even the weather, sometimes fickle at that season, was perfect, providing a clear sky and light warm breeze for the opening pageant of the Pleasures of the Enchanted Isle.

The carrousel began with the now familiar fanfares, pages, heralds-at-arms, with contrasting interludes of strange wild bagpipe music and violins, and laudatory verses by Périgni and Benserade inscribed on the shields of the contestants. Arabesqued copies of these had been handed out to the spectators, and small localized disturbances of laugher met, as always, the lines assigned the Marquis de Saucourt, whose faunlike nature could not fail to inspire a *double entendre:*

. . . His lance for some encounter
Held always in arrest.

Under triumphal arches at the end of one of the new park's avenues sat the Queen and three hundred favored ladies. Before them paraded the four ages of gold, silver, steel, and iron, the signs of the Zodiac, the seasons, and the hours, following a gilded car twenty-four feet long and eighteen high; then shepherds arraying the lists.

The King, as Roger, had all the crown jewels on his person and the housings of his charger. Saint-Aignan, wearing his new ducal honors lightly as the plume of his helmet, rode as marshal with De Noailles, judge of the courses, and behind them came a formidable band of princes in the tinsel of antique raiment and improbable names: Aquilant le Noir, Griffon le Blanc, Renaud Brandimart, Richardet, Olivier, Ariodant, Roland. Strikingly out of place in this august company, the young Marquis de la Vallière, as Zerbin, carried a shield blazoned with a phoenix on a pyre ablaze with sun and the device *Hoc juvat uri* — happiness to be burned by such fire. If his sister felt a certain lack of taste in this, she had only smiles and praise for him later in the day when he carried off the first prize, a gold sword set with diamonds, its buckles and cross belt alone very valuable.

At twilight the King's guests approaching the banquet space saw four thousand giant torches flower abruptly into fire around a vast crescent of tables served by dryads, nymphs, and fauns, while Pan and Diana descended to greet them from a moving mountain. Beyond the golden balustrade, beyond the arcades of the theater lit with countless green and silver girandoles, an orchestra began to play.

The Pleasures lasted for six days more, surfeiting the Court with a succession of games, feasts, masques, and comedies. Molière's *Princesse d'Elide* was performed, with its bold celebration of the King's passion, and on following days the first three outrageous acts of *Tartuffe,* soon to bring down on the playwright's head the fury of the fanatical. Before the end of the celebrating, Louis had decided to let Mansard lay foundations for a new palace.

As the summer advanced it became clear to everyone what the King desired for Mlle. de la Vallière — friends, recognition, respect. Secrecy was out of date. Some kind people always appear when it may be to their advantage, and soon one of these began visiting Louise. Mme. de Brancas, wife of the chevalier of honor to the Queen Mother, was, like D'Artigny, a woman of rather mildewed reputation. She and her husband had been in the pay of Fouquet, and with his fall found their fortunes in disrepair. Anne reproached Mme. de Brancas for her overtures to Louise, and the lady went to the King in tears. Her troubles, she said, the wages of her affection for Louise, could be blamed on the Duchesse de Navailles, who talked too much. Louis was angered. Navailles was undeniably a storm center and should be removed for the peace of the whole Court.

The Comtesse de Soissons gave him his excuse. Driven to recklessness by the failure of her efforts to ruin Louise, she took direct action. Making a private appointment with Maria Theresa, she proceeded to recount to her the whole history of His Majesty's adultery and suggest methods of revenge on his brazen concubine. Wholly unnerved, the Queen locked herself up and sobbed for hours.

Olympe delayed only long enough to get settled into another role, and went to see the King. This time she was a friend torn between two loyalties; however, she dared not waver long, she said, because of the gravity of her news. His Majesty should know that, in spite of all warnings, Mme. de Navailles had been rousing the Queen against La Vallière. It might be better, Olympe added, not to mention any of this to Her Majesty herself, since she was distraught with grief and could only cause a scene.

Louis was almost pleased. With the speed of a descending axe he severed the Duchesse de Navailles from her duties as first lady-in-waiting, and replaced her with a woman of more sophisticated moral outlook, Mme. de Montausier, who was also one of Louise's new friends.

The Duc de Navailles protested his wife's treatment, and he too was banished from Court, his post as governor of Le Havre taken away and given to Saint-Aignan. No more protests were heard from any quarter.

One of the unlucky Duchesse's last official acts had been the appointment of a new attendant to the Queen, Mme. de Montespan. Louis was still cool toward her because of her tricky behavior with Madame, but there was no real reason for removing her from her new post, so he let the appointment stand. This new lady-in-waiting was a great comfort to the unhappy Queen. She was very, very religious, always first to be ready for Mass, quick with a sweet smile and her mistress's prayer book. And endearingly bad at cards was Athénaïs — the only attendant Maria Theresa had ever been able to win money from. Furthermore, the Queen had by chance overheard her criticizing La Vallière for her wickedness. Yes, this beautiful saintly young woman was nothing less than an ornament to the Household.

IX

THE PRETTY AMAZONS

A DEATHLY SICKNESS fell on the Comtesse de Soissons. In her feather beds, in the summer heat, she shivered and sweated and thought of eternal damnation. Flies clustered on the bedposts and a stagnant-river stink haunted the chamber. After a day or two without relief she sent for Madame and confessed everything she could think of concerning her own wickedness and a little about De Vardes's. Henriette could scarcely believe that all this was more than feverish imagination, but she thanked Olympe, forgave her, and talked to her consolingly for a long time. From now on, however, she would certainly keep guard on her own secrets.

In Poland the Comte de Guiche had once again narrowly escaped death. A ball striking him in the chest shattered the miniature of Madame which he wore. It was an incredible adventure, quite in keeping with Armand's character. Now he was back in Paris, but had not yet succeeded in arranging an accidental encounter. His permission to appear at Court, Louis had made clear, depended on good behavior, and Henriette herself was glad for this stricture, since she had no wish to be seen by the beautiful Armand in her present condition, swollen and awkward. Her son was born in the middle of July, and celebrations were held all over France. A boy! Monsieur preened himself, and the Queen Mother offered prayers of thanks for this little Duc de Valois. Her other grandson, the Dauphin, was a skinny child, often sick, and therefore an uncertain stake in the game of dynasty.

The Pope, after two years or so of delay, finally gave in to Louis on the Créqui affair. He had supplicated mediation by the world's Roman Catholic princes, but Germany was busy fending off the Turks, and Spain unsuccessfully at war with Portugal. By now Louis's troops were landing in Italy, and there could be no doubt that they meant to lay hands on Rome. Peevishly complaining, the Pope had a few people killed or banished by way of reparation, and then sent his nephew off to France with gifts of paintings by Titian and Leonardo and a memorized apology.

This Cardinal Chigi turned out to be a seductive-looking man of thirty, tall, with an air of distinguished suavity. The Court, charmed with him, began to arrange a series of parties. Chigi admired *La Princesse d'Elide* extravagantly and asked that Molière be presented to him, showed a discerning taste for music, and on a hunt with His Majesty skillfully killed three hares and a partridge.

> *His favorite [the King's] in the matter of government is Colbert [Chigi wrote home] of whom we shall say more later. The Duc de Saint-Aignan occupies a great place in the King's credit, which comes to him not from his participation in public affairs, but because of the part he takes in the diversions of the Court, of which he is promoter and organizer. It is through this seigneur that the King learns what the Court thinks. But the person who enjoys his favor more than any other is Mlle. de la Vallière.*
>
> *He had the flower of her virginity; she was one of the ladies of honor of the young Duchesse d'Orléans. She is of noble race. The name of La Vallière comes to her from a castle of which she is marquise. She is scarcely twenty years old. She is of more than average height; carries herself well; her face slender; her hair blond; the whiteness of her cheeks allied with pink; and she is well proportioned with great harmony of form . . . in summary, her beauty much surpasses that of the young Queen . . . She has never shown herself proud of the favor of the King, who goes regularly to see her every day.*
>
> *She loves French poetry very much and those who cultivate it . . .*

Comes now the young Queen, little . . . a face small, deli-
cate, and very white, to which art has added a certain rose.
The length of her nose offers some disproportion with the rest
of the face. The affection of the King, very lively at the be-
ginning of their marriage, has diminished since being shared
with her and La Vallière. She never intervenes in public af-
fairs and knows nothing of them, except for what she learns
from little confidences of the Queen Mother.

Chigi's eventual departure left the French quite melancholy. To
raise their spirits they packed their boxes and left for trips to Vincennes and Versailles, where building was again under way.

Louise was never far from the King that summer. Her chamber
was in the main part of the castle; she rode beside him on the
road, and walked the terraces with him after dinner every day, followed by the princes of the realm.

"She was most brilliantly beautiful," says the Grande Mademoiselle.

Philippe, pink lips pursed, asked whether Louis would make his
devotions at Pentecost. "No," Louis said, "I have no intention of
being a hypocrite like you, going to confess because Mother demands it."

The battle between Anne and Louis had been fought to a silent
impasse. Meeting, they never spoke. The courtiers, inquisitive and
amused, watched for some climax. On a certain morning mother
and son surprised each other in an otherwise empty salon. Would
either begin a conversation? Distant observers paused and speculated. Louis strolled to the window, gazed out, returned, made a
profound bow, and left. Poor Anne could not hide her tears, and
it was remarked that she ate no dinner that night. Señora Molina
walking through her oratory, later, stopped as the Queen Mother
looked up and sighed, eyes red, "Ah, Molina! These children!"
Finally Anne's confessor stepped in with some advice. She must
humble her pride and speak first, he said.

Louis was easily melted, and in the emotion of reunion confessed himself guilty and a fool in every respect. Pressing her ad-

vantage, Anne reminded him of the duties he owed his high worldly position and the terrible danger to his soul, and urged him passionately to break the chains of his bad habits. In a rare mood of frankness, Louis answered that he was often sensible of pain and shame — but, he said, in avowing his passion to God, it became all the stronger; he could not resist it, and furthermore no longer had any desire to.

Anne searched herself for an answer to this candor and found none. But Louis, never content with repelling an invasion, proceeded to counterattack. "For a long time," he said, "I have disputed with myself whether to ask women of quality to attend La Vallière, but now I have resolved that this must be, and pray you not to oppose me." Totally beaten, Anne was forced to fall back on God, who had for some time taken little apparent interest in her problems. Still, religion was something to keep her occupied. As for Maria Theresa, she was silenced even more easily than her mother-in-law.

Toward the end of September, Louis was invited by Philippe and Henriette to spend a few days at their country estate, Villers-Cotterets. It was to be an intimate family party, and he decided to bring Louise.

The Queen, almost immobilized by another advanced pregnancy, learned of the plan and retired to the oratory, that convenient refuge, to cry. Kindly reasonable, her husband urged her to be brave and cheerful. He pointed out that in only four years he would be thirty, and surely that was soon enough for a man to settle into habits of sobriety. In four years he would give up all thought of mistresses and become a model husband. Her outcries reduced to a muffled snuffling, Maria Theresa sat and listened to his athletic springing steps going away down the corridor. So, dressed in the most elegant taste, followed by respectful ladies of high rank, Louise entered Madame's house and was presented by the King. In this same house, so short a time ago, she had been a timid girl both dreading and hoping for notice from a jealous mistress. Now she was courted, amused, and complimented.

Humiliations for La Vallière were now unlikely. The only persons in a position to deal them were the queens, who by looking the other way and keeping to their rooms at certain hours of the day could avoid the sight of the lovers walking together through the gardens. But, Louis decided, even the queens must be brought into line.

From Villers-Cotterets the Court returned to Vincennes. On an October evening when Anne's friends were gathered at the game tables in her apartments, Louis led his mistress in with an utterly casual air, and sat down with her at Philippe's table, claiming him and Henriette partners by the act. After an instant of shock, all players took up their cards, dice rolled again, and the conversation got on somehow, in spite of the faces of the two onlooking queens. It was a surprise assault carefully calculated by the King for a time when his wife and mother would be together. They had thus, in effect, formally received Louise de la Vallière. What she herself felt about this evening was never said, though the observant guessed it was more painful for her than for the reluctant hostesses. Certain it is that only Louis was pleased with his surprise.

Back in her own room, Maria Theresa groaned from the depths of her outraged feelings and sent Mme. de Motteville to confer with Anne of Austria. The vivacious Mme. de Montausier, a declared partisan of Louise, met Motteville in a corridor, and the two fell on the subject and took it apart with great dispatch. Cried Montausier, "The Queen Mother has done an admirable thing in seeing La Vallière. It was the act of an able woman and a good politician. But she is so weak we can't hope she'll sustain her attitude as she should."

Some protests were heard. The Duc de Mazarin — who had married one of the Cardinal's nieces and adopted her more illustrious name — was a man well known for his piety. He sought a private audience with the King and announced that he felt constrained to tell His Majesty of the great scandal his conduct with Mlle. de la Vallière was causing. The King, having heard him out, asked, "Have you finished? For a long time I have known you were damaged up here." With a finger he tapped his own brow. The Jesuit father Annat, Louis's confessor, failed even more embarrassingly. He presented an ultimatum — either Louise or himself. He would leave Court unless the King gave up sin. Louis continued in sin, and Annat developed something of a tendency to skulk.

As far as society was concerned, Louise was a radiant success. No other royal mistress had ever gone so far so modestly, and she was given a name and a description — the Scrupulous Beauty. The Grand Condé, who had come to know her well, wrote, "One could not be more loved than Mlle. de la Vallière is at Court, never doing ill to anyone and always doing as much good as she can."

To the criticism parroted among her enemies, that La Vallière was too gentle — in fact, lacking spirit — there was vigorous contradiction on all sides. "A humor sweet and free," wrote Bussy-Rabutin, and amplified the remark with a quatrain:

> *A spirit fine and fiery*
> *Which gives a swift reply,*
> *And never has she said a word*
> *She later would deny.*

"It was necessary to amuse the King in order to hold him," Saint-Simon commented later. No woman could have kept that restless man in love so many years without wit and personal variety. But the recurrent sight of "that girl" in her own palace was too much for the Queen to bear. Personal injury might in Christianity be accepted, but not such flouting of conventional rules. She became nervous and lost sleep, developed a facial twitch, got violently nauseated, and a month later gave birth prematurely to a daughter. This infant, fearfully dark in color and hairy as a little marmoset, died almost immediately.

Yet Louis was grief-stricken. A man of strange contrasts, increasingly callous and brutal to people who crossed him, he still showed himself tender where his children were concerned, quickly touched, embarrassed by tears but unable to prevent them.

The Queen, too, would die, the physicians said. She had bled too much; her lips were white and her breathing shallow. She held the crucifix in her puffy little claws and spoke with rare, odd dignity. Her only regret, she said, was for the King, whom she had loved faithfully in spite of everything, and for his mother — moving a finger toward Anne who was bending over the bed to catch her words. She would die at peace, she continued after a pause, if Louis would grant her last request. Moved, Louis bent his head in what seemed assent. The request was that he find a husband for La Vallière and get her married without delay.

Maria Theresa had already received the last rites. Her features were pinched with the look of death. It was doubtful how much awareness remained. Yet her round blue eyes were fixed on him relentless as stones. Louis muttered that he would not oppose her. "They can find someone," he said. Who was meant by this distracted "they" nobody knew, but the promise was made; and with a sigh the Queen closed her eyelids and went to sleep, as a first step toward recovering her health.

Incongruous, everybody agreed, that His Majesty's choice for La Vallière should be, of all the men in France, the Marquis de Vardes — he, with his pretensions and sarcasms, the exact opposite of the proposed bride. But Louis knew what he was doing. De Vardes had no love for Louise. If he should agree to marry her there would be no sudden surge of husbandly jealousy for the King to contend with.

The Marquis, however, declined this match in spite of the promised dowry and political advantages. Like a wolf, he scented the concealed trap. As soon as the Queen was recovering comfortably, Louis hurried to the Palais Brion to see whether Louise was angry with him for trying to sell her. There was a certain distance in her manner which checked his ardor and finally he gave up trying to embrace her and began to justify himself. If he had permitted any talk of marriage, he said, it was only because he had been sure she would refuse absolutely. There was a long silence before she looked up to answer. "I tell you," she said, "it would be an easy thing for me to die — but to escape from an engagement as strong as ours — impossible. So love me. If you stop, I know very well there

could be nothing more for me in the world." Humbled and overcome, Louis promised that nothing in life should ever, even for an
instant, distract from her his passionate devotion. Whether she believed him or not was little to the point. It was at least three
years too late for the luxury of doubt. She knew she must try to
keep her mind serene, lest, as the Queen had done, she kill her
child by bringing it too early.

Once more it was time to shut the doors of the Palais Brion and
let down the curtains against the stares of the inquisitive.

Two eminent ladies came to call on Louise that winter, Mme.
de Sévigné and Mlle. de Scudéry, the author of those romances
which had thrilled the schoolgirls at Blois. They were there to
enlist her as an ally. Would she try to gain the King's clemency
for Fouquet, now at last coming to his trial, probably his death?

She would. But as soon as she mentioned Fouquet's name, Louis
let her know how much he disliked women's meddling in official
matters. First his mother had pestered him about this man, and
now Louise. He changed the subject.

It was not until December 20 that the prisoner's friends and
enemies learned the judges had, after all, withheld the death pen-
alty. Fouquet was to be allowed to live on in captivity as long as
he could. Mme. de Sévigné wrote that day to a friend, "Praise
God, Monsieur, and thank Him: our dear friend is saved — he
passed the thirteenth vote . . . I am so happy I am beside myself."
At the fireside of the Palais Brion, the King said, "I wouldn't have
stopped them if they'd sentenced him to death." Louise did not answer. She may have been wondering whether it was a trick of the
fire that made his face so hard.

Just after Christmas, late at night, Louise was roused from sleep
by her little favorite dog. Warm against her feet, he began vi-
brating with growls like a teakettle coming to a boil, then broke
into hysterical barking. Louise sat up, calling in alarm for her lady-
in-waiting in the next chamber.

No disturbance was heard from marauders either inside the
house or out, but on opening the window of their mistress's bed-

room the servants discovered a hook in the sill, and dangling ropes. Louis had a thorough investigation made next day, but could learn nothing more. From then on a strong guard was assigned to the Palais Brion, and a maître d'hôtel was appointed to taste Louise's food, for fear of poison.

On the coldest day of that unusually bitter January, the accoucheur Boucher entered a now familiar door, one giving on the gardens of the Palais-Royal. Precisely at noon, as the clock tower tolled, the King's third son slid into his crimson hands. At nine that evening the baby entered a process becoming routine — out of his mother's warm bed, into the respectful arms of the minister Colbert, off to a waiting carriage and the dim faces of strangers; next day, at the church of Saint-Eustache, a name which made him a person, Philippe, son of François Derssy, citizen, and his wife. It was all a great deal of bother for a child to endure who had, anyway, less than a year to live. He and his brother Charles, whose horoscope was scarcely more promising, were never even to meet.

Armand de Guiche, still romantically, hopelessly, persistently the lover of Henriette, began uncovering De Vardes's treachery. One clue pointed to another, and one day De Guiche challenged his old friend either to fight or confess his guilt. Instead, De Vardes went that afternoon to Madame with a letter in his hand which he said was from De Guiche. Something in his look alerted her, and in a nervous reaction she refused to accept it. At this, to her astonishment, he suddenly fell at her feet, groveled, wept, and asked for her pardon. Disgusted at the sight of this great cavalier in such a condition she looked away and left him to get out of the room as quickly as possible. Within a few minutes Louis had replaced him, wearing a somewhat grim smile.

De Vardes had shown him the alleged letter from De Guiche and promised, by putting it in Henriette's hands, to prove that she was a liar betraying the King's orders. His own ruin or hers had depended on whether she would accept a message from her foresworn lover. Thus De Vardes lost, dramatically.

"Leave the matter to me," Louis said calmly.

Henriette spent the rest of the day writing a long letter to her mother and Charles, giving a detailed description of her harrowing escapes. But weeks passed without any sign of resolve on Louis's part. De Vardes was still at large, evidently unscathed, and Madame's bitter enemy. De Guiche tried to see her, but she was too terrified — perhaps of the King, perhaps herself. His letters came back unopened. He begged the Comtesse de Gramont to intercede for him, and paid her daily visits in the hope of meeting Henriette there by chance. It was no use. But coincidences lie in wait for such men.

The Duchesse de Vieuville gave a masked ball. To create mystery, all guests came in hired coaches and without attendants, and mixed quickly with the crowd to prevent being identified through the company of a spouse. Entering the house, Monsieur presented his hand to an unknown lady, and Madame was claimed by a masked man prowling leopardlike on the stair. As they climbed toward the ballroom, she glanced down at the hand near her own — scarred, the thumb crooked and drawn — a familiar ugly hand. At the same time the man recognized the perfume that only she, the individual princess, wore; and they reached the top of the stair without daring to speak. Armand was the first to find presence of mind. Talking rapidly in a low voice, he told her what she had to fear from De Vardes, and recounted with some chivalrous excisions the slanders already current. Across the room Monsieur came shimmering, and the Comte turned away. Blinded by the tears running down inside her mask, Henriette stumbled on the step and fell — into Armand's arms. He held her for an instant which seemed long to both of them, while bystanders exclaimed that she had been saved a nasty accident.

Two weeks later the English ambassador, Lord Hollis, wrote in a dispatch, "The Marquis de Vardes has been ordered to surrender himself to the Bastille, to expiate some unbecoming words of which it is said that Madame has complained to His Majesty."

De Vardes had been observing with some amusement the progress of an affair between Mlle. de Fiennes, one of Henriette's maids of honor, and the Chevalier de Lorraine. "Why bother with that girl," he had asked, "when you could have her mistress just as easily?" This casual question earned De Vardes two years of confinement in the dreary village of Aigues-Mortes, and nineteen more of banishment from Court. Execution would have been kinder.

A long time had passed since Olympe could lay claim to being this man's mistress, but his fate disturbed her mind. Or perhaps it was submerged hatred of Madame, who had distracted De Vardes's speculative eye from herself. In any case, she lost all sense of caution and began telling a series of wild and contradictory lies. To Louis she said that Madame's loyalties were still with England, that the Comte de Guiche had advised her to take possession of Dunkirk in her brother's name, and that to help her he had placed the regiment of guards which he commanded at her disposal.

Such a calumny, easily proved absurd by a few words from the accused, seems to show that something was going wrong with the fine fittings of this typically Mazarin mind — secret drawers sticking here and there, keys refusing to turn, ink blots on certain important papers.

Louis's patience had come to an end, and her family name was not strong enough to protect her this time. He knew she had fooled him often in the past years, informed the Queen, and worked against Louise; he suspected in fact, that she knew something about the attempted invasion of the Palais Brion. Both Olympe and her comparatively innocuous husband, Eugène, were banished.

What seemed like strength in Henriette, and was praised by her friends, was only despair. She kept her promise to the King and refused all letters or messages from De Guiche, though it was not kept from her how he waited in corridors and courts, how thin he was getting, and how he had refused the advances of Molière's wife, the pretty prostitute Béjart. To see him would only stir up more plots against their honor and safety. Besides, they would soon be parted again, in any case — England and the States-General had finally begun their long-threatened war, and French soldiers were off to join the nearest campaign.

On the day before the scheduled departure for Holland, De Guiche was in bed with a fever. But he was desperate to see Henriette once more, and so got up and borrowed a gray linen livery from one of La Vallière's lackeys. Wearing this, he stood in the court-yard to watch her pass in her sedan chair from the Palais-Royal to the Louvre. It was a long wait and he was weak; he came up to her window, spoke, became suddenly very pale, and fainted. The sedan chair moved away as servants rushed forward to carry the rash lover back to his bed. Henriette and Armand were never to meet again.

She had occupations. The post brought diplomatic commissions from England every week; and now Louis, too, was beginning to consult her — a strange departure for the man who never permitted any other woman even to mention politics in his presence. And she was helping the Duc de Saint-Aignan compose the winter ballet, *La Naissance de Vénus* (*The Birth of Venus*), in which she herself as the Goddess of Beauty was to rise from the sea on a mother-of-pearl throne, attended by twelve Nereids. Louise was one of these, and so, according to the critics, threw the rest of the scene into eclipse.

Louis was successively Achilles, Hercules, Jason and Alexander, and the poets compared him very favorably with the originals in every case.

In England preparations were under way for the forthcoming war with Holland. Charles spoke of it in a letter to Henriette dated February 9, 1665.

> . . . *We are useing all possible diligence in the setting out the fleete for the spring. My Ld Sandwich sett saile two dayes since, with 18 good ships, to seeke out a squadron of the Duch fleete, wch we heare was seene upon the north coast of England, and if he had the good fortune to meete with them, I hope he will give a good accounte of them. I am very glad to heere that your indisposition of health is turned into a greate belly, I hope you will have better lucke with it then the Duchesse heere had, who was brought to bed, monday last, of a girle. One part I*

shall wish you to have, which is that you may have as easy a
labour, for shee dispatched her businesse in little more than an
houer. I am afraide your shape is not so advantageously made
for that convenience as hers is, however a boy will recompense
two grunts more, and so good night, for feare I fall into nat-
urale philosophy, before I thinke of it. I am Yours. C.R.

The child just borne by the Duchess of York was Princess Anne,
later to become Queen of England. With the arrival of good
weather, the rival fleets began maneuvers, watched with anxiety on
both sides of the Channel. Henriette wrote her brother nervous
messages; by return post he spoke gaily and evasively of other
things, and forwarded the latest compositions of his favorite guitar
player, Francesco Corbetta, who had lately made guitars a fashionable craze at Whitehall. But in spite of Charles's nonchalance,
everybody knew the forthcoming battle would be decisive.

In early June it happened, off Lowestoft. Charles and Henriette
heard first that their brother, the Duke of York, had been killed
when his ship, the *Royal Charles,* was blown up. The report, however, was false. The Dutch admiral, Opdam, died with five hundred
of his men in the explosion of his own flagship; seventeen other
vessels were sunk or captured, and the remnants of the fleet fled
home to the coast of Holland. It was a flamboyant victory for the
English.

The news of York's death threw Madame into a state of shock,
from which she went into convulsions. Lord Hollis wrote his
master, "If things had gone ill at sea, I really believe Madame
would have died." A later post, however, brought the full story
of the Dutch defeat, and Henriette recovered sufficiently to write
Charles.

Never has such a crowd been seen here, as Monsieur and I
have had to congratulate us on this occasion. The Comte de
Gramont was the first to bring us the news . . . We were at
Mass, and there was quite a sensation. The King himself called
out to his ministers who were in the tribune, "We must re-

*joice!" which I must say surprised me not a little, for although
at the bottom of his heart he wishes you every possible success,
I did not think he would care to declare this in public, owing to
his engagements with the Dutch.*

The French Court was summering that year at Saint-Germain,
their pleasures damped at intervals because of the Queen Mother's
recurrent illness. Louis, walking alone on the terrace at dusk one
day, saw a dim red light playing around the distant towers of
Saint-Denis, neither sunset nor St. Elmo's fire. Out of its center
rose a dark cloud which gradually took form as a hearse, and above
it, shifting but definite, the arms of Austria. He knew there could
no longer be any doubt that Anne was dying. Twice in the next
week she received the last sacraments, but still, somehow, hung on.

Grave reports came from abroad. The Black Plague had broken
out in England and was killing the London population with horrible speed. Charles moved to Hampton in the hope of escape, and
the French ambassadors, having complained crossly of the local
fogs, were now terror-stricken at the prospect of something worse.
From Kingston, where he had fled, the Duc de Verneuil wrote
home, "Yesterday I . . . while taking my daily walk along the
road, found the body of a man who had died of the plague."

A further flight to Salisbury proved they could not escape; one
of the King's servants came down with the symptoms, then a
stranger dropped dead not two hundred yards from their door. "A
bad habit," Courtin remarked, "which is, I fear, beginning to
spread."

Mme. de Sablé, a Paris lady as well known for her dread of in-
fection as for her intellectual gifts, sent the ambassadors some of
her personally concocted disinfectants, but even the moral courage
brought by these was insufficient, and when they heard that the
number of dead in London was nearing the ten-thousand mark,
they begged to be allowed to come home.

Madame's mother, herself sick with a lung complaint, set sail
for France in July; her doctors thought a trip to France might save

her life if anything could. She arrived in Paris to find that Henriette had just been delivered of a stillborn girl.

The Court in summer, however, had little time for brooding on unpleasant subjects. With his reproachful mother confined to her bed most of the time, the King took Louise with him almost everywhere but to the Council Chamber. Trips to Versailles were more frequent than ever, and sometimes Maria Theresa was allowed to come along, to accustom her to the presence of La Vallière.

The rapid embellishment of the palace was a pretext for all kinds of parties, outdoor theatricals, picnics, and suppers in the Labyrinth. But hunting was the diversion of the season. Mlle. de la Vallière's riding struck the other ladies with amazement and envy. "And," said the Grande Mademoiselle, "the dress of an Amazon suited her ravishingly; the large cravats made her appear fatter."

Condé writes, "In their embroidered jackets, these Amazons are the most piquant in the world, and particularly Mlle. de la Vallière with one of Madame's girls. They never leave the dogs, and it is impossible for any man to go faster."

These successful costumes appeared even at balls in the evenings. Reports the observant Condé, "The ladies showed themselves in jackets and those sorts of vests that are seldom worn nowadays . . . but above all Mlle. de la Vallière wears this fashion so well that one can imagine nothing prettier. She has been extremely gay on this trip."

The Abbé Locatelli, a tourist from Bologna, writes of a sightseeing expedition he made to Saint-Germain that summer while Louis was in residence. Visitors were permitted to roam the grounds from daybreak until sunset; and owing to the laxity of a sleepy concierge, Locatelli and his friends were admitted a little before the appointed hour.

In returning by galleries covered with verdure, at the moment the sun rose, we found under a tunnel of laurel Mlle. de la Vallière. She was in the company of some ladies and gentlemen, occupied with her coiffeur . . . Perceiving us, His

Majesty, who was with the Maréchal de Gramont, made a sign to us with his hand to approach. Immediately the Abbé became very pale, going quickly to throw himself at his feet. After bending the knee, following the custom, and kissing the border of his cloak, he rose at a sign from His Majesty, who asked him how he got there, and who was with him. The response heard, the King signed me to come also — I approached at once, and after having saluted the sovereign in the same fashion, I answered in my best French the questions of His Majesty. The King: "Where do you come from, Monsieur?" "From Bologna, to serve Your Majesty." "You are from a bad country." "Why, Sire? Bologna is the country of numerous saints, among whom one adores the incorruptible body of Saint-Catherine." At this name, His Majesty removed his hat, then added, "You undertake a difficult thing in trying to defend a place where men butcher other men." This was the reputation the Bolognese had then. At these words, I remained mute and my face was covered with blushes. The King turned his back to us, laughing graciously. Thus dismissed, we went out by the little gate where we had entered. The concierge almost died of chagrin . . . it had been forbidden him to let anybody enter . . .

La Vallière "was of very ordinary beauty, medium tall, a little lame, with eyes very beautiful in all truth." Locatelli remarks that the King, being then in a period of peace, was giving himself with passion to the pleasures of the chase, and that among the professional hunters themselves there was none who knew better how to load and fire a pistol or to mount a horse than Mlle. de la Vallière. "I saw her one time (at the Tuileries)," he adds, "bringing up a rough barb horse, leap straight onto his back while he ran and reared, aided only by a silk cord passed through the horse's mouth in the guise of a bridle." But, he concludes, it was also "by her grace, her spirit, her address in needlework, her talent in music and singing that she has conquered the heart of the King."

That summer, in spite of the fearful inconvenience it always entailed, Louis managed two or three short vacations alone at Ver-

Cinquieme Journeé.
Feu d'artifice sur le Canal de Versailles.

Dies Quintus.
Jocundum luthorum e igne pulvere super litusum Versaliarum.

FIREWORKS AT VERSAILLES
from an engraving by Le Pautre
(British Museum)

HENRIETTE, DUCHESSE D'ORLÉANS
from a painting by an unknown artist
(National Portrait Gallery, London)

sailles with Louise, to walk the abandoned paths and enjoy the park, so fast becoming the most beautiful in France. On such days Versailles once more seemed to Louise what it had been at her first sight — what it could never be in times of festival — a summer legend, a true palace of Alcine, through whose ethereal walls time could never break.

Louis's expansion program was proceeding satisfactorily. The colonnades of the Louvre, opposite the church of Saint-Germain de l'Auxerrois, were rising now, and he was much pleased with Colbert's new bas-relief, molded from Trajan's Column in Rome. The square was crowded all day with people from everywhere in the world watching the workmen swarm over their scaffolding a hundred and twenty feet high. But even more impressive than this evidence of the French love for sculpture, Louis thought, was the subtle reminder that the prince who could command all this also commanded a hundred thousand soldiers. Now at last he had the War Minister he needed for his fighting forces — Louvois, bright, brutal, singleminded.

Already, a year before, Louis had invented the officer's confidential report, which was a wedge under the old corruption. This year, on the death of the Duc d'Epernon, Colonel-General of the Infantry, he had seized the post, and now, with the help of young Louvois, he was undermining the posts of Grand Master of Artillery and Colonel-General of Cavalry. He hoped that these appointments would soon be purely decorative. He himself would then be in complete control, as a king should. He had an interest in most of the current world conflicts, having recently sent reinforcements to the Emperor of Austria, who was fighting the Turks, and dispatched an expedition to Cyprus under command of the Duc de Beaufort. An exceptionally hardy man was Beaufort, and possessed of a strong stomach. During a recent sickness he had received a deputation of fishwives from Les Halles in his bedchamber and let them all kiss him. They had wanted to look at his golden head on the pillow and assure their idolatrous sisters of the Guild that he was on the way back to health. But the palace smelled of eels for the rest of the day.

After the building, military, and diplomatic schemes came myriad minor concerns — the organization of an Indian company, the sending of shiploads of horses to New France, the purchase of the Gobelins for tapestry manufacture.

And with Louis's growing sense of personal dignity came symbols of formality. The Knights of the Holy Ghost, a newly created group, wore a uniform exactly like His Majesty's own — seventy gentlemen authorized to go with the King on hunting parties and drives, all in blue outer coats embroidered with gold and silver, worn over vests lavishly beribboned. To go with this, a shoulder belt with sword, muslin throat band edged with fine lace, and broad-brimmed beaver surmounted by a double row of plumes. This was a fashion which would soon sweep all of Europe, except such dark barbaric countries as Spain and Poland.

The year 1665 was a good one for the Bastille, which received for safekeeping four eminent men, Fouquet, Bussy-Rabutin, Péguilain, and Sacy.

The Comte de Bussy-Rabutin, cousin, friend, and would-be lover of Mme. de Sévigné, and wielder of a too-sharp pen, made a serious mistake. A scurrilous little pamphlet which he had intended only for the amusement of his friends, *Histoire Amoureuse des Gaules* (*An Amorous History of the Gauls*), got into the hands of a treacherous mistress and thence into print. In this fanciful version of bedtime life at Court, La Vallière was treated with respect, but Madame and many other important lovers were sullied. Louis, apoplectic, sent the author to prison for twelve months, just as a beginning.

Little Péguilain, recently come into his title of Duc de Lauzun, but still fierce as a hornet, had loved his beautiful cousin, De Guiche's sister, ever since childhood. When she married the Prince de Monaco, he had dressed in a postilion's garb and followed her honeymoon carriage clear across France as a sign of brokenhearted fidelity.

Now Mme. de Monaco was back at Court, accompanying her husband on a business trip, and showing herself somewhat bored by a devotion threadbare as Lauzun's. To his jealous eyes it was clear that she wanted another man — and that man none other than

Louis himself. Her seductions were subtle, the King alert. Lauzun, quick as a rocket to fizz and explode, commanded the Princesse to stop her shameful flirtation. To emphasize his disapproval he stole some compromising letters of hers, and she, enraged, complained to Louis. A terrible scene ensued. Questioned arrogantly by the King, Lauzun answered even more arrogantly. Louis could not draw his sword and run a subject through, though both men rather thought for a moment that he would. He had only one recourse.

Sacy was the smallest fish in the net, having been merely a religious dissenter too insistent on his own point of view.

Somehow the thought of this silent quartet damped the vivacity of those still at liberty around Court, and pointed a definite moral — it was no longer safe to contradict His Majesty in matters of finance, gallantry, or Church doctrine.

On the feast day of Sainte-Anne, July 26, the Queen Mother lay worn out with the long labor of her death. Inside the *ruelle* of her bed stood Maria Theresa and Mme. de Motteville. The Queen was complaining about her husband. "But," she murmured, softening to vague tears, "my troubles are nothing, if God will only preserve my mother," and turning to Motteville, "If I lose her, what shall I do?" There were no new words of comfort for the dying woman to say, though the old ones recited over again usually helped for a while. But who was to help Anne herself? Not Louis, who had in other days stayed beside her, anxious as a daughter, covering her when it got cold at night and sleeping on a trundle bed within call.

This was her Saint's day, too — and he had taken Louise to Versailles on a pleasure trip. When he paid a dutiful visit to his mother next morning she would scarcely speak to him. Her night had been sleepless with pain and bitter thoughts, and it was not hard for Louis to guess her feelings. He was subdued and guilty and begged her pardon. After all, it was obvious the old Queen must soon die in spite of her astounding tenacity. In justice he should, he realized, restrain his pleasures for a time, stay home and practice filial respect.

Consequently, the Court moved for several days at a slowed

pace. But the great turning wheels of the realm could not be stopped even for Anne of Austria; there was the grueling work always. And a man soon to be orphaned needed to forget his worry, needed a cheerful mistress more than ever. Louise had no idea, he thought, how mistaken she was to show signs of melancholy at such a time. Occasionally there was even a hint of reproach in her eyes. A slight coldness came into their association, until she abandoned what he called her pseudo-pious affectations and began amusing him again.

The marital squabbles of Philippe and Henriette were frequent and spirited, that year.

"You could never be King," she told him one day.

"And why not?"

"You're too little."

Philippe brooded on this wound to his vanity and ended by ordering a pair of boots with very high red-lacquered heels. He tottered proudly in to supper only to discover that Louis still loomed above him. His Majesty wore an ill-concealed smile and a duplicate pair of red-heeled boots. Monsieur's irritation was obvious to all. He never would learn that it was useless to compete with such a brother as Louis XIV.

The whole trouble, Philippe thought, was Louis's total lack of consideration for others. For instance, knowing full well that none of the Court might put on a hat until he chose to don his, Louis often kept everyone standing around in the evening air in danger of neuralgia or worse. On occasion Philippe had been forced to lay his gloves across his head for protection.

Louis was violent, too. Once when they were boys he had poured a whole bowlful of *bouilli* in Philippe's hair just because he had reached for a piece of meat, forgetting it was Lent.

Madame had less time than her husband to meditate on personal wrongs, past and present. As mediator between Charles and Louis, she was greatly worried by her two countries' strained relations. Her long-worked-for treaty seemed certain to miscarry.

Charles, frankly irritated by the continual delays and slippery policy of Louis, wrote that month,

. . . Standers by say these Ambassadores are kept here only till France can agree with Holland upon what termes they shall helpe them, on which, if they agree, I shall be necessitated to take part with Spaine, and to your exception thereunto, lett me minde you that, according to the course of the World, those are better frinds who see they have neede of us, then those whose prosperity makes them think we have neede of them.

The English ambassador, Hollis, forwarded his own comment on the ominous situation in a report.

. . . When the King of France went away, I had an interview with the Queen Mother afterwards, and took the boldness to ask her how she found things. She said they had been all the time within talking over these businesses of Holland, and that Louis XIV told her he had made King Charles some propositions, which were very fair ones, which, if he refused, he must take part with the Hollanders.

A little later Hollis's dignity was hurt by an insult from the Princesse de Carignan — one of those savage little struggles for precedence which so constantly enlivened the courtiers' day. His carriage on its way to the Louvre was stopped by her servants armed with clubs, and made to wait until hers had entered the gate. The fiery, morose old Puritan refused to accept either Henriette's apologies or those of the Princesse herself, and became absolutely intractable. It was impossible to make further use of him as a mediator in the English-French crisis.

All during the autumn Madame and the Queen Mother carried on negotiations, but with failing hope. Charles himself now saw clearly that war was inevitable. In October the English Parliament met at Oxford, and the French proposals were formally rejected. Now war lay in wait along all horizons, giving an occasional thunderous mutter, but its actual outbreak was delayed by Anne's torturedly slow dying and her constant prayers to Louis to prevent this ultimate horror. They moved Anne in a litter from Saint-Germain to Paris, journeying toward the end, toward the royal vaults of Saint-Denis. Unknown to them, however, another death had taken precedence of hers — that of her brother, Philip IV of Spain.

Louis was gratified when the news arrived. Fate's neat gambits had a way of leaving weapons in his hands, almost as if some co-operating genius were at work. Now was the time for advancing formal claim in his wife's name to the sovereignty of Flanders.

As Mazarin had foreseen, Maria Theresa's dowry had never been paid in full, and so the rest of the contract might be regarded as waste paper. To Louis the dowry was a negligible matter. He much preferred Flanders — and would take it.

X

SORCERY AT COURT

"DO NOT BELIEVE," she said, "that my mirror has failed to teach me the truth. I have lost almost everything that can please, and I am afraid that, your eyes not being satisfied, you will search among the beauties of your Court to content them. But, do not deceive yourself — you will never again find what you find in me."

The King, says the chronicler, looked long and searchingly at his mistress, and reassured her with the power of words which he knew how to wield so well. What he esteemed in her more than the freshness of that color, more than the brilliance of those eyes, was her spirit and her heart — qualities so beautiful that they could end only with her life. And the woman, embracing him, said, "You are good, my prince, to comfort a heart that fears too much because it loves too much."

The pageantry of that Christmas season, though planned in the intervals of Anne's illness, was more marvelous than ever before. Under the music, the cadenced tread of squadrons; around the King a cloudlike darkness from which rays came, such an aura of power and danger as gods have and use for making worshipers out of men.

Maria Theresa, in deep mourning for her father, did not attend Madame's fête on the eve of the Three Kings; but Louis came, through the great gallery of the Palais-Royal, his progress between the exclaiming mirrors, under the crystal conflagration of the chandeliers, stopping all voices. He wore a suit of violet velvet seeded with pearls and diamonds, and walked already like a conqueror.

Nobody could doubt that this ominous year would deliver itself to him like a woman.

The program for the evening read, "Concert in the great gallery of the Palais-Royal. Comedy in the small. Supper. Ball." The comedy, Molière's *Le Médecin Malgré Lui* (*Doctor in Spite of Himself*), was to become the winter's most popular play in Paris. Delighted courtiers, hearing the King's uncontrollable fits of laughter, were even more amused by the disgruntlement of His Majesty's physicians. In the opinion of the medical fraternity, it was a play in very poor taste.

"So the world laughs at doctors who kill folks with impunity," said a moralist.

A few days later, Louise's flighty little follower, Mlle. d'Artigny, was married in the greatest style to a rich man, the Comte du Roure. Louis, who never forgot a promise, had arranged it, and the ceremony was performed in Madame's apartments by her particular friend, Daniel de Cosnac, Bishop of Valence. The King and Philippe helped the bridegroom into his nightshirt and put him to bed, and Henriette and Athénaïs de Montespan honored the new Comtesse in similar fashion.

This was an event full of possibilities for the gossipers. Such unheard-of condescension from royalty to that cheap little D'Artigny, such favor from His Majesty, could only mean that La Vallière's power was growing. Soon, they said, she would control the giving of public office. But the gossip was wrong. That evening Louis looked up, laughing, across the marriage bed, and saw with some surprise how fabulously beautiful Mme. de Montespan was.

Maria Theresa hung around the chambers of her mother-in-law, complaining as usual. No queen in history had ever endured such insults as she. How dared His Majesty shower on servants of La Vallière honors reserved for princesses of the blood royal? One must be a Christian, said Anne patiently; a wife must forgive a young husband his youth. A wizened little smile showed for an instant through her agony, like a flower in a thicket. Just before she completed her tedious dying she spoke separately for a while with Louis, Maria Theresa, Philippe, the Grande Mademoiselle, and Henriette. Something had revived her old affection for Madame, who was now to receive the crucifix Anne held and many of her most valuable jewels.

An express had been dispatched for the sacrament, and while waiting the mourners retired to the adjoining cabinet. There they settled all questions of ceremonial and other business matters, including the division of Anne's apartments at Saint-Germain.

Louis decided that he should leave for Versailles at the moment of her death, and Philippe might go to Saint-Cloud, if he wished. This left the Grande Mademoiselle in charge of the funeral arrangements, an idea which she was forced to accept, though not without a certain amount of carping.

Difficulties arose at the approach of the Archbishop of Auch and his almoners with the Holy Viaticum. How far should the party advance to meet this procession? Mme. de Motteville, always helpful, remembered that when Louis XIII lay dying his mourners had gone as far as the outer door of the palace. The Grande Mademoiselle, glad to encounter a problem she could grasp, objected. This was too much honor for simple churchmen. It was her privilege to walk first, and she would not go one step beyond the middle of the court of the Louvre. All agreed.

Receiving extreme unction, Anne lay apparently unconscious, but as a priest bent to anoint her ears with oil she stopped him and made Mme. de Flex, one of her women, raise the lace borders of her cap to prevent their being smeared. As soon as the ceremony was over, the King fainted and was carried into the next room.

Philippe, tethered all night to his mother's bed by some belated filial feeling, was the only family member to witness the last frightful phenomena, which came at six o'clock. He was so upset he refused to stay another second, and hurried away to Saint-Cloud before the sun rose. Mme. de Flex carried the dead woman's keys to Louis, and her will was brought out and read before the remaining family by the minister Le Tellier. Immediately afterward the King took carriage for Versailles.

Business got under way. Anne of Austria had wished her heart to be buried at Val-de-Grâce, her own church built in thanks for Louis's birth. This relic was escorted there by three dutiful ladies, Mme. de Longueville, the Princesse de Carignan, and the long-suffering Grande Mademoiselle, dressed in a very fashionable mourning cloak. She waived her right to sit beside the royal heart, "because," she said frankly, "of the malady from which she died." A man of the cloth, supposedly less susceptible to the contagion of breast cancer, took her place.

Next evening solemnly at seven, the body itself was borne from the Louvre to Saint-Denis. There the mourners packing the church listened for an hour and a half to the traditional harangue of the Archbishop, on delivering up the corpse at the portal, and the prior's replies. Obsequies went on until two in the morning.

Simultaneous rites were in progress at Notre Dame, where the royal family appeared, with Madame as chief mourner in a train seven yards long.

Six days after Anne's interment, Louis declared war against England, first with an intimation to the ambassadors and then publicly with the reading of an official proclamation and flourish of trumpets.

Sermons, always epidemic at that season, set in now with unusual severity. In addition to the regular Lenten weekday course in the chapel of Saint-Germain, there were plagues and plethoras of funerary dissertations. Only one man's voice rose clear and significant above this windy oratory. Bossuet, newly appointed Dean of Metz, made Sunday a civilized day for the Court's more sensitive listeners. That winter of 1666 marked the beginning of his friendships with the two women most greatly envied, most deeply troubled, at Court — Henriette and Louise.

For comfort after Anne's death, Philippe fled home to the arms of his dearest friend, the Chevalier de Lorraine — a blond, rather fat younger brother of the Grand Equerry, M. d'Armagnac. His cherub face had won Monsieur, and the bond had been tightened, if anything, by Lorraine's notorious affair with the maid of honor Fiennes.

Monsieur, roused to desperate jealousy on this occasion, was willing to promise Lorraine anything in return for his exclusive attention. What the Chevalier wanted, it soon became clear, was plenty of money and complete control of Monsieur's household. Now it seemed that, in spite of Madame's bitter opposition, he was on the verge of success. Servants loyal to Henriette began to disappear mysteriously from the staff; her orders were countermanded. Between her and this tenacious house guest raged a silent war, while Philippe kept busy with his endless trivia. He refused to hear a word against his friend — not a word! Everybody knew what a surly disposition Henriette had, anyway.

More and more often the Court was treated to the sight of Philippe hanging girlishly on Lorraine's arm at parties, a dainty figure with a waist undeniably as small as Mlle. de Fiennes's, and with much prettier eyes.

Louis congratulated himself on his past self-restraint and tact in the matter of his mother and Louise. "I have the consolation of knowing that I never disobeyed her in anything of consequence," he said with perfect sincerity. But now Anne was gone, and the old-fashioned at Court were no longer to be humored. As the first example of his changed regime, he gave the Queen a new attendant, Mlle. de la Vallière.

Before the end of January a reception was held for a large deputation from the Parliament, come to "make compliments to the King on the death of the Queen Mother." At the mass which followed, the astonished eyes of the magistrates were turned magnetically toward La Vallière, close beside Her Majesty.

D'Ormesson, peering through spectacles of moral outrage, wrote, "In spite of her very handsome eyes and color, this damsel does not seem beautiful to me. She is skinny, mouth and teeth ugly, the end of her nose big, and her face too long."

Louise certainly was not at her best that afternoon, suffering nervous strain at this prominence which was for her a pillory. She was, besides, in the first tremulous, pallid days of morning sickness. Sometimes such desultory comment as D'Ormesson's will forecast not only a change of weather but a new season. The King was not noticeably cool to his favorite — if anything, he was more ingenious than ever in finding ways to honor her. But someone had expressed surprise on finding the famous belle "so little beautiful." There it was. Within a few weeks it would become, curiously, almost universally in style to speak of La Vallière with pity and disparagement. Ignorant as trees in a grove, which are however never mistaken, shedding their leaves obediently in unison at the end of summer, the Court whispered. Louise heard the rustle, falling, falling, and was inexplicably cold. One thing brightened her during that Lent of universal mourning; she was able to see her firstborn son often after the death of his infant brother, Philippe. Charles had been brought to the Tuileries by his father's order and established in a fine nursery befitting his position. He was becoming quite handsome, much like Louis, with dark eyes, and an air of absurd pomposity that dissolved his mother in love and amusement. She had never dreamed that a two-year-old could be so definitely a person and such fascinating company.

Jean-François de la Vallière was not so much in favor as he had been. He could scarcely be blamed for the fact that his wife was plain and grave, but when he became attracted to Mlle. de Fiennes and consequently fell afoul of the Chevalier de Lorraine, the King's reaction was astounding. "It will give me pleasure if you will have no more business of this nature with that girl."

Anyone would suppose, huffed the red-faced Marquis in private, that the King himself was some irreproachable old churchman.

Philippe, all mixed up, not knowing quite where to pin his rancor, decided on the Marquis, since it would never do to accuse Lorraine — he might get cross. Consequently, M. de la Vallière sensed himself somehow less charming than he had been for the past year or so. He took the occasion of Anne's death to address his individual condolences to Louis, and may have allowed himself some quasi-fraternal expression. In any case, the King's response was extremely dry. "Monsieur le Marquis de la Vallière, what I have suffered in losing the queen, my mother, surpasses all the efforts of your imagination, and, to answer you briefly, know that only

the Hand which dealt me such a wound is capable of healing it."
Very soon the snubbed one left for Holland at the head of the
Dauphin's Light Horse, probably grateful for the chance to forget
Court life in his duties as Captain-Lieutenant.

Péguilain, or Lauzun, as he must now be called, was out of jail
again, looking for trouble. His love for Mme. de Monaco had not
perished in the Bastille, but it had changed, gone quite mad. She
was terrified of him and hid whenever possible. Slight as her reward had been for last summer's pinches and asides with the King,
she was compromised, and it was obvious from Lauzun's harsh
witticisms, piercing glares, flaring nostrils, that he would like to
complete her ruin himself in some publicly humiliating way. Who
had stolen the key with which she was to have let herself into
Louis's chamber, and then stood hidden and grimly smiling while
the thwarted pair whispered through the keyhole? Ha!

On a hot afternoon at Versailles a gambling game for a jewel
worth two hundred pistoles was in progress. The ladies in their
summer gowns sat for coolness on the floor. The King stepped
back two paces in order to see better, and those between him and
the wall had to move aside.

One of these, Lauzun, planted his sharp lacquered heel in the
open palm of Monaco's hand and twirled on it. She screamed with
pain, and everyone cried out sympathetically. Lauzun declared himself horrified, devastated, and aghast at this clumsy misstep, but his
curled fierce mustaches were quivering all the time like those of a
cat who has just landed a fish and is watching it leap. Louis was
very much annoyed.

The Prince de Monaco found his honor involved in the matter,
and saw no way out except to go to Holland and consult with his
brother-in-law, the Comte de Guiche. Arrived in the Low Countries, he found the French camp a rather pleasant place, char-
acterized by an atmosphere of amiable buffoonery. One day
De Guiche challenged his friend the Marquis de la Vallière to a costume contest. He himself shortly appeared before the unbelieving
eyes of the sober Dutch dressed in an outfit part Greek, part

Roman, with strong suggestions of the Spanish, Italian, and Hungarian.

La Vallière had not been able to rid himself so effectively of all French influence, but was highly ridiculous, just the same. While they argued over the prize, an innocent visitor appeared, the Comte de Louvigny, dressed merely as himself, a noble gentleman of the French Court. De Guiche and La Vallière conceded defeat at once and awarded him the crown. Even more surprising than all this, to the good citizens, was the subsequent spectacle of costumes being flung off by the young lunatics as they got back into military harness. The Prince de Monaco was much warmed by this company, and after a few days decided to stay and join the Dutch fleet. It was better than life at Court.

"The Queen of France," an English correspondent wrote in June, "perceiving Mlle. de la Vallière big with child, hath forbid her to appeare before her any more, and disgraced some of her ladyes of honor, who deluded Her Majestie, that there was nothing but a meere friendship between the King and her."

This act, in spite of its humiliation of Louise, brought longed-for relief. The entertainments of Court were beginning to seem a little mechanical, the inexorable routine very tiring. Because of the growth of the Royal Academy of Painting and Sculpture, she was forced to leave her little Palais Brion. Louis gave her instead a tall house near the Tuileries, its front windows looking down the Rue de l'Echelle — an establishment more suited, he said, to the dignity of her status. Dignity was a word he had begun to use often, and sometimes Louise felt when he looked at her that he saw not herself but some half-symbolic figure, the mistress of the King of France. It was as if a barrier had come up between them through which they could speak and touch, but to no effect, all signals become empty of meaning, bringing the wrong response, or none. For pleasure and occupation she spent hours every day with little Charles. And then there appeared in her salon a new amusing companion. Not new, really, but rediscovered — Athénaïs de Montespan. In the old days at Madame's court both had been too full of girlish whimsicality, too self-centered, to make company of each other. Now, Louise thought, they were mature enough for a genuine friendship.

Athénaïs came by every afternoon, full of spirited advice regarding the furnishing of the new house, piquant gossip about the people they knew, and anecdotes concerning the poor Queen's daily gaffes. And how unfailingly exquisite Athénaïs was; if she were to wear a wreath of pea vines in her hair all other styles must at once become obsolete, pretentious, and worthy of ridicule — if a crown, she was Diana and all other women hairy-legged provincials. This individuality was laid, furthermore, on everything she touched, so that it became funny or glamorous according to her mood, the way a witch's finger may turn an empty box into a mud turtle or a bowl of potpourri. She was two years older than Louise, but looked, it was said, four years younger. Married and already the mother of two sons, one would have taken her not for a woman but one of those strange young girls who disturb the mind with doubt as to whether they are naïve or provocative, so sweetly slanderous are their words, so innocent the glance of their slightly upslanted eyes.

Tactfully, Athénaïs refrained from mentioning these daily visits to Louise in the Queen's presence. It could only upset poor Maria Theresa, who looked on Madame de Montespan as a comfort sent her from heaven. Every evening in Her Majesty's bedchamber, Athénaïs presented commentary on the day at Court in the form of sharp little impromptus as good as Molière's. Plenty of men pursued her with clever or clumsy blandishments, and every word they said, every roll of the eyeballs, was naughtily parodied for the Queen's benefit — and the King's. The anecdotes repeated again and again a subtle message for him: "See how I reject all other men. I am waiting . . ."

At first His Majesty was present only occasionally, sitting on the *ruelle* and smiling in the shadow of the curtains. Then, as the weeks passed, he began coming almost every night. Maria Theresa was delighted with this development and proud to have such a chance for showing her cynical husband how virtue may exist side by side with beauty. For Mme. de Montespan, by her own testimony, was a devoted wife, pious to the point of saintliness, and nobody else at Court was so outspokenly critical of sin. In fact, Maria Theresa wished Louis could overhear some of the cutting things Montespan said about La Vallière in confidence. But of course it would never do to repeat them, or he'd banish her the way he had Mme. de Navailles.

Athénaïs went several times that winter and spring to visit the sorceress La Voisin. Her request was an old story to the wise woman. For years before this, Court ladies carefully masked had been coming at night to ask help in getting rid of the King's mistress. There had been the Comtesse de Soissons and that abortive assassination at the Palais Brion. And, more recently, the Comtesse du Roure — Mlle. d'Artigny, she had been — who wanted La Vallière poisoned. But such things were not easy to compass, not easy at all, even for a conscientious practitioner like herself.

None of these other ladies, however, had shown such persistence as Mme. de Montespan. It was barely possible she had that rare nerve necessary to bring about a successful stroke of chiromancy. First there were the ordinary preliminaries — reading cards, studying the palms, and looking into the eyes; then incantations, and love powders blended in a chalice. Athénaïs found it was a lot of trouble to get these powders introduced into the King's food, and the results were maddeningly slow — imperceptible, in fact.

The sorceress was at last obliged to hold a meeting with her colleagues, the priest Mariette and another by the name of Guibourg, called The Prior because his legitimate church was the priory of Bois-Courtilz. Guibourg was a sinister man in appearance, dark-skinned, with a cast in one eye. His mistress was a noted poisoner. The couple's talents lay rather in murder than contraception, and none of their numerous offspring had lived long. It was decided among this group that the importance of Mme. de Montespan's problem justified strong measures. Accordingly, on a fine day of early summer, a carriage rolled out on the road to Orléans. Half a league from Paris lay the medieval Château de Villebousin, surrounded by a deep stagnant moat and thus proof against surprise.

Not even crows scattering cinderlike over the sky could see into the small darkened chapel where, an hour later, a young woman came barefoot over the cold sweat of the stone floor and stretched out on the altar. She should have been naked, but her high rank had won some modification of the rules. Instead she lay with a sheet over hips and legs, face covered by a scarf. Between the rows of lighted candles Guibourg approached in his priestly robes, carrying a white cloth and chalice. These were arranged on the bare belly of the supplicant, and the Black Mass began. It was a long ritual, seen mostly as shadows by the young woman peering from under the edge of her scarf.

At the moment where a ritual kiss is commonly given the altar stone, Athénaïs received it on her flesh and betrayed her feelings by a tightening of the toes and fingers, but still maintained utter silence. Now it was time for the consecration. Usually a stillborn child was used, but today all things must be well done. The baby, a thin, thumb-sucking boy, was carried to the priest who received him reverently.

"Astaroth, Asmodeus, princes of friendship and love," went the conjuration, "I conjure you to accept this sacrifice which I present you, this infant for the things which I ask. I conjure you, spirits whose names are written in these papers, to accomplish the will and design of the person for whom this mass has been celebrated."

The woman on the altar took her cue. "I ask the love of the King, and that I obtain all that I ask of him for me and my parents . . . that he leave and see no more La Vallière."

After a pause Guibourg, precise as a surgeon, stuck his little knife into the child's throat and let its blood pump into the chalice. The body was then carried away for a more leisurely operation, the removal of heart and entrails. These would receive a second oblation before being burned and reduced to a powder for the use of Louis XIV.

Nobody was ever quite sure why Charles, who had been such a sturdy little boy, died that summer. Some said it was from fright at a sudden cannon salute — he might have had an unsuspected weakness of the heart. But from whatever cause, he died like a snipped flower in the July heat, as was so often the way with children. It could not be helped; one had to be philosophical. The Court was at Fontainebleau holding its midsummer revels at the time, and Louis sent Colbert home to the Tuileries to take care of funeral arrangements. Bleary-eyed with weeping over the little boy who had been so like himself, the King nevertheless could not endure Louise's company very long. He wanted comfort and distraction, not a constant reminder of loss brought by the sight of other people's tears, deathlike faces, and disheveled hair. To grieve was natural, he thought and said, but prolonged melancholy was selfish and unattractive.

It was astonishing how understanding Mme. de Montespan was to the King during this time, with her tender humor and a certain look of sympathy he kept surprising on her face. Louise was no less grateful for Athénaïs's company; to have her in the house was to create an illusion of her own gaiety. Charm and light were necessary to the King — and could it matter so much, for a little while, which woman was their source? "Help me amuse him," she asked with a little rueful smile, and her friend consented very graciously.

In society, war was the fashion of the day. A military camp had been established at Fontainebleau, where Lauzun cavorted at the head of the royal dragoons. Consistently out of step with life, the Grande Mademoiselle had noticed and admired this fiery pipsqueak, and was at last, at age forty, suffering the embarrassing pangs of adolescent love. Other Court ladies, too, attended the military reviews, riding behind His Majesty to Compiègne and Vincennes. But Louise, awkward in advanced pregnancy, could not ride. There was little to do but sew, walk in the gardens, and read — always books that might make diverting discussion with the King. But now they were seldom long enough alone.

In late summer the Court moved to Vincennes. It was an uncomfortable palace to live in, meant only for public affairs and parties, built in the antique style without corridors, but with labyrinths of rooms; no place for the indulgence of sickness or gloom — certainly no place for the bearing of a child. But Louise was surprised there by untimely labor on October second, and Boucher, hastily summoned, was late arriving. Lying on her bed to rest at intervals, or walking her chamber with white lips and the sweat of the second stage beginning, she would hear her door open and have to turn a face of civil greeting toward ladies and gentlemen passing through on their way to other apartments. Some hours passed, and then, finally Boucher, just in time for the final throes. Louise was well trained; there must be no crying out as the astonishing pains clamped her in two. But she did groan, gasping for breath.

At this moment the door opened again and Henriette advanced with little steps into the room. "What's the matter?"

"Ah, Madame! I have the cramps. I'm dying."

With a glance of contempt Henriette passed on.

"Hurry," Louise said to Boucher. "Hurry, for God's sake. I want to be delivered before she comes back."

This time she had a daughter, delicate and small as a wax doll. Louise was given only a glimpse of her before the high furious cry was stifled in linen and shawls and smuggled away. There was no time for holding her in such a public place, not even the meager three hours which had been allowed before.

All precautions were as usual futile. Everybody at Court knew within an hour or two that the King had another bastard, and fell with vengeful willingness into the expected pretense of ignorance. Many ladies, exclaiming concern for La Vallière's undiagnosed affliction, flocked to her room all afternoon and evening to study the patient and visit. Louise had roused from her trance of exhaustion, with some instinct of self-defense, and ordered the room filled with plants and flowers. And now, powdered and perfumed, her hair brushed back into curl, she chatted and played the hostess. There were card tables and refreshments, and at midnight a *médianoche* speedily devoured by the rapacious guests. The ordeal lasted twelve hours.

Louis was one of the few who did not call that day on the new mother. He was at Versailles in the morning, and stopped on the way home to buy some presents for various ladies he knew, for various reasons.

XI

THE TASTE OF DEATH

T H E R E W A S a feeling of disaster in the air despite all the carnival. London lay in ashes after its great fire in September. None knew the extent of the loss yet or could feel anything but awe and regret, though England was, at the moment, an enemy.

At midwinter Monsieur's two-year-old son was taken with fever and convulsions. He was a promising prince, handsome and doted on. His father decided in a panic that he must be baptized at once — a ceremony usually put off until age twelve. Accordingly the small Duc de Valois was taken from his bed to church and thoroughly doused with cold water. His death the following evening was looked on at Court as a national calamity, because of the delicacy of the King's only son. It was said by those with an ironical turn of mind that if young Philippe-Charles had been a common citizen's son instead of Monsieur's, he would have lived.

The heart was taken to Val-de-Grâce, the body brought late on a December night to the tombs of kings at Saint-Denis, through the dark streets in a slow procession of princes and nobles bearing lighted torches. Henriette's friend, Daniel de Cosnac, the lovable, swashbuckling Bishop of Valence, spoke the funeral discourse.

Madame was too numbed by shock to hear the sympathetic speeches addressed to her by the world. Monsieur was also deeply distressed, almost without intermission, for two full days. Then his mind was mercifully invaded by anxiety over securing for himself the reversion of the allowance his son had received from Louis.

All winter the King danced as if love and war were not enough for his superhuman energy. The great performance of the new year, *Ballet des Muses,* was repeated several times. Rather more subtle than usual, Benserade's verses hinted at new things in the lives of the dancers.

Louis, a shepherd, was styled a destroyer of wolves; and Athénaïs, who had been allotted a very routine verse the year before, now was permitted a certain note of impertinence which must have been disturbing to her somber young husband the Marquis.

Louise, a stylish shepherdess, was joined by the King as the dance ended, to form a charming pastoral picture, poised and smiling — a couple marked, nonetheless, for ruin by the powers of hell. Louise's verse was to be her last public tribute. Its respectful gentleness is typical of the tone Benserade always took with her, contrary to his slanderous nature.

> *Young shepherdess in whom heaven has put*
> *All it gives its best friends,*
> *Of beauty, heart, and wisdom —*
> *And — to believe your eyes — of tenderness,*
> *You seem the ornament of the village,*
> *And I love to see in an object so handsome*
> *Perfectly both these things assembled:*
> *So much glory and so much modesty.*

Maria Theresa, pregnant again, kept to her apartments and out of the way; and Louise, too, wryly recognized the familiar symptoms in herself, though her latest baby, Marie-Anne, was not yet four months old.

To crown the Carnival season, Louis threw open the doors of Versailles for a week, and here the forecasters were regaled by the sight of Mlle. de la Vallière and Mme. de Montespan seated together at one of the four principal tables, "incessantly served with an equal abundance and politeness."

Here on one of the ethereal green days of April, belles and cavaliers rode out for an equestrian meet, all admirably equipped, conducted by Madame dressed in a vest of ruby-red velvet and mounted on a white horse covered with a cloth-of-gold brocade stiff with pearls and stones. Louis in a stylized version of Hungarian costume rode like Attila, all gold lamé and diamonds. But this tournament was not exclusively antique in tone. Besides swords and lances, pistols were brought in and fired, some with perfect success. The lanterned fabulous park was open to the public, and all who came in masks were allowed to join the dancing. "All Paris was there," a correspondent wrote, "and four thousand partridges were served at supper."

Five days after the Queen was brought to bed of another girl, writes D'Ormesson, "the ballet given at Court, full of the buffooneries of Molière and the Italian comedians, showed us the King and La Vallière side by side."

The observant Prince de Condé remarks, "In the middle of these diversions there were a million intrigues among the women. They were bitter in their hearts; all were extremely jealous of Mlle. de la Vallière; there were very few who did not envy her."

Condé, being a man, was wrong, however, on the significant point. There was, indeed, universal jealousy among the women, but it was jealousy of each other, rather than of La Vallière. They circled her in speculative unrest, as if she were an image from which the magic had gone. She was finished, they knew by the myriad tiny signs which, in total, men call intuition. Which of them would topple her from the pedestal and take her place?

Rumors grew like fungus. It was said the Duc de Lauzun would be married to La Vallière. The Duc d'Aumale, rather. No, neither of these, but De Vardes, after all, who had been forgiven by the King and would soon appear at Court again. Nobody knew better than Louise what nonsense rumors usually are. She heard and believed each one of these in turn.

Athénaïs, still faithfully joining Louise every evening to help amuse His Majesty, was an interested observer of the signs by which the royal mistress betrayed her state of mind. Louise, she said, grew suddenly jealous, and one evening burst into tears. " 'For Heaven's sake, my good friend, do not steal the King's heart away from me!' " But, says the good friend, "her star had set . . . I would willingly have broken with the King, but that would not have revived his dead love for her."

With the first wild flowers of spring came the usual anonymous verses, slipped from hand to hand. One said:

> *Be lame, be sixteen,*
> *No bosom, very little sense,*
> *Parents? God knows. Get your children in an*
>   *antechamber.*
> *On my faith, you will be the first among lovers,*
> *And La Vallière is the proof.*

Taken as poetry it might be disregarded; thrown as a rock, it bruised. Athénaïs had often hinted more wittily than this at the comparative humbleness of Louise's lineage.

It seemed that season that fun was impossible without the presence of Mme. de Montespan. She wore invisible ermine and let fall sayings as pretty and *outré* as pickled rosebuds. She moved as if her skin had been newly fitted by God and breathed the air as if it were something delicious. She was extremely happy; her husband had gone to his estates in the bleak Pyrenees. He had tried to get Athénaïs to accompany him, but that was of course out of the question. It was much better this way — his tastes were those of a peasant, and Court life beyond his talents. She hoped sincerely that he would find satisfaction in his rural projects — road building, windmill and bridge construction, vineyard planting, and the eternal repairs of that leaky old castle.

At Easter everyone's eyebrows were raised when the King took Communion in his parish church of Saint-Germain de l'Auxerrois, something he had not done for a very long time. Did it signify the uprooting of a deep and long-lived sin?

Always a critic of royalty, Olivier d'Ormesson croaked, "Here in Paris there are few masques, and few people who have the heart to be joyful."

Patin reported, "All around me people complain loudly of their misery . . . Well, this Carnival at least is over! The doctors complain that they have no patients and no money. Only comedians have a good time of it. *Tartuffe* is all the rage. All the great world goes there. We need not wonder. Human life is like nothing so much as a comedy." It was evident even at Court that the French were tired of taxes, tired of war.

Well, Louis agreed, it was time he gave them more for their money. This fruitless war with England was delaying his conquest of Flanders, and it caused perpetual trouble among the ministers. Colbert, obsessed with the problems of his budget, would place his mountainlike weight against the vigorous demands of Louvois for funds to support an army increasingly well trained, well disciplined, magnificently equipped, and therefore expensive. This fighting force must soon justify itself with some showy and profitable victories. As soon as possible a secret treaty was arranged with Charles. The islands of the Antilles were to be given back to England, and in exchange England pledged to refrain from helping Spain for a full year. On May 8 these terms came to light. Louis wrote, "Peace is signed in reality, and all the plenipotentiaries who meet at Breda will have to do is draw up the treaty on paper." As soon as it was signed, Turenne marched to the frontier with an army of fifty thousand men.

Mme. de Sévigné complained, "Paris is a desert. All the youth of France is gone to fight in Flanders, and I shall go back to the country, preferring solitude there to empty streets here."

Few courtiers visiting the camp near Fontainebleau failed to thrill to the sight of plumage advancing like surf, the noise of trumpets and drums, and the smell of gunpowder in the spring air. Women honored with the royal nod had their camp costume, as brilliant as any designed for masquerades, and rode out to play at the military life in the dyed and pennoned tents dressed for His Majesty's party.

Mme. de Chatrier, one of Condé's household, described the scene in a letter.

I saw a great plain with a huge quantity of tents placed symmetrically. That of the King, which I visited, was composed of three rooms and a chamber with two cabinets, all gold; the whole place furnished in Chinese satin. It was full of cavaliers of very good aspect, more proper to entice the enemy than to cause fear. This group, of whom His Majesty was chief, was composed of Madame, Mlle. de la Vallière, Mme. de Montespan, Mme. du Roure and the Princesse d'Harcourt, who remained in the tent during the heat of the day and ate there; it was not the repast of war, but of great magnificence. In the evening the ladies mounted horse with His Majesty, the troops putting themselves under arms and discharging their muskets, without, however, killing anybody.

All this was play, but Louis would soon leave for Flanders, and some few women would be chosen to go with him. It was said that Mme. de Montespan had already been invited. Louise had not. A year before, she would have thrown herself into Louis's arms and demanded a musket of her own, for the fighting. This year she could only wait, at first in anxious humiliation — at last in bitterest certainty that she was to be left behind. But she would soon be compensated for what the world regarded as a loss of face, and very handsomely.

On Wednesday, May 13, 1667, the assembled chambers of Parliament received such a letter-patent as had not been seen for half a century.

Louis, by the grace of God King of France and of Navarre, to all present and to come, salutations.

The benefits which kings exercise in their Estates are the exterior mark of the merit of those who receive them and the most glorious praise of the subjects who are so honored. We have no power to express better in public the particular esteem we have for our dear and well-loved and very faithful Louise de la Vallière than in conferring on her the highest titles of honor that an affection very singular, excited in our heart by an infinity of rare perfections, has inspired for some years in her favor. And although her modesty has been often opposed to

*our desire to elevate her earlier to a rank proportional to our
esteem and her good qualities, nevertheless the affection which
we have for her and justice do not permit us to defer evidence
of our recognition for a merit so well known to us, nor to refuse nature longer its effects of our tenderness for Marie-Anne,
our natural daughter begot on the person of her mother. We
have acquired for her the lands of Vaujours, situated in Touraine, and the barony of Saint-Christophe in Anjou, which are
two holdings equally considerable by their revenues . . .*

*But reflecting that it would lose something of our grace if
we do not enhance the value of these lands by a title which
can satisfy together the esteem which provokes our liberality and
the merits of the subject who receives it, taking also into consideration that our dear and well-beloved Louise de la Vallière
is the issue of a house very noble and very ancient, of whom the
ancestors have given on many important occasions signal marks
of their zeal for our State, and of their talent and experience
in the command of our armies, in consequence, the lands of
Vaujours are raised to a duchy, to be enjoyed by the said damsel, Louise-Françoise de la Vallière, and after her decease,
Marie-Anne, our said daughter, and the children male or female descended from her, which we have declared and will
declare legitimate and capable of all honors and civil effects . . .*

Parliament's predictable conclusion to this document was summed
up by the Procurer-General. "The said letters-patent shall be registered . . . to be executed according to their form and tenor."

Louis had expected no opposition, and there was none. He was
certainly no less a king than his grandfather Henri IV, and flattered himself that he had handled the matter with more finesse than
Henri, whose blunt recognition of his mistresses and bastards had
often verged on the socially offensive.

To universal surprise, Maria Theresa accepted the title of the new
duchesse quite graciously. Louis had promised to give up other
women by his thirtieth birthday. To his wife this act signified

preparation for the happy day — a proper provision of economic security for his old responsibilities.

Louise herself was at once surrounded, fawned on, and overrun by a mob of ravening congratulators when the news was made known. The Duchesse de Vaujours! Now, everybody exclaimed over and over, she would have the courtesy title "Madame," an equipage emblazoned with a ducal crown, and the coveted Tabouret — the right to sit down in the Queen's presence — even to ride in her carriage. Even her mother was there, the old Marquise de Saint-Rémi, curtsying like the rest, but with a strange expression on her small soft face, as if she came not to congratulate but to comfort.

All day a parade of relatives Louise had never even met moved through — swept there, they said, by an impulse of unselfish joy at her great fortune. The King himself arrived at last to be thanked, and, on the strength of his recent generosity, announce his formal intention of leaving her out of the Flanders expedition. The whole thing was absolutely impossible, he said. Had she forgotten her condition? He was concerned only for her safety. Madame, too, was pregnant, he pointed out, and he had ordered her to stay home at Saint-Cloud.

Yes, Louise burst out, but Madame was delicate, whereas she herself was so strong. Only four months pregnant was not much. She begged, pleaded. Absolutely not, Louis said stonily. She was to be sensible and wait at Versailles. She bent her head.

On May 24, Louise, accompanied by her faithful little sister-in-law Gabrielle and the somewhat sardonic Comtesse du Roure, took the road to Versailles, just as the Court rolled out toward Amiens and its first night's lodging. The weather was gorgeous, and the King on horseback galloped past the giant coach where Maria Theresa sat with the Grande Mademoiselle and Mme. de Montespan, and swept off his hat with his famous graceful gesture.

"Venus accompanied Mars," said one of the poets. There was no need for subtlety. Everybody at Court knew by now who Venus was — except Her Majesty, of course.

After a few days Mars left Venus, still unconquered, with the rest of the ladies at Compiègne and rejoined his army at Charleroi. He felt frustrated but on the whole rather pleased. What towers of fine resistance she erected for his demolition! Soon. Yes, very soon.

The Flemish strongholds made less resistance than Montespan. Louis entered Charleroi as if it were Paris. Ath and Tournay yielded in two days; and he moved on and through an equally submissive series of other towns — Furnes, Armentières, and Courtrai. It was almost too easy.

At home Philippe had caught the war excitement like a bad cold. He was narrowly observed by the Bishop of Valence, Henriette's friend, who was always hanging around the house to give her practical as well as spiritual advice. Perhaps it was not too late, the Bishop thought, to make a man of Monsieur — or a man of sorts.

This was not the first time the Prince had shown a military interest. Not long since, he had listened to proposals made by some Neapolitan nobles, and had actually put himself at the head of a revolution they were plotting against the Spaniards. He learned by accident, however, that Naples was close to Vesuvius, which sometimes erupted, and so hastily changed his mind.

But the Flanders campaign was another matter. From all indications the enemy were prepared to fight according to gentlemen's rules, holding out just long enough to satisfy the demands of honor and then surrendering with a good deal of fanfare and pageantry. It would be a shame, Philippe confessed, for the King's own brother to stay home and miss all the fun and rewards. Fine! said the Bishop heartily, they would go together to the front.

On the morning of his departure, Monsieur took a dignified and tender farewell of his wife and mother-in-law and was pleased to notice that several of the attending ladies shed tears. He mocked their anxiety, cocking his hat casually like Captain Tréville. Was he not a grandson of the ferocious Henri IV?

The ensuing weeks turned out to hold more fighting and fewer laurels than Philippe had expected. The Bishop stayed doggedly at his elbow to urge him on, rather annoyingly, but also saw to it that the Court gazetteers kept full record of his master's prowess under fire. Thrilled and unbelieving, Henriette learned that her husband had been seen in the trenches at Tournai and Douai, and had distinguished himself by his courage and coolness.

Louis was not quite so charmed. Military ardor was not a quality to be encouraged in kings' younger brothers; in the past it had only led to trouble. He was not at all sure he liked this Bishop who had got Philippe out of petticoats. But he might have spared himself his worry. Before long the siege began to seem monotonous to Monsieur. It was all so dusty, and one never got a minute's peace. He fell back on the decoration of his tent, making it sumptuous with crystal chandeliers and plenty of ornately framed mirrors. Then, before this palled, fate provided another diversion. He learned to his relief that Madame was dangerously ill from a miscarriage, and so hurried back to his warrior's welcome, envisioning the waving of laurels in many fair hands at home.

A few days later he wrote a note to his brother-in-law King Charles.

Madame begs me to ask Your Majesty's pardon for not writing by this post, but she has not the strength to sit up, since the accident which happened to her a week ago, after which she was thought to be dead during a quarter of an hour. This has obliged me to leave Douai, before the entrance of the King, my brother, to whose arms the town surrendered three hours before my departure.

Lauzun had shot to prominence as a national hero and was once more the King's dear friend because of his picaresque effectiveness on the battlefield. At the head of his dragoons, dressed like one of Mazarin's monkeys, and abristle with paraphernalia, he smote the Grande Mademoiselle with timorous love. She would wait patiently in the heat for him to parade past, hands sweating and a mottled color coming and going in her face so like an indecisive combination of the classic masks of tragedy and comedy. Mostly he ignored her. This great princess, meant by birth and inclination for roles of heroic drama, had again fallen somehow into the lead of the season's best farce.

To Mme. de Montausier
  Superintendent of the Queen's Household

24 *May* 1667

Madame, the new inquietudes caused by my new grandeur put me so far from the tranquil state I had thought to reach by that elevation that, finding it impossible to hide them longer, I have recourse to your confidence and wish to communicate to you my heart, the reflections I have made.

It is a custom among honest men in making changes among their servants to prepare for parting by paying extra wages, or by recognition of their services. I fear that it is the same with me, and that the King, by this great honor, thinks to tame me to retreat, and to throw me into so much vanity of spirit that, ambition overshadowing my love, I may suffer less from this misprizing . . .

Most people know that my love in its birth and progress has been disinterested, and that in considering the King, his crown, among his other qualities, has seemed the least lovable.

The new rumors I hear of marrying De Vardes with me justify my apprehension and suspicions: the welcome and the good countenance I have from the Queen appear to me a tacit request for consent to this. But she knows not that my heart has a repugnance to this greater than dislike, and that I am incapable of breaking the vows I have made, never to change from loving and never to marry.

I bear the title of Duchesse de Vaujours, I have the tabouret in the Queen's presence, I walk in the rank of duchesses. I have ceased to be La Vallière. The King has recognized the fruit of our embraces: my daughter is legitimized. It remains only for me to choose a husband for her to make her one of the kingdom's great . . .

But what will become of the royal blood which I sense with this fifth month moving in my flanks? You know — I revealed the secret to you in the time of conception. The King knows, and he has promised a boy, without having done anything for the child . . . What a difference between brother and sister! One, a legitimate duchess, the other an unrecognized bastard . . .

I have all the need in the world of your help and of your wise counsel . . . You have and will always have occasion to remember that I am, my very dear madam, your very faithful friend and servant,

LA DUCHESSE DE VAUJOURS

After writing the letter, Louise sat for a long time with the pen drying in her hand, looking out across the vast deserted terraces and summer gardens. Somewhere beyond, in another world, was a tree where she had sheltered once from the rain. Never again could she go home to that cool green tree . . . Daphne who yielded to Apollo.

Fifteen days of battle had opened enough cities to make possible a respectable triumphal progress. The Queen must see her new subjects. Louis ordered her and the other ladies to meet him at Avesnes.

News of this reached Versailles at a time when loneliness and despair had brought Louise to a crisis of desperation. She had never been good at self-restraint and the long-range plan, and now she felt that to wait any longer would result in madness or suicide. Any folly was better than this nightmare of inaction. She ordered her carriage, threw a few belongings into her traveling boxes, and set out next day for Flanders with Gabrielle de la Vallière on one side, rather apprehensive, and Mme. du Roure on the other. She made the coachman drive on all night, sitting sleepless through the dark country, like a soul escaping from one part of hell to another. Her companions dozed and fitfully complained.

Meanwhile, the obedient Maria Theresa had left Compiègne in her convoy of coaches loaded with beds, boxes, curtains, costumes, lackeys, armchairs, dogs, prayer books, priests, crockery, fans, and sets of viols, like the slow sailing of a great fleet. By the 20th of June she was at La Fère, halted and installed early in quarters for the sake of a peaceful card game with her women. Continually appearing messengers brought news of arrivals and departures, and on this evening, Mademoiselle prowling around the rooms was the first to learn the shocker.

"Mme. de la Vallière is going to arrive this evening," said a face at the door.

Card playing ended on the spot as Maria Theresa's placidity curdled like milk in thundery weather. She screamed, sprang up, and ran around the room slamming things. Nobody could calm her — Mme. de Montausier, the Princesse de Bade, not even Athénaïs. Mademoiselle said in a certain tone of admiration for the unbridled scene, "She vomited her dinner and cried with rage."

Early next morning Mademoiselle, passing through the outer chamber toward the little cabinet where the Queen was being dressed, saw three women seated wearily on a chest, Louise and her dusty fellow travelers.

"Have you seen Her Majesty?" she asked. They said no.

Maria Theresa, afflicted with her old facial twitch as the result of not having slept all night, eyes filling occasionally, insisted on keeping the besiegers out.

Cried Athénaïs in tender indignation, to heaven and all bystanders, "Look what a state the Queen is in!"

At the hour of Mass, Her Majesty made undignified haste to the tribune of the church and slammed the door lest the Duchesse de Vaujours should try to claim her right of entry. Louise, however, remained below in the nave among the crowd for whom all this was less church than theater. Mass concluded, she stood waiting for the Queen to come out, and made a profound Court curtsy. Without bowing or speaking a word, Maria Theresa bounced on into the carriage with her three attendants and Mademoiselle, urging them with elbows and audible hisses to close the space.

These ladies, during the day's journey, left few aspects of Louise's strange behavior unanalyzed. As usual, Athénaïs led the discussion. "I certainly admire her courage in daring to present herself before

MME. DE MONTESPAN
from a painting by Mignard
(Bowes Museum. Mansell Collection photograph)

LOUISE AFTER BECOMING A CARMELITE NUN
from a painting by Mignard
(Marseilles Museum. Bulloz photograph)

Her Majesty without having been summoned." And then, piously, "God preserve me from ever becoming the King's mistress! But if I were, I certainly would show more shame in the presence of the Queen." Much gentle applause at this, with tears again from Maria Theresa at such welcome sympathy, and punctuations of agreement from Mme. de Montausier, with whom Athénaïs was becoming very friendly.

Louise, having seen them together, gave up whatever hope she may have had of friendly support from Montausier, or even an answer to her recent letter.

Maria Theresa now saw that fate had presented her this opportunity to discipline Louise. Never before had there been such a chance. Louis was far away, and at last everybody was blaming that brazen girl as she deserved. To humiliate her was really a Christian duty. That night at dinner Louise arrived to find all seats filled. She returned to her chamber as unobtrusively as possible, but not before catching sight of a few odd expressions around the Queen's table. M. de Villacerf, maître d'hôtel, had been forbidden to give the Duchesse anything to eat. He was a kind man, however, and understandably reluctant to starve the King's mistress. After some delay a sort of picnic was smuggled into her room.

At Guise, the next night's stop, Louise failed to appear among the company at all. Somewhat disappointed, the Queen had to be content with the gossip, increasingly scathing and free, which flourished in her enemy's absence. Now they were on the road not far from Avesnes, and word came that the King's party had been sighted on rising terrain ahead. Excited and strict at the prospect of a drama to be played, the Queen gave orders that all other carriages were to hold back while she advanced alone to meet His Majesty.

Louise saw through the summer field mist the King's unmistakable horseback silhouette come over the hill and stay like a piece of memory against the sky. He was the same — nothing had changed. He was her refuge and love, and they had been apart in some sickness which could be cured by being close together, only to touch and look — as always before.

Something broke and suddenly her eyes began weeping. "Drive!

Drive!" she yelled to the coachman, beating her knuckles on the panel. The whip cracked; the carriage left the delaying curve of the road and lurched out over the plowed ruts of the field, creaking and laboring, footmen clinging to their pitching roost.

The Queen began shrieking in a frenzy, ordering everybody to stop that coach, commanding her driver to make speed or be killed. The entire Court, becalmed, helpless, and aghast, watched the unseemly race. The Queen was as usual far outclassed. None of them saw the meeting between Louise and the King. But even Maria Theresa would have been satisfied. Even Athénaïs.

Louis sat at the head of his silent escort and watched the woman alight, come toward him with her little limp over the rough ground, and bow.

"What, before the Queen?" was all he said, with utter coldness, and after a moment turned away to let her rise, as a door may be opened for a cat. And she knew that she had been mistaken after all, and that this king was no man she had ever seen before, or could ever come to know.

XII

LOUIS THE GREAT

TOWN AFTER TOWN opened its gates and the Court poured through to startle and awe the Flemish burghers.

One of them wrote, "All you have heard of the glory of Solomon, and the Emperor of China is not to be compared with the pomp of warlike array which surrounds the King. The streets are full of cloth of gold, of waving plumes, of chariots and superbly harnessed mules, of horses with gold and embroidered trappings, and of sumptuous carriages."

And another, "La Vallière is playing the Grande Duchesse at the camp, and Monsieur is gone with a fine courage to join the King at Arras."

This observation of Louise was superficial, but justified to some extent by appearances. As the King had commanded, she played her part in public, and all outer signs of discord disappeared from the Queen's entourage.

On the morning following their meeting on the hillside, Louis sent Mme. la Duchesse to Mass in attendance on Her Majesty, and then, as Maria Theresa took her place in the somewhat crowded royal carriage, he invited Louise also to enter with a gesture at once courteous and commanding. All the ladies moved over, stepping on one another's feet and wrinkling their skirts in the crush, but forced to smile. The King liked only cheerful faces around him. This act set the pattern for all his future arrangements — simple, neat, almost intolerable for everyone else involved. Only the gay nonsense of Mme. de Montespan held off alternate grimness and hysteria in the close quarters of the Queen's Household.

Athénaïs had good reason to be gay.

*The King saw Mme. de Montespan every day in her cham-
ber, which was below that of the Queen [wrote the Grande
Mademoiselle]. One night, at dinner, I heard the Queen complain to the King that he had not come to bed until four in
the morning, and, as she then wanted to know why, he replied
that he had been working very hard on dispatches. And, in
saying these words, he turned his head aside not to let her see
him laugh. I, in fear of doing likewise, did not raise my eyes
from my plate.*

But Maria Theresa did not believe him. Far from it. She knew
very well he had been with La Vallière — he needn't think he
could ever deceive her again.

News of the surrender of Montespan to the King's arms caused
as great a stir as anything else that had happened in Flanders. As
soon as it was learned at Versailles, the English ambassador sat
down and dutifully relayed an account to his government. "Mme.
de Montespan is the beauty of the day on this journey and gives
great fear to the deserted lady . . ."

Louise, at sixteen, had given herself to the King in a scant six
weeks. Athénaïs had delayed more than a year, promising and with-
holding. Was her body, at last, as delightful as she had hinted? The
King seemed to think so. Rich in her glamorous accomplishments,
he did not appear to notice that she was quite incapable of feeling
love.

After six days, Louis left to rejoin the army at Charleroi, and the
Court withdrew again to Compiègne. At Notre-Dame de Liesse the
Queen halted to make her devotions, and Athénaïs invited Louise
to join her at the confessional. They went arm in arm as any friends
might, one bright-faced, composing her manner to sobriety for the
occasion; the other hollow-eyed and abstracted as a sleepwalker.

Louise had little to confess. She had long ago served her prescribed penances for the child beginning to be so heavy and vigor-

ous in the womb. What had been a secret would soon be common knowledge, as always before. But there was a difference — this child, nourished on grief and desperation, was hers alone. She would take him home to Paris and wait for his birth.

The rest of the Court stayed on at Compiègne until the end of July. During this period Louis decreed for the army a rest from conquest and went himself to visit Madame at Saint-Cloud. Her recent miscarriage had been dangerous; for ten days she had lain with the scale tipping delicately toward death before it balanced back, but at last her physicians declared her saved.

Monsieur was full of ennui again and ready to return to the army now that the surrendering was going forward with such dispatch. He got back to Flanders in time for the fall of Oudenarde, still dogged by Henriette's pesky Bishop of Valence, and even let himself be urged into the trenches at Lille.

Rumors began: Monsieur was to receive the post of Lieutenant-General of the Army and would command an expedition the following spring to Catalonia. It appeared that inscrutable fate was about to create a career for Philippe after all. Unfortunately, one day the Chevalier de Lorraine came riding into camp slightly wounded. Philippe paled, shrieked, and hurried to retire with him to the rear. Battle-blackened soldiers witnessing this spectacle of wifely solicitude exchanged glances. After this episode Monsieur spent more time with Lorraine and less time besieging Lille.

Louis was enjoying the war, which was proceeding in the grand tradition. At the outset of the attack on Lille, the city's governor, the Comte de Brouai, sent to ask the King which quarter of the camp he occupied, in order to withhold fire. Louis answered, "All quarters." This bravado proved ill-advised; the defenders peppered the besieging troops on all sides, and behind His Majesty in the trench a page of the royal stable fell dead. A soldier grabbed Louis and dragged him down; the veteran Marquis de Charost tore off the King's plumed hat and traded his own, saying, "Sire, the wine is drawn and it must be drank."

The siege took nine days and went according to gentlemen's

rules. The chivalrous Brouai, hearing that there was no ice in the King's camp, sent a ration to him every day. Louis asked the messenger to increase the amount, and was answered, "Sire, he is chary with it because he hopes the siege will be of long duration, and he is apprehensive that Your Majesty may ultimately suffer for the deprivation." But the odds were too great for a long siege. Lille's Spanish garrison was only eight thousand men. Of this, the vanguard was cut to pieces by the Duc de Créqui and the rest retreated to find refuge under the walls of Brussels and Mons. The speed of this victory sent shafts of alarm into Brussels, and the population began packing frenziedly. Valuables were shipped to Antwerp and all roads out of town swarmed with escaping citizens.

All Flanders could have been stripped like a wheat field then; but Louis had too few men to garrison every village in the country. Louvois advised him to be content instead with leaving large bodies of men in the towns already taken and to concentrate on fortification. Louis agreed, and turned the problem over to one of his new genii, the engineer Vauban. Then he rode home to Paris, to a populace made maniac with rejoicing. The great days had really arrived — a cloud of glory had opened and was pouring gold on a France destined to subjugate the world.

At Villers-Cotterets Monsieur was playing war games with Lorraine, ranging tables and chairs the length of the salon to represent fortress walls, and sticking up mirrors as outposts. On these he advanced with brandished sword, outwitting their tactics and breaching their defenses — there, and there, and there! The Bishop of Valence watched, disgusted and melancholy. Philippe had just informed him of his intention to keep his dear friend Lorraine henceforth forever near and to have no secrets from him. On their return to Paris the Chevalier's belongings were accordingly moved into the best rooms of the Palais-Royal, very near Monsieur's.

Soon Philippe began to complain that the Bishop was too much devoted to Madame's service and too intimate with her faithful servant Mme. de Saint-Chaumont. Worse, he had been spying on the Chevalier de Lorraine. There was no help for it, Monsieur said, that fellow must go. But first the Bishop obtained a parting audience from the King, saying afterward to the Duc de Luxembourg, "I have just seen a great man who has disgusted me more than ever with the little master it is my misfortune to serve!"

Said Louis, "My brother never had but one able man in his service, and he couldn't keep him long." He had forgotten for the moment that great soldier and scholar Tréville, captain of Monsieur's musketeers, who would have retired to a monastic life years earlier if it had not been for his devotion to Madame.

After the banishment of the Bishop de Valence, Henriette wept in private. She had very few friends left. Her nightmares were of being bound hand and foot in a giant web, under the china-blue eyes of a spider with the cherub face of the Chevalier de Lorraine. Where would it all end? Charles's letters from England had almost stopped coming, too. He was suffering from insult and a broken heart that season.

Frances Stewart, the tantalizing maid of honor sent his wife by Henriette, had kept her bedroom door locked all this time despite his proclaimed passion, and now had put herself permanently out of reach by marrying the Duke of Richmond.

Charles was not to be distracted, either by Nell Gwynne, impudent in her jockey's trousers of a morning, or the regal Lady Castlemaine. He moped.

Early in summer from his eyrie in the Pyrenees, the Marquis de Montespan wrote enthusiastic, tender letters to his wife. The mountains were beautiful, the vineyards thriving, the air pure. There she could be the queen of a small but loyal realm and forget with him the miserable petty follies of Court. He would deck her bower with fresh flowers every day; they would eat fruit from their own orchards and live forever like a couple in a romance. He was increasingly impatient and insistent.

This menace had to be met somehow. A life among peasants and country nobility would have been inconceivable to Athénaïs at any time, and particularly now. She wrote evasively to the Marquis, sprinkling the message with big and little lies. The Queen, she said, needed her too badly right now to grant her a leave of absence; five or six other ladies were away. She gave her word of honor that she would join him later in the year, after the Court's return from Fontainebleau.

Before long an answer came, so wild and acid that Athénaïs was almost frightened for the first time in her life. The man called her a liar, said he knew she had been spending three hours every night for the past year in La Vallière's apartments with the King, posing as a purveyor of news and gossip. Furthermore, only one of the Queen's other ladies had been absent — not five, as she claimed. He announced his intention of collecting all possible documentary evidence against her and bringing legal action, charged her to give up his son, the Marquis d'Antin, into the hands of the valet Dupré until his own return, and ended with a threat to shut her up in a convent.

That night, Athénaïs's memoirs record, the King observed her distracted air, "his glance searching though very sweet. 'Something troubles you — what is it?' " and he felt her pulse. She showed him the letter from her husband, and Louis changed color. "It is a matter requiring caution and tact. At any rate we can prevent his showing you any disrespect. Give up the Marquis d'Antin to him. He is useless, perhaps an inconvenience to you; and if deprived of his child he might be driven to commit some desperate act."

"I would rather die!" cried Athénaïs, and turned on him eyes which held the beginnings of a great grief glittering attractively on the lashes. She allowed her hands to be held.

"Very well, then," Louis said. "Keep him yourself and don't give him up."

But Louis was thrown by this event into a condition bordering on nervousness. He saw a threat in this unreasonable Marquis de Montespan — not to his will, which was above the sticky touch of controversy, but to his dignity. And by now, to Louis XIV, dignity had become the most important thing.

The Queen also received a letter about this time, full of interesting information, and unsigned. She read it several times and then summoned Mademoiselle, Mme. de Montausier, and Mme. de Montespan. "I have received a letter which tells me many things," she said in a worldly tone, "but I don't believe them. Someone says the King is in love with Mme. de Montespan and that he doesn't love La Vallière any more; and that it is Mme. de Montausier who leads this affair — that Montespan is fooling me . . . In short, everything is said to make me hate her. I absolutely don't believe it, and I'm sending this letter to the King."

The Grande Mademoiselle, uninvolved, said only, "Your Majesty has done well." Montausier, guilty as charged, austerely denied any part in the affair. From among her busy thoughts Montespan produced a reply of sorts consisting of testimonials regarding her obligations to the Queen, and kindnesses received, and ended typically with a narrow-eyed pounce on the significant thing. "I know where that letter came from!" The Queen closed the matter on a note of self-congratulation. "I see many things," she said. "I am not such a dupe as everybody thinks, but I have prudence." The only result of this meeting was Louis's prompt dismissal of Mme. d'Armagnac, on whom Athénaïs put the finger of suspicion for the letter's authorship.

"He is the most modest man in the world," Mme. de Longueville said when Louis returned to Saint-Germain in September. "The appearance of a conqueror, which he could affect, is increased by his lack of conscious pride." Her discerning feminine eye noticed something else at this time, unremarked by the purely political. These days, Louis did not seek out the company of women; the old frank pleasure in their company seemed entirely gone. His civility lacked address and gaiety — some nods, bows, an honest response when they spoke to him, but nothing more. "In the old days it was not so; he began, he sustained the conversation, like any other man." Simply, Louis's youth was past. He would never see the morning star again over the woods at Fontainebleau or ride bareheaded in the rain beside the carriage window of any girl, no matter how pretty, or climb among the chimneypots of a roof at night.

On October 2, Louise gave birth to her fourth child, a son. As before at Vincennes, her indisposition was the occasion for a large supper party lasting very late and attended by all courtiers of sufficiently high social position. The baby had been taken away immediately by Mme. Colbert to be brought up with his sister, and the chamber hastily set in order. "Everybody suspected her childbirth," Mademoiselle wrote. "Everyone knew it. But she would not show anything."

Because he had desired this son, the King came and visited the mother on several consecutive afternoons. His manner in her presence was easy, friendly, as it might have been toward a favored sister-in-law. It told her without words that she could rely on his help and protection.

Athénaïs had just confided to Louis her moral certainty that this child was not his, but Lauzun's; but Louise would never learn of this confidence if he could prevent it. Already he knew the Marquise de Montespan and her little stories better than she would have liked to be known. But she was safe enough. Liar or not, loving or grasping, she was the most beautiful woman in France and the most dangerous, and it was fitting she should belong to the King. That winter she made the Court spin and glow with the vitality of her astonishing queenhood. All the women hurried to copy the styles of her gowns and coiffures, and behind them a few months later came the envy-eyed fashion-aware females of the rest of the civilized world. She could command with a look and make obedience seem pleasure.

This reign began in November with six days' celebration of the feast of Saint-Hubert.

Louise was spared the sight of Athénaïs's first public triumphs. She had not regained strength as quickly as usual, after this birth, and spent her days sleeping in a sort of imitation of death, or in trancelike meditation on the random evidences of the year's end. Was that dry leaf, scratching over the sill, a note to her from one particular tree — a tree in the park at Versailles? But by now, surely, it would be cut down to make room for the next year's formal garden.

Back to Paris for Christmas, and a new guest brought novelty to the winter fêtes, Charles II's illegitimate son the Duke of Monmouth. He was a handsome and engaging young man who had been recognized at his father's court for a long time. Henriette received him with delight, gave a course of balls in his honor, and soon aunt and nephew had introduced a brief vogue for English country dances.

Louise, in attendance everywhere as was required of a lady of her rank, followed the prancing figures of the dance with her memorizing eye, but did not move from the stool where she was now privileged to sit, within conversing distance of Maria Theresa.

Philippe was piqued at young Monmouth's popularity, and the Chevalier de Lorraine said he should also be jealous of Madame. Didn't she talk with the Duke in English, and obviously prefer his company to that of her own husband?

Henriette, reacting in the familiar pattern, complained aloud of Lorraine's insolence and rudeness in her house.

Monsieur flounced out shouting counter-accusations over his shoulder. His nerves were on edge anyway; the Chevalier, he had good reason to suspect, had been seducing that Mlle. de Fiennes again. In a sudden fit of fury he ordered the girl off the premises for good. Soon Madame, wondering where her maid of honor had gone, was told by the bland Lorraine that he himself had sent her away as a friendship sacrifice to his dear Monsieur. The quarrel got completely out of hand. Comfortable Mme. de Saint-Chaumont, who loved Henriette and was a careful governess to her daughters, thought it was high time the Chevalier was dislodged, and went to the King with her version of the whole tangled story.

Louis admonished Monsieur, who suddenly turned nasty and vengefully forced Henriette to leave Court in the middle of the party season and bury herself with him and Lorraine at Villers-Cotterets. There she stayed for several weeks of snowy solitude, condemned to watch the friends amuse each other at a distance, like two girls snubbing a third. Madness cocked a bright vacant eye in all the empty mirrors of the castle.

The King was having intermittent vapors and sensations of nausea. Athénaïs had begun visiting sorcerers again and experimenting on him with their prescriptions — ashes of toads' bones and moles' teeth, human dust, and a curious concoction of dried prunes allied with cantharides and lime.

Louis, being a true Bourbon, was exceedingly lustful even without these stimulations, but the new mistress was beset with feelings of insecurity. Never having experienced an authentic passion herself, she was skeptical of its existence in other people. In the King it was a mysterious source of benefices which might be withdrawn capriciously at any moment, and needed constant tending. Also, she was still paying the sorceress of the Rue de la Tannerie for charms designed to kill Louise, though these were expensive. One of them, for which results were promised, involved the burying of pigeons' hearts, with incantations, in the Bois de Boulogne.

Whether the aphrodisiacs misfired, raising instead His Majesty's warlike spirit, or merely some wish to be in the field where the food seemed to taste better, that winter brought another defeat for the Spaniards.

Louis and the Prince de Condé swept down and conquered the whole province of Franche-Comté in less than a month's time. Only the intervention of the Triple Alliance forced Louis to call off his armies. Ralph Montagu, the new English ambassador, and Sir John Trevor, sent over by Charles, proposed the terms of agreement between France and Spain which would be finally settled in April. Louis was not happy; he had to give up Franche-Comté in order to retain those towns in Spanish Flanders taken in the previous campaign. But he was halted only momentarily. There lay Holland like a great roasted pig with an apple in its mouth, ready to be seized, defended by no fortifications of any consequence. He saw now, however, that his first act must be to detach England from the Triple Alliance; he could not defy a united England, Holland, and Sweden. He called accordingly on his most useful statesman, Henriette. All spring, in spite of recurring sickness, she kept up a busy correspondence with the most important Englishmen — her brother Charles, Buckingham, Arlington, James Hamilton — and became an authority on matters at Whitehall.

Meanwhile the King pressed forward his plan for invading the Low Countries. He was proud of France's strength. Previously dilapidated and deserted seaports were now walled with defenses; in their cannoned harbors rode nearly sixty ships of large tonnage, capable of being converted to men-of-war. And limitless material resources came pouring out of the new booming colonies in America, Africa, and the East Indies.

At Court amusements continued as usual. Molière's *Tartuffe* had caused loud shrieks of wounded sensibility from all the clergy of France and their pious supporters, with recommendations that the playwright be burned at the stake, and was banned from further production. Henriette defended both author and play and had it performed privately during the season. As a result it triumphed at last, and now in the spring was again titillating the worldly.

Amphitryon burst forth in music and color the same month. The plot, so marvelously parallel to scenes of contemporary palace life, might have been created to order for that year instead of merely adapted from Plautus. Jupiter, the King, plays out his night-long adulterous love with the help of a thinly disguised Duchesse de Montausier and many other well-known minor characters.

Nobody supposed that Maria Theresa was learning to understand the language of symbolism, but sometimes she looked at Mme. de Montespan in a very unnerving way.

Louise had begun to spend part of almost every day with an old acquaintance who, in her time of despondency, was becoming a close friend. Gigault de Bellefonds was a serious man in his late thirties, a marshal of France, and a distinguished military commander. He had overcome most of his youthful frivolities, including a passion for gambling on the horses, and had recently discovered religion as a way of life. With the enthusiasm of the newly converted, he worked on Louise's mind and emotions. She smiled a little wearily, but let him talk. His presence was a genuine comfort, conversation aside.

In spite of all he had done for the country, Louis was not universally liked. His critics, who had endured patiently enough the King's love affair with a shy unambitious girl, were somewhat less touched at the sight of this new haughty mistress wearing their tax money around her neck in the form of emeralds. They said that the King at thirty was getting old enough to know better. He sensed this hostility, though no courtier in recent years had been brash enough to reprove him openly. Increasingly politic, Louis felt that there could be no gain in antagonizing his subjects by exhibiting Athénaïs more than was necessary, and therefore began exercising a sort of crooked discretion.

Montespan and La Vallière should live together, to create an impression of comradeship — family even. Everybody knew about Louise, and perhaps they would let themselves arrive gradually at the feeling that here in the royal Household was a harmony almost as good as innocence. At least, under such an arrangement, nobody would be able to prove that Athénaïs was anything but a confidante and attendant of the official mistress. He therefore commanded the two women to become bosom friends.

In His Majesty's absence with the army the Queen waited at Saint-Germain. Caught in the machinery of routine, Mme. de la Vallière and Mme. de Montespan performed the duties of their charge and rank. They could not have separated any more than those small painted figures who come out to strike the hour can mutiny against the clock. The courtiers, always avid for surprise, fell into groups of silence at the spectacle of these two ladies walking around together in apparent amity. There was something in it of almost Roman decadence.

The Peace of Aix-la-Chapelle, forced on Louis though it was, became the excuse for a great party, and Versailles was readied for an eight-day dissipation. The forest had gone down like wheat in all directions, and everywhere the ravished stroller came on new bowers, porticoes, and statues. The orangery, called by La Fontaine a very garden of the Hesperides, opened its waxy blooms and languishing perfume to the July heat, and from the menagerie came the whistles and purrs of barbaric African and Asiatic birds. And there was the great grotto of Thetis with its colossal bas-relief of a golden sun, Louis's device, setting in the waves of the sea, surrounded by Tritons and Sirens gushing with streams of water, and the walls holding life-sized statues of Apollo and the Muses.

At midday the guests were summoned from the outlying gardens to the dining hall. Its walls were verdure continually refreshed by water spray and its pillars five long rows of trees, each bearing a different kind of fruit. In the center five vast buffets held a profusion of architectural pastries, partridge in cabbage, spiced fillet of duck, galantine of chicken, rabbit and cucumber, salads, veal quarters, melon; hors d'oeuvres of fried sheep testicles and roast beef spread with kidneys, onions, and cheese; colored sugar confections, and cakes of all kinds. The ladies seated themselves informally without regard for rank, the Duchesse de la Vallière among the crowd, between her sister-in-law Gabrielle and Mme. de Villacerf, the Marquise de Montespan at the Queen's table under a neighboring tent. Afterward, says the chronicler, the guests embarked in carriages behind Her Majesty and drove through the umbrageous avenues of the park, coming by many charming detours to a little leafy theater hung about with tapestries.

The play was *Georges Dandin,* Molière's treatment of a subject he knew very well from personal experience, the jealous husband. But he never forgot himself as the artist, who must let his own irony merely enhance the result as a slight vinegar flavor does the taffy. The King and Court were very much diverted. Between the acts were pastoral interludes hinting broadly at current events, and a ballet afterward, Lully's *Le Triomphe de Bacchus.*

Dinner was served by torchlight in view of cascades bursting from a rock surmounted by a silver statue of Pegasus and porphyry vases of evening-scented flowers. Five services were offered, each of fifty-six plates, and when the guests rose from table His Majesty ordered the gates thrown open to the public, who made short work of the remaining food, demolishing mountains of pastries and castles of marzipan, to the entertainment of courtiers now loitering toward the ball beginning indoors.

Under a dome of blossoming branches, to the music of violins and hautboys, the King led the dancing. The hall was a stylized forest with foliage through which appeared the smooth marble limbs of statues, and fountains filled the air with spray from their braided falls, sheafs, and showers. At the darkest hour of night, shortly before dawn, the Court gathered on the ramps which rose to the grand terrace; the populace crowded together in the gardens below, and all waited for the final spectacle.

> *By a prodigious change* [Félibien *wrote*], *the castle appeared truly a Palace of the Sun. All the casements appeared full of antique statues diversely colored. In an instant, all the balustrades were lined with flamboyant vases which decorated and revealed at the same time the vast extent of the superb park. Suddenly one heard, by the sparkling noise of a thousand music boxes, a heroic harmony which was followed by a thousand plumes of fire surging from the fountains, the woods, and the bowers, and jetting from the mouths of the lizards, frogs, and other bronze animals which ornamented the basins.*

Next, on the horizon broke forth a confetti of sparks, multiplying and showering over the still black mirror of the canal —

> *and shooting from a single jet an infinity of huge rockets; then, marking the cipher of the King in their turn and return, tracing in the space double L's, all bright with sharpness and purity. Finally, all these lights extinguished themselves, and, as if they had obliged the stars of the sky to retire, one perceived that the day, jealous of such a beautiful night, was beginning to appear.*

Four years before, such a sky had been lighted for Louise. Now, before her dazzled eyes, the ghosts of linked L's floated down, disappearing among treetops, leaving nothing but the sharp dead odor of gunpowder. They were gone, now . . . now they were nowhere.

XIII

A HUSBAND SPEAKS

THERE WAS no holding him back — before long the Marquis de Montespan returned to Paris. He moved with the terrifying purpose of a panther — confronted his pale and speechless wife, called her a string of coherent names and smacked her face — went to the authorities of the Châtelet and registered a case against her — and bearded the King one afternoon at Saint-Germain to deliver a forceful unfaltering sermon to his victim's unbelieving ears. He poured out scriptural quotations, citing David in particular, and ended by suggesting that Louis surrender the Marquise to him at once, and fear God.

"You are crazy!" squawked the Grande Mademoiselle when he told her later of this event. He also went to Mme. de Montausier and accused her of pandering, in terms which sent her to bed sick with shock. She had not seen her little services to Athénaïs and the King in this light. "I praise God," she said to Mademoiselle afterward, "that there were only women here, for if there had been a man, someone would have been thrown out the window!"

Athénaïs soon recovered her poise, and in a sumptuous undress of diamonds received guests in her boudoir with whom she laughed merrily at her husband's clowning. However, no man could safely make Louis XIV look ridiculous, and a *lettre de cachet* was signed before long in the hope that a spell in prison would quench the Marquis's nonsense. But the arrest must somehow be justified.

Among Mme. de Montausier's rewards for her sympathy and tact had been the appointment of her husband to the post of governor of the Dauphin — a position which Louise's friend M. de Bellefonds had hoped for. The King decided to allege that the Marquis de Montespan had treasonously criticized this appointment, and accordingly had him thrown into a cell at For-Leveque for eight days.

Mme. de Montespan's memory of this period proved to be full of curious gaps. In later years, in gentle self-approbation, she wrote, "Not being naturally of a bad disposition, I would never allow M. de Louvois to send him to the Bastille. On the contrary, I secretly paid his debts, which amounted to more than fifty thousand crowns, very glad to do him this service in return for the evil which he said of me." The records of Crespin and Carré, notaries of Paris, show that this year Mme. de Montespan was herself so short of money she found it necessary to borrow fourteen thousand livres.

Hard beset to find a legal reason for detaining his prisoner, Louis was forced to let him go. On the morning of the release His Majesty somewhat ignominiously departed for Chambord, a Renaissance castle at some distance from Paris. Significantly, it was not accessible to the public, as the other royal residences were, having high and well-guarded walls all around the park.

Louise, whose company had been requested for the expedition, looked out from one of the upper windows over the dreaming summer landscape where the Loire wandered among trees. There was Blois, deserted all these years, like a small dark city. The King came up beside her and for a moment stood looking too at the far-off towers. On the glass before them was a verse, scratched some other year by an unknown idler.

Vary woman must;
Place in her no trust.

Louise with lifted forefinger touched the period and smiled, with a little questioning look. The King walked on. Next day the verse was gone, replaced with a new unflawed pane.

The determination to be quiet, to hold to pride no matter what it cost, had sustained Louise for a long time. The Maréchal de Bellefonds helped with his easy friendship and obvious respect, and Bossuet, too, could with an occasional bit of wisdom loosen the knot of her inexorable pain and give her a period of rest. But as she and Bossuet began to know each other he stirred in her another sort of trouble — the beginning of a fear, a conviction, that her penance was well earned. She was guilty beyond any doubt, beyond hope of pardon, but repentance could not come until passion was overcome; and that never would be. Her mourning should have been for the state of her soul. Instead it was for the denial of an earthly, dark, deep-rooted, physical love. She knew how useless words would be now with Louis, once so sensitive to the shades of meaning in everything she said. Still, they were always there, violent and bitter, pushing off the lid of control and sense while she slept, so that she woke sobbing like a madwoman into her wet pillow.

Sometimes she wrote to an old adviser in the Church, less in hope of reaching his understanding than in the need of expression.

Ah, my father, do not rebuke me for this; it is too small a thing. It mortifies only my flesh because it has sinned, but does not touch my soul, which has sinned more. It is not these sins which kill me, it is not these which take away all sleep, all repose; it is the cowardly desire to add to those I already have. And, don't I see them every day? Don't my eyes follow their eyes? Am I not seated beside my rival while he is beside her also, but far from me? Have I not seen? Have I not heard? Ah, my father, God punish me if I blaspheme — I do not know what hell is, but I cannot imagine anything more terrible than this which holds my heart, where it remains nevertheless, where it complies — for not to see him would be another hell to which it could never become accustomed.

The day came when, alone with Louis, her reserve broke. She began by asking simply what his feeling might be for her, if any remained. He answered coldly that he was too sincere to deceive her. It was true, he said, that he loved Mme. de Montespan, but he retained for Louise a great deal of affection; he would do many things for her happiness; he did not believe she could desire anything more. He added, after a pause, that she must surely realize that a king of his character could not accept restraint.

A dry, perhaps unnecessarily hard reply, which touched something Louise had thought beyond further hurt. Suddenly she wept, begged, reminded him — hopeless, helpless, making a fool of herself while he listened with an expression of justified distaste. Finally he interrupted. If she wished the continuation of his affection she must demand no more than he could give freely, of his own will. For the rest, he desired that she continue to be sensible about Mme. de Montespan as before. If not, he would be forced to take other measures, in case she showed herself disobliging or lacking in courtesy to the Marquise.

A writer commenting on the days which followed says:

> *Mme. de la Vallière, who is the best soul in the world, renders obedience, and regards the will of the King as the rule of her own. She lives with Mme. de Montespan in a manner which one could not reasonably expect of a rival. And as everybody thought the King was tired of La Vallière, and thought to break completely with her, and give himself wholly to Mme. de Montespan, everybody admires her sweetness and submission.*

Louise never complained to the King again. Only one remark remained — a sonnet, its contemplative music suggestive to the reader of harpstrings struck beyond some corridor of late afternoon. Its last lines speak not so much to Louis as to the poet herself.

> *. . . Love, to whom I owe my good and ill,*
> *Would you had given him a heart like mine,*
> *Or else made mine a heart more like all others.*

Big crude beautiful Beaufort was gone. After commanding an expedition to Gigeri he went to Cyprus, disappeared battling amid a rabble of Turks, and was not seen again. All France presumed him dead except the salty fishwives of Les Halles to whom he had been son and hero. They took the money their granddaughters made in prostitution, set the price of eels a little higher, and pledged his ransom. An English observer reports that the collection came to about seven crowns apiece for the entire Guild. But Louis felt sure of his death. This left a post vacant, and he had a man in mind to fill it — his most recent son, now sixteen months old. But how should the candidate be named? Louis, Bastard de Bourbon, Comte de Vermandois? Or simply Louis, Comte de Vermandois, Admiral of France? The latter form sounded more impressive, somehow.

The young Comte had recently been legitimized in letters-patent to Parliament (". . . Our natural son whom we have had of our dear and well-loved cousin, the Duchesse de la Vallière . . ."), and now his financial future must be planned. Louise's fortune was, after all, more apparent than real. Vaujours, like most of the old country estates, was falling to ruin, inefficiently run, and producing little. Most of the peasants were wretched, and their new mistress was already showing an unrealistic inclination to intercede for them rather than force payment. No, Vaujours could not be expected to support both her son and daughter. Furthermore, the King had noticed that Athénaïs was too big with child to dance as a nymph in the winter ballet. The end of this would be, if a son, another tactical and economic problem.

There were worries of other kinds, too; strange hints occurred that the fickle French, always unpredictable as animals, were turning against him. Sometimes insults were yelled at him through the palace gates, and unpleasant incidents occurred. One day a woman, half mad as the result of her son's death in the labor of Versailles, shoved close to Louis and screamed obscenities, calling him a filthy tyrant. "The King could not believe his ears; he asked whether she was speaking to him, to which she answered yes and went on." The creature was seized, whipped publicly, and thrown into jail.

But in spite of this example a foul-mouthed man waylaid Louis not much later in the same way. He got his tongue cut and went to the galleys.

To compound trouble, the Marquis de Montespan was still around Paris making a nuisance of himself. He had requested papal consent to his divorce — which would of course never be granted — and then climaxed everything by an act of unbelievable audacity. He dressed himself and his servants in the deepest mourning, hung funeral emblems over the entrance of his house, draped his horses and carriage in black, and had horns symbolizing his state of cuckoldry painted over the armorial bearings on its doors. He gave orders for the performance of a funeral service in his parish with the whole town and suburbs invited. "My wife," he said, "is dead of an attack of coquetry and ambition." Both Louis and Athénaïs met this with contemptuous disregard. But what would the maniac do to celebrate the birth of her child in March? The prospective parents were most uneasy.

Further scandal must be suppressed. It was important that Louise should remain, in public opinion, the royal mistress; therefore she and Athénaïs were assigned adjoining rooms wherever the Court wandered. To reach Montespan's bed, the King had to pass La Vallière's. To describe this situation, a courtly euphemism was coined. "His Majesty has gone to The Ladies," everybody said. Their apartments at Saint-Germain were on the east, overlooking the old pavilion of Henri IV, and reached by a little spiral staircase to which Louis carried the only key. Each of The Ladies had two spacious rooms opening onto a balcony.

Out of the vast trash basket of the past fall some slips of paper.

Feb. 1, 1669

Presented by Jean Marot, architect to the King . . . to Mmes. the Duchesse de la Vallière and Marquise de Montespan . . . living in lodgings of the Tuileries, for building four grottoes . . . two for the said lady Duchesse de la Vallière and two for Mme. de Montespan, all in their apartments at the château of Saint-Germain-en-Laye . . .

The document is signed in a manner characteristic of each woman — "L. de la Vallière" and "The Marquise de Montespan."

Again, "Fountain ornaments, furnishing of basins and water conduits made for balconies of the apartments of the said ladies." This was not for bathing, but to please the King's taste for hydrology. On the terrace below he had built a fantastic grotto with marble walls and statues of Neptune and Tritons, echoing with cascades which fell among mosaics of shell and coral branches in various colors.

Athénaïs was criticized by some. "A new mistress not very delicate," Mme. de Caylus said. "She lives with the declared mistress — same table, same house. She likes this very well, because she hopes to fool the public and her husband, and her pride makes her taste the pleasure of seeing constantly humiliated a rival from whom she has nothing to fear."

Early in the spring of 1668, Montespan gave birth to a son. Palace organization took charge immediately; Lauzun, who had been waiting impatiently in the antechamber for some hours, received the royal child and carried him across the courtyard to the arms of his nurse. This Mme. Scarron was a widow of thirty-five. Born Françoise d'Aubigny, a girl of good family, she had endured hard days as the wife of a crippled penniless poet. Since his death she had been one of the little charities of Anne of Austria. When Anne died, however, her pension stopped, and all subsequent petitions for its renewal had been ignored.

In her own need, Athénaïs remembered this irreproachable woman and offered her the position of governess to her children, but Mme. Scarron's prudery exceeded her penury. She refused, "saying that she preferred not to bring up the children of Mme. de Montespan, but if they were those of the King, and he wished it, he might ask." The King did ask, not without a certain raising of the eyebrows at this woman's calm self-assurance. He was repelled from the first by her severe manner and her cheap black gowns; but no doubt she was reliable.

Athénaïs, who frankly disliked children, was well satisfied to hand over the keys to the house at the end of the Rue de Vaugirard. Any young widow would have felt such an establishment meant good fortune. Now Mme. Scarron had at her command a staff of servants, carriages and horses, and there was nobody to question her authority. She had personal assets, too — intelligence, a cold handsomeness, and some taste. It would indeed be strange if she could not use these advantages to surprise His Majesty a little on his first visit, she thought. How Mme. de Montespan would have laughed if she had suspected her servant of such notions!

Madame was busy with the preparation of a secret treaty between her two countries. Charles, at first unwilling to acquaint even his own ministers with any details, gradually let Arlington and Buckingham learn a little. As a first term he promised to join Louis in the invasion of Holland and co-operate with both land and sea forces. In return he was to get large yearly subsidies while the war lasted and a share in the final spoils. Next, he was to make public confession of his conversion to Roman Catholicism.

This was the point most desired by his loving Minette, though it was a dangerous act certain to enrage his subjects. However, said Charles to the French ambassador, he had long ago come to the conclusion that no other creed agreed so well with the absolute authority and divine right of kings. But all these questions suggested a meeting between brother and sister, and Charles was much disappointed to find that Henriette was too sick to make the trip that year. "I must confesse, I would rather have had you stayd some monthes before you had been with childe . . ." The baby, another girl, was born at Saint-Cloud in August.

In Paris, where the Court had stayed, the same month brought the Queen a son, the Duc d'Anjou. Rejoicings were prolonged and drunken throughout the kingdom. But before Madame was out of bed she learned of her mother's death at her country house, Colombes. The old queen had not been well for a long time, and a concourse of royal physicians had prescribed opium to help her sleep. The queen objected at first that her old doctor Mayerne had warned against narcotics. "Besides," she said with a deprecating smile at her ladies, "an astrologer told me years ago that a grain would be the cause of my death, and I fear that M. Vallot's prescription may be that fatal grain."

Nevertheless she submitted, and in the morning was found comatose and dying. Father Cyprian, her confessor, hurried the last rites, but she could not respond. The Grande Mademoiselle observed caustically, "She could not sleep, so the doctors gave her a pill to send her to sleep, which it did so effectively that she never woke again."

Immediately Monsieur called his lawyers and laid claim to all the dead woman's possessions in his wife's name, though Henriette protested that she would wait for her brother's decision. The English commissioners soon arrived and drew up formal inventory. Most of the jewels and the Titians, Holbeins, Correggios, Vandykes, and Guidos were taken to England, but the furniture and all paintings affixed to the walls were left. House and lands at Colombes were handed over to Henriette as His English Majesty's free gift.

After paying Madame a visit of condolence, Louis and Maria Theresa took carriage for Chambord. Philippe packed hastily and went too. Left to her loneliness and grief, Henriette sent for Bossuet and gave him her mind as an experiment in the growth of grace. They spent whole days together, to the satisfaction of her more religious ladies such as Mme. de la Fayette. On the whole, Bossuet found her a less complicated subject than his other experiment, the repressed and passionate Duchesse de la Vallière.

In time even the Chevalier de Lorraine began to seem less important in Madame's life as she listened to "the most honest and straightforward of men, the gentlest and frankest speaker who has ever been known at Court."

In November he preached a delayed funeral sermon in the chapel at Saint-Germain, before the assembled great of France and England. He reminded his listeners of the past, of the royal child snatched from disaster by a devoted lady-in-waiting, brought to her exiled mother's arms to become her consolation in sorrow, her joy in ruin — the same princess who sat among them in the freshness of her beauty and youth that day.

No prophet turned in the pause to look at Madame, but Bossuet himself all through that Lent spoke of mortality and the brevity of human joy. Everywhere death cut down the young and the clever. "Now," he said, startling the congregation with his touching and impressive words, "now is the axe laid to the root of the tree." Six months from that Sunday Henriette would be in her grave.

During the summer Louise began some changes in her way of life, carefully, not to rouse the King's opposition. Self-love numbed by a shocking disillusion begins to return at last with little tentative demands. Some relief must come, if she hoped to survive, from the harness in which as one of The Ladies she pulled the carriage of Louis's conceit. She bought a little house at Carrières on the Seine and furnished it with whimsical rusticity. There was a little outdoor bathing room with tables and chairs of turf, and after floating in the river she could sit and eat brown bread and cream bought in the village. It was a condition almost like peace.

Unused inclinations were taken up for the first time in her life. She bought in a sudden mood of extravagance the jewels of the Duchesse de Mazarin, who had recently fled France, and wore them with imagination and taste. Said Mme. Scarron, who seldom paid compliments, "She dresses magnificently." And her mind, waking to restlessness, led her into avid but disorganized study. She had read romances and histories before; now in addition there was philosophy, the dry spice of Descartes and Aristotle.

Close friends and cousins often came to visit, charmed as could be with the elegant naïveté of the Duchesse's arrangements. Most often there was Bellefonds to make check on the state of her spirit and give rueful report of his own difficulties as one of the King's chiefs of staff.

Louise was even beginning to know her mother, the Marquise de Saint-Rémi, who after all these years had begun giving advice. Louise and she should retire to the Vaujours estate, she said firmly; she herself would think it pleasant to help with the education of her two pretty grandchildren whom Court life and their father were already beginning to spoil. But all other advisers disagreed. Wasn't Louise a duchess, trained to love fine and sophisticated things, still handsome, and only twenty-five? Too young, surely, to bury herself in the country. She would soon die of boredom.

Mme. de Sévigné, who had always liked Louise, observed from a distance her life with Montespan and predicted nothing but evil. "The Rose and the Torrent," as she styled The Ladies, "are allied in reciprocal confidence and see every day the Fire and the Snow (Louis and Maria Theresa). You know that this ensemble cannot last long without great disorders."

Strife and nonsense muddied the year 1670 for those at Court and afield. There was no longer, as in previous reigns, any life for a man of birth away from the King. His avowed purpose, to break the ancient power of the nobility, was almost realized. Money and prestige were not to be found in the land but in the royal service, from either military or political appointments. Louis liked to see the faces of his subjects gathered around when he rode, walked, ate, went to bed, rose, worshiped, or took medicine. Asked a favor for some stubbornly provincial gentleman, he would remark, "That is a man I never see," and so end all hope.

By this stage of the reign the business of being a courtier demanded a man's whole energy and concentration. His life was uncomfortable, anxious, and boring, beginning in the dark drafty pre-dawn and ending late after a day of waiting on aching feet for the King's signal to move to a new location.

New courtiers, particularly, were bedeviled by the formality. Most had to wait years for a coveted room in the castle, living meantime in expensive quarters in the town never seen by daylight. The lucky ones lived in the master's garrets in matchboard cubicles baking for part of the year and freezing the rest, noisome with hints of old chamber pots. The greatest reward was to be chosen by His Majesty to hold the candle as he undressed for bed, or to be bidden to join him in a promenade.

Of all the royal residences the Louvre was the worst, exposed as it was to the explorations of the Paris public, and this year so overcrowded that even those allowed to live there had begun to mutter complaints about the dirt and disorder.

Louis promised that Versailles should be different. He announced that there he expected everybody to observe a private-house standard of cleanliness. For one thing, there should be no more urinating in corners and behind doors — a revolutionary idea which was, however, generally approved.

Henry VIII of England had broken up church lands and used the pieces for buying his barons' allegiance. A serious mistake, Louis thought — like killing the goose that laid the golden eggs. He himself remained a loyal son of the Pope, protecting the monasteries and other properties, keeping them rich in potential revenues, and appointing his friends to superintend them. Men of this sort, mere tenants of the King's good will, were not likely to relax their fidelity to the crown. They watched him anxious-eyed as dogs who see the master put his hand in the breadbox.

Struggles over precedence became, naturally, more bitter than ever before. Great ladies squabbled and set their lackeys on each other; scenes occurred in chapel over certain cases of unauthorized inching-forward of prayer cushions. Louis smiled and said nothing.

But there were some disputes which he was forced to contemplate seriously. Philippe had learned with glee that the doddering Abbé de Langres was sick, and, ever the constant lover, promised the Chevalier de Lorraine that he should inherit the income of two abbeys which this death would leave vacant.

The Abbé duly expired. On January 30, Philippe presented his petition to the King and was flatly refused. Monsieur's disappointment was nothing compared to that of Lorraine, who gnashed his teeth and snarled that it was time for a little self-assertion on Philippe's part. Scared, Philippe returned to the royal chambers and told Louis he absolutely insisted on this indulgence for Lorraine. He had promised! Louis refused in an even more peremptory manner, adding a few words of brotherly criticism. At this, Monsieur flew into a tantrum, yelling that he would not stay at Court another minute, and flung back that if only he had a house a thousand leagues from Saint-Germain he would go there and feel overjoyed never to see his brother's odious face again.

The King, more taciturn than of old, replied only by ordering Lorraine's arrest. He was tired of this baby-faced troublemaker who was always trying to build his fortune on Philippe's — and all the others like him, Beuvron, for instance, and the worthless Chevalier de Rémecourt. Maybe arresting Lorraine would put down a few of the others for a while.

Recently Philippe had surprised him by asking for the government of a province. Louis refused; he knew how such appointments can breed civil war. Their father's brother, Gaston, had used just such a chance to levy men and money for opposing the crown. "Silence your evil advisers," suggested the King, and Monsieur, disconcerted, stammered that the idea had been his own. Louis was incredulous. Who, he asked, had led Monsieur to insist on a seat in the Privy Council, which he quickly lost by betraying the proceedings? Philippe, trapped, said in a huff that he would certainly be less mortified by this unexpected refusal if Henriette, who was after all the daughter of a crowned head, might have the privilege of an armchair in the Queen's salon. This, too, was denied. Louis was becoming utterly inflexible in matters of etiquette.

And now this matter of the abbey. Lorraine was carried off by the royal guards to Pierre-Encise, near Lyons. Philippe, on learning of this tragedy, toppled over in a dead faint, revived, hurried to Louis, and begged him while walking around the room on his knees to countermand the order. It was no use.

Monsieur went home again and ordered his apartments dismantled. Mademoiselle, perpetually at hand, commented on the nastiness of his language and his rudeness to Henriette. Madame in response treated him with the gentleness one may give a hurt child, saying that though she had little reason to like the Chevalier, she was sorry for the grief his arrest was causing. Next day they left for Villers-Cotterets. All indications pointed to a long period of sulking.

After a month Colbert went out for a visit to see what might be done to salve the situation. But there would be no terms, Philippe said, stubborn and mean, unless Lorraine were recalled. Louis was greatly irritated at this message, and learning that letters were passing between Philippe and the prisoner, had him removed to the fortress of the Château d'If at Marseilles, and forbade all communication. Such gossip sprang up at this open quarrel between the brothers that Louis was forced to send special messages to his foreign ambassadors in explanation of the matter. Paris and the provinces were full of wild talk, and journals and letters spread erroneous reports. It was also said, truthfully, that Monsieur and Madame had "parted beds." All sympathy was with the poor wife, chained like a slave to this frivolous tyrant's chariot and dragged into the thistled desert of Not-Court.

Relief was coming, however. Before long an English envoy, Lord Falconbridge, arrived with a formal invitation to Henriette from Charles II. Next day Colbert followed with a carriage full of presents — jewels, lace, perfume, diamond garters, gloves, and twenty purses each containing a hundred louis d'or. These were from the King, who could not get along without her help in the tangle of international relations. He had drawn tickets for her at the Court lottery, or so he said, and they had won these prizes.

At the same time the French Secretary of State requested Monsieur, in His Majesty's name, to return to Court, saying that Lorraine had been freed and allowed to go to Italy on condition he keep out of France.

Grudgingly, then, Monsieur let himself be coaxed from his retreat. But nobody need try to impose on his good nature. If Madame thought he would let her go to England, she was quite mad. It was most unseemly, in the first place, for a woman to be trusted with State affairs — and now it appeared there had been secrets! He was mortified and vindictive. Somehow Henriette always got all the glory and attention. But after a week of concerted cajolery, the wronged husband relented a little. He said Madame might visit her brother in Dover, but he himself would cross over with her so that she would not get all the honor of the treaty. There the matter rested for a few more weeks.

In the meantime, far from being discouraged by Lorraine's example, several secondary contenders came forward in the hope of taking his old place in Philippe's heart and purse.

At present [Henriette wrote], his chief friends are M. de Marsan, the Marquis de Villeroy, and the Chevalier de Beu-

vron. The Marquis d'Effiat is the only one of the troop who is perhaps a little less of a rogue, but he is not clever enough to manage Monsieur, and the three others do all they can to make me miserable until the Chevalier returns. Although Monsieur is somewhat softened, he still tells me there is only one way in which I can show my love for him. Such a remedy, you know, would be followed by certain death!

All these problems were hard enough for Louis to contend with, but now life in his own ménage was upset in spite of all his care and commands.

Athénaïs was frequently drunk and always behind in her gambling debts. And she was not as even-tempered as she had seemed at first. Sometimes he found himself answering her virago shrieks with shouts that, he realized later, had certainly penetrated the bedroom walls. Her famous wit, which had beguiled him like the dance of a little dagger, was not so amusing when in private she turned its point against him. She made him feel at times like a rather slow-witted bourgeois husband, plain Louis de Bourbon. On March 31 she gave birth to their second son, Louis Augustus, Duc du Maine. The forms of secrecy were duly observed; Mme. Scarron was waiting in the antechamber with swaddling clothes ready, and took the Duc straight home to his nursery.

Louis was grateful for this air of efficiency and calm, so rare a thing in women. He was beginning to think his first dislike of Mme. Scarron had been ill-considered.

XIV

THIS SINNER

THE PIGEONS' HEARTS, frozen underground all winter in the Bois de Boulogne, thawed with spring, and the Marquise de Montespan remembered the incantation of the witch La Voisin. At last it was taking effect as promised. The physicians of Mme. de la Vallière could not agree on a name for her disease, but concurred in the opinion that it would prove fatal. Called on for consultation, the King's doctors took up their vigil, giving an occasional experimental purge and observing with clinical interest the swift decline of the patient.

After a time priests were sent for, and these, specialists in symptoms of another kind, took up position on the opposite side of the bed. In Louise's sight all these faces were clouded, cleared away by other pictures and presences — there were measureless spans of darkness, a spinning thread of fever — the real chamber again, voices, and suddenly, horribly clear to her consciousness, the meaning of what they were saying.

"The priests on one side, the physicians on the other, spoke with as little hope of my soul as of my life. Like a poor beast, I could do nothing for my salvation." How could she have forgotten about hell? What might hell be, after all? What but this life again, continuing without hope of change, worse than the traditional rapacity of that fire that burns without flickering, so lovingly described by the Lenten sermonizers — her individual self, Louis, and Athénaïs, doomed to the pattern they had set, mirrored and mirrored again inescapably down eternity? And in hell there could be no respite such as came to her here, sometimes, when the weary body claimed periods of sleep, dragging the mind down with it into blessed nothing.

Yet she had asked for death. She felt the last of life drain through her like sand through an hourglass, and called to the only one she could think of — "Mercy. Mercy." No answer came except a motion of priests toward her head, ready with the crucifix; but she was only unconscious again, not dead. The doctors, next morning, marveled at the strength of her constitution, and the priests, talking of divine intervention, went away satisfied that they would not be needed.

Within a few days, swift as it had come, her malady disappeared. Louise, no more than comfortably weak, thought about the condition of her soul, which still lay in desperate danger, spotted, she now knew, with deceit and vanity, riddled with cancerous sin. She must have help if it was to be saved. An indulgent confessor might easily be found, to admit her to communion — but hasty absolution would do no good in a case so aggravated. Its peace would be false.

The way, God, to offer you a pure sacrifice agreeable to your eyes, with a spirit full of the world's vanities and a heart full of passion? The way to lodge you without profanation in the same dwelling whence, with such trouble, I have driven your greatest enemies? Give me a contrite heart . . . Inspire me by your grace . . . Look on me sometimes, approaching you, a humble stranger . . . Regard with pity this sinner who, all on fire with passion, asks . . . a drop of that living water with which you quench together in the soul the source and the thirst of guilt. But above all, look on me as on Madeleine, and allow that like that penitent saint I water your feet with my tears, and that in trying to love you greatly, I begin to efface my many crimes. God, who takes away the heart of him you will, change all my loves . . . For you know, God, how easily I am impressed by the things I see and the people I frequent, with what facility I do good with the good, and practice evil with the bad . . . Save me from the sweet poison of pleasing this world and loving it.

A second envoy came from the King of England, eager to see his sister and conclude the Secret Treaty.

Philippe remained adamant, but now Louis was tired of humoring him. This mission he said, was for the good of the State, and according to royal command. There was no more to be said.

On April 28 Madame set out for Flanders with a large company of ladies and gentlemen confused as to the expedition's purpose but in holiday spirits. The royal coach, gilded outside, embroidered inside, was like a room on wheels, fitted for sleeping, eating, and games.

"The King left today from Saint-Germain with one of the most beautiful and sumptuous suites one can imagine," the ambassador from Turin wrote. "There were eight in his coach — himself, the Queen, Monsieur and Madame, Mlle. de Montpensier, Mme. de la Vallière, the Marquise de Montespan, and the Marquise de Béthune." Mme. de Béthune later gave up her seat to Gabrielle de la Vallière. They were attended by a cavalry escort led by Lauzun, brilliant as a bantam cock out there in the blowing April day, and the rest of the Court followed in a line of conveyances strung out for miles across the landscape.

Mademoiselle alternated between rapture and misery. She, who had been sought by the eligible princes of the world — Charles II himself, the King of Portugal, the Duc de Lorraine — and had refused them all, was now palpitating with the desire to become a wife. But the man of her choice ignored her timorous confidences. No doubt he was afraid of her fabulous name and fortune, as well he might be. Or — agonizing doubt — was he in love with someone else? She had to know. She evolved a scheme for getting him into conversation, at the same time observing his unguarded response.

At Noyon, gripping her courage as an inexperienced rider takes the reins, the Grande Mademoiselle posed her question. Would M. de Lauzun, out of his experience of the world, advise her regarding the selection of a husband? His answer was not discouraging; he said he would give the matter his consideration during the course of the journey. But now a new alarm struck her. There were rumors once more that Lauzun had been assigned to marry the Duchesse de Vaujours. Certainly it was possible. If the King had made up his mind to dispose finally of Louise in this way, nothing could change it. In a jealous agony she waited for news. None came. At last, coming as near sidling as a big-boned woman can, she approached the Chevalier de la Hillière, lieutenant of Lauzun's guards. "What's all this," she said, "this noise going around that he's going to marry Mme. de la Vallière?"

"He mentioned it to me yesterday," La Hillière said, "and told me 'I'm furious against people who spread that story. The King has never dishonored anybody — he wouldn't begin with me.' "

So Mademoiselle was saved temporarily, but she still watched Louise with hard and suspicious eyes.

Everywhere they stopped, Senlis, Compiègne, Saint-Quentin, Arras, rooms were taken and an imitation Versailles set up by speedy scene arrangers. Balls and fireworks greeted the King's arrival in every town, and in exchange all the important local ladies were given presents. But the weather changed; it rained, and plumes and uniforms were drenched. Some fabrics faded disastrously. The majestic coach lurched and sank with sucking sounds into the mud, fording innumerable streams; and Mademoiselle, who shared with the Queen a hysterical dread of water, joined her in screaming until the King was ready to kill them both.

Half a league from Landrécies the bridge was washed out by the flooding Sambre, and the Court waited cramped, damp, and without food or drink for twenty-four hours. Finally some chickens were procured, half cooked over a fire of wet sticks, and torn to pieces by the hands of the famished royal party. The Queen was given some watery soup from the remains and complained to everybody while drinking it. Nearby there was a leaky barn, to which toiling lackeys, slipping in the ancient mire, hauled mattresses and covers; and the King announced bedtime, restraining his natural irritation with God and the women.

"What!" Maria Theresa shrilled, "sleep all together? How horrible!"

"You have only to leave your curtain open," His Majesty said rather acidly. "You will see us all."

Scarcely comforted, the Queen arranged herself behind her

drapery, and the rest lay down with a certain amount of muttering and shoving — Monsieur and Madame on the far side, then Louis, Mademoiselle, Louise, Athénaïs, and Gabrielle. Some slept as the night rained on. Louise lay awake listening to rat noises in the rafters and the running water. The human body could learn to rest on such a bed as this; convent pallets were even harder. In some strange way she welcomed the discomfort and even the proximity of Athénaïs's perfumed hair, as if by hoarding up penances she could buy her freedom. But how long the night was . . . and gradually all other thoughts were forced away by the awareness of Louis's presence. Or could she think of him as present? Between them on the mattress lay not Mademoiselle, but a continent.

The triumphal journey continued, to the fascination of the new Flemish subjects who crowded the streets to see Louis calmly riding with his "three queens."

"Louis XIV had no modesty," says Lamartine. "There was so much distance between monarch and subjects that morals and religion scarcely dared to grumble. One respected the prince in spite of the scandals; they were part of the Divine Right."

Madame was not in good health. She retired to her bedroom at the end of every day's journey, and the Court commented on her thinness and pallor. In the coach one afternoon Monsieur sat staring at her speculatively. An astrologer had once told him, he said, that he would have several wives, and this prophecy seemed likely to come true. It was plain Henriette would not live long.

"This seemed to me very hard," Mademoiselle said, "and the Queen and I showed by our silence what we thought of his conduct to poor Madame."

Henriette took all this patiently; she was used to it. Philippe did not travel with her often, anyway. He had decided to charge through the towns at the head of his regiment, sword bared, in commemoration of his own warlike deeds, and so was kept busy.

At Lille the King and his company turned back, while Henriette with his commissions and a retinue of two hundred and thirty-seven went on to Dunkirk. There Charles's ships rode at anchor, ready to ferry her across to England.

Next day, the 25th of May, with Dover in sight, a boat appeared rowing toward the fleet, and Henriette weeping on deck with joy was soon embraced by both her brothers, the King and the Duke of York. Behind her, with a tear on her lashes, too, stood a pretty girl, Louise de Kéroualle. Within two minutes after boarding the ship Charles had marked her with his practiced eye.

The treaty was complicated, the celebrations were prolonged; and consequently Henriette overstayed her husband's leave by several days. On May 30 she told the French ambassador that she had almost persuaded Charles to declare war on Holland immediately, and was trying to remove the obstacles to the conclusion of the commercial aspects of the agreement. Finally, June 1, the Secret Treaty was signed and delivered to the ambassador, who set off in haste for Boulogne.

In parting, Charles gave Minette six thousand pistoles for building a chapel to the memory of their mother, and filled her lap with rings and brooches for herself and her friends. Then, smiling, he asked her to leave one of her own jewels as a souvenir. She sent her little maid of honor, Mlle. de Kéroualle, for her casket, opened it, and told Charles to choose. "This," he said, taking the girl's hand. "Let her stay in England." Henriette laughed and frowned. Impossible, she said. She was responsible to the girl's parents and must take her back to France. So she sailed June 12, in salubrious weather, carrying a copy of Edmund Waller's newest ode.

> . . . *No wind can favor us. Howe'er it blows,*
> *We must be wretched, and our dear treasure lose!*
> *Sighs will not let us half our sorrow tell,*
> *Fair, lovely, great and best of nymphs, farewell.*

Charles told his sister goodbye three times, and each time returned to put his arms around her again as she wept. Never was there such a sorrowful leavetaking, said the wondering historians who stood around to record the scene, and the tears never dried from this princess's face the whole voyage, till she heard the guns at Calais firing in her honor.

Saint-Germain was no longer a pleasure palace for Louis; it made him melancholy. He could not avoid looking toward the threatening towers of Saint-Denis, though there were certainly enough other views to attract the eye. Worse, he could not keep them out of his dreams. On a June night they rose above his deep sleep as ship masts rise over the ocean horizon, wavering through a mistlike fire. Something formed in the center of the fire and held — a skeleton with lifted hands from which spilled a woman's jewels. The King woke, sweating. He never had such nightmares anywhere else. It was another reason, if he needed one, for hurrying completion of Versailles. There, at least, he would be able to sleep.

"Madame bears death plainly written in her face," the Queen said calmly, startling the whole company. It seemed at times that her words came not from observation, but from a knowing of the blood — that same Spanish blood that makes soothsayers of gypsies.

But nobody agreed with her. Madame was restored to health and vivacity. Not even Philippe's petty persecutions could cause more than a momentary shadow, a certain expression of weariness — and, heaven knew, his constant talk about Lorraine had the same effect on everybody else.

It was hot beautiful weather reminiscent of that best summer in time, 1661, Henriette's bridal year. Against the advice of her doctor, Yvelin, she went bathing in the Seine on June 29 and came out feeling faint, weak, conscious of a nagging pain in her side. Next day she complained again of the same sensations, but entertained friends as usual and paid a visit to the chamber where an English artist was painting her elder daughter's portrait. About five o'clock, after dinner in Philippe's apartments, she spread some cushions on the floor as was her habit, lay down, and dozed lightly for a time, watched by her quietly gossiping women. Madeleine de la Fayette, who had often seen her sleeping face, remarked a strange alteration, an almost gray pallor, and Monsieur agreed casually that she certainly looked unwell.

Henriette woke, wandered out into the hall, and stopped to speak for a few minutes with Boisfranc, the household treasurer, meanwhile holding a hand to her side. Back to the salon, and she asked Mme. de Gourdon to bring her a drink. It was iced chicory water, which she drank slowly. No more than a minute later she gasped, and cried out as if stabbed, "Ah, what a pain! What shall I do? I must be poisoned!" Her frightened attendants hurried to help her upstairs to her chamber, where they unlaced her gown, took off her shoes, laid back the bedcover. Tears stood in her eyes; a new onslaught of pain rocked her back and forth on the bed; she could not lie down. Feet came running from all directions, servants, two or three low-ranking medical men who did not dare open their mouths, and finally M. Esprit, physician extraordinaire. Madame was suffering from colic, he said, that was all. But the word poison came again from Madame's grimacing lips. At this, La Fayette looked closely at Monsieur, who seemed utterly unmoved and only remarked that in that case an emetic had better be tried, and some of the chicory water given to a dog. Mérille, the first valet, accordingly brought an emetic, but its only effect was to bring on a renewed attack of the pain which had already exhausted the patient, leaving her wrung and trembling.

Mme. de Gamaches stepped forward and felt her pulse. There was none, she said, and Madame's hands and feet were getting cold. Now Monsieur became upset and began calling for action from the doctors. Esprit responded unctuously that there was no danger and that he would answer for Madame's life. Philippe reminded him unkindly that he had also answered for the life of his son, the little Duc de Valois, who was now dead.

From the church of Saint-Cloud came a deep tolling of bells, calling the canons together to recite prayers for the sick. Three hours passed. The household priest arrived, and close behind him M. Vallot, the King's physician, who had been summoned from Versailles. Henriette was confessed and bled. Afterward she turned her disheveled head on the pillow and beckoned her husband close. "Monsieur, you have not loved me for a long time, but this was unjust; I have never abandoned you." He turned away, evidently moved.

The chamber was gradually filling with people. The Prince de

Condé came near, gravely inquired how Madame felt. She said she was dying and hoped soon to be out of her pain. "Not so!" said the doctors, coming out of their consultation with smiles of encouragement. Another bed had been made up with fresh sheets, and in a momentary lull of pain Henriette rose and crossed the room. At Vallot's insistence she drank a little soup and then was convulsed again. By now the smiles of the medical men were a little forced. One of them admitted that the numbness of the arms and legs was a bad sign. The ladies, who had been intermittently whispering to Madame that Monsieur would be certain to treat her better after all this was over, ceased calling her attention to his spouselike anxiety and now stood around in silence, looking at the twisting shape on the bed.

At nine the Duc de Créqui had taken the news to Versailles. "Madame is dying," he said bluntly, and the King and Queen rushed at once into their carriage. On the stair at Saint-Cloud they met Vallot, still announcing his diagnosis of simple colic to any who would listen; but none who saw the patient could believe him. She lay with her hair matted and wet with the sweat of prolonged agony, her nightdress unfastened, her features pinched. "My nose is already sunken in," she said in a tone of wondering sadness. "She had already the air of a corpse," Mademoiselle agreed, standing aghast behind Their Majesties.

For a minute or two Henriette spoke affectionately to both Louis and Maria Theresa, and then as the King, not even trying to hide his tears, bent to embrace her, she said, "Kiss me, Sire . . . do not weep for me, or you will make me weep too. You are losing a good servant, who has always feared the loss of your good graces more than death itself."

The Grande Mademoiselle, who had a horror of such things, stood at the foot of the bed pretending to be too overcome with sorrow to approach any closer. Beside her was the Comtesse de Soissons, just back from exile, her eyes glittering with some unreadable emotion. Out of the night, rustling up the stair, came others of the Court, some pressing unobtrusively against the walls, others making their way toward the bed.

Outside in the corridor those on whom the time had begun to

weigh heavy whispered jokes and hushed each other's laughter. Among all the faces was one Henriette had never seen so clearly before. His look made an island in the crowd, telling her he loved her and would have given his own life to save hers. Answering, she smiled and said, "Goodbye, Tréville — goodbye." And there were The Ladies as if in church, Montespan and La Vallière, and the Maréchal de Gramont, proxy for his son Armand de Guiche, who would be the last to learn that Madame had left him for good.

Montagu, the English ambassador, arrived, and spoke softly with her for some time. She said, "I beg you to tell my brother . . . I have always loved him better than life itself, and now my only regret in dying is to be leaving him."

Montagu asked in English whether she believed herself poisoned, but was interrupted by the priest Feuillet — "Madame, you must accuse no one, but offer your life as a sacrifice to God."

After a pause she answered. "If this is true, you must never let the king, my brother, know it. Spare him that grief at all events, and, above all, do not let him take revenge on the king here, for he at least is not guilty."

Business matters were discussed with one and another person; letters were called for and entrusted, messages sent, servants commended to Charles's care. Late at night the crowd thinned, going home to bed. Monsieur, crying, came to kiss her again, and she dismissed him gently.

Still another famous doctor appeared and bled her in the foot while she waited in terrible anxiety for the arrival of Bossuet. There was not much time left.

"My God, when will these fearful pains cease?"

"What, Madame," said the stern Feuillet, "are you already impatient? You have been sinning against God for twenty-six years, and have only begun to do penance in these last six hours."

She moved her head from side to side on the pillow and asked at what hour Christ had died on the Cross.

"At three o'clock."

"Perhaps he will let me die at the same hour."

Extreme unction was administered, and at the same moment Bossuet came into the room. "Hope, Madame, hope!" he said, knelt, and gave back the crucifix which had fallen out of her hands. Surrounded by the kneeling few who were left in the chamber — Montagu, Mme. de la Fayette, Mme. d'Epernon, the Maréchal de Bellefonds, and M. de Tréville — he prayed for the passing soul. Agony convulsed her again and the death sweat broke out on her upper lip and forehead. Bossuet urged her to offer her pains to God in union with those of Christ on the Cross, and she said faintly, "That is what I am trying to do."

He held the crucifix high before her eyes and she was released for the moment, lying back exhausted. Bossuet retired to the window seat, apparently to pray alone and give her a few minutes' rest. In the interval she beckoned her maid with a lifted finger, and whispered in English, "Give him the emerald ring which I have had made for him, when I am dead."

In a moment she said, "It is all over . . ."

Bossuet leaned over her, seeing in her eyes the austere blind look which is like a climax of passion. "Madame, you believe in God, you hope in God, you love God?"

"With all my heart," she said, and the crucifix once more slid down her breast out of her relaxing fingers.

It was exactly three o'clock on the morning of June 30.

The Bishop of Valence wrote, "Thus this great and royal hearted princess passed away, without ever having shown the least sign of trouble or weakness in this awful surprise . . ."

"I pray that God may receive her in His mercy," said Feuillet, "and all you, who read these words, pray for her also."

An hour later, Ralph Montagu wrote the King of England a report of his loss and dispatched it immediately. ". . . Excuse this imperfect relation, for the grief I am in . . ."

Sir Thomas Armstrong, after a long look at the dead face lit by the thin dawn light and a ring of wax candles, took Montagu's letter, rode for Calais and never stopped until he reached Whitehall.

The French royal family, assembled in Louis's chamber that morning, heard Bossuet describe Henriette's dying. "Madame was gracious to death, as she was to everybody."

"The King's grief has been . . . so excessive," Lyonne wrote, "that I am very anxious for his health. He is going to sleep at Saint-Germain tonight, saying that he cannot remain in this house of pleasure while he is so overwhelmed . . .

Even so, business matters had to be considered. Taking Mademoiselle aside that day, Louis said, "My cousin, here is a vacant place. Will you fill it?"

"You are the master, Sire," she stammered, but turned a little green in the face. Even in the old days she would never have chosen Philippe as a husband.

The widower himself achieved emotional calm faster than anybody else at Court, and did not waste the day. He took Henriette's official letters and the money she had set aside for her servants, and hurried off to Paris. There he devoted himself with a free mind to mourning arrangements and receptions. His daughter and her little visiting English cousin, Anne, were dressed in trailing mantles of purple velvet; and visitors at the Palais-Royal were sent to pay their formal condolences in the nursery, not only to these two but to the baby, Mlle. de Valois.

But, the English secretary, Vernon, remarks, Monsieur wearied of "walking in the shade of melancholy," and two weeks later joined the Court at Saint-Germain, in fine spirits and done up in mourning of supreme elegance. He told Louis he would like to marry Mademoiselle, because at her age she would be unlikely to bear children, and he would thus inherit her whole fortune.

In early August, Vernon wrote, "Monsieur is in amours again, and if he be not shortly married to Mademoiselle, all the world is in a mistake. He follows her, he courts her, he is at her toilette, and waits on her as she dresseth herself."

Tréville, led home in the dawn of that last June day, was so numb with sorrow that his friends were afraid he would sink into madness. He went on at Court performing his duties well enough, however, until after the funeral; then he gave up his post and entered the Jansenist retreat at Port-Royal, to spend the rest of his life as a scholar-recluse.

Mme. d'Epernon, who had also been at Madame's bedside, retired before the end of the year to a convent.

Cosnac, the Bishop of Valence, remembered that summer long

afterward. "I cannot describe the state in which I found myself. Since men have been known to die of grief, it seems a crime on my part to have survived that day . . . My strength resisted the shock. I was not even ill, but from that day, my life became so sad and dreary that it was little better than a living death."

To Louise the words spoken in her own mind so short a time before returned with shaking significance. "Oh death, your approach is cruel to those who have never thought on you, and who put all their hopes in the world's things. Oh death, your sight is terrible to those for whom you end all pleasure . . ." But there are many kinds of death. Some kill by degrees, as blight does a tree. Was not Madame, after all, to be envied?

The news broke in London like word of some national disaster. Charles, sobbing in wild grief, cursed Philippe with every name in a soldier's vocabulary. ". . . But, Sir Thomas, I beg you, not a word of this to others." In spite of this cautionary afterthought, it was too late to stop the rumors. The word "poison" slid around Whitehall like a snake. Buckingham raged like a lunatic and wanted to declare war on France. In the city a mob gathered, yelling for French blood. The ambassador's life was threatened, and a detachment of the royal guard had to be sent to protect his house.

In France, likewise, few doubted that Madame had been murdered. It was said the Chevalier de Lorraine had sent the poison from Rome, and his accomplice, D'Effiat, rubbed it on the silver cup their victim habitually used.

Louis ordered a post-mortem, which was held the evening of June 30 in the presence of the English ambassador and a number of other officials. English and French physicians found no trace of poison and drew up an official statement declaring that death had been owing to cholera morbus. But, says Boscher, one of the English surgeons, the autopsy had been performed most unskillfully, "as if the surgeon's business was rather to hide the truth than to reveal it."

Nothing remained but to get on with the funeral, which Louis decreed should have all the ceremony usually reserved for crowned heads. The corpse lay in state for two days, surrounded by lighted candles and sprinkled with holy water by the King and Queen; then, in fulfillment of Henriette's old promise to the nuns, her heart was taken in a silver casket to Val-de-Grâce.

On the night of July 4, the body was removed to Saint-Denis by torchlight, followed by Mademoiselle and all the princesses of the blood, a procession slowly winding down the avenues of Saint-Cloud between the dark-arching summer trees, across the Seine, and up the quiet streets of Paris, until the gates of the chapel were reached at two in the morning. Here the coffin was set down in the Abbey of the Kings under a black velvet canopy, to be watched night and day by Monsieur's guards while monks chanted masses for the dead.

Two days before the funeral, Saintôt, the King's Master of the Ceremonies, followed by heralds and criers with bells, marched in procession through the streets and knocked on the doors of the Parliament and Council Chambers, proclaiming in a sonorous voice, "All noble and devout persons pray for the soul of the most high, powerful, virtuous and excellent, Princesse Henriette-Anne de'Angleterre, daughter of Charles I, King of Great Britain, and of Henriette-Marie, daughter of France, and wife of Philippe de France, only brother of the King . . ."

On the morning of August 21, representatives from all the Corporations, from Parliament and the Law Courts, and a huge crowd of nobility poured into the Abbey of Saint-Denis. The Queen sat in a tribune with the King of Poland, the English ambassador, the Duke of Buckingham, Lord Sandwich, Lord St. Albans, Lord Arundel, James Hamilton, and the Comte and Comtesse de Gramont. In came the chief mourners, a long parade, and last the members of Monsieur's household carrying burning torches.

The coffin lay in the center of the choir, mourned over by allegorical statues of Youth, Poetry, and Music, and covered by cloth of gold edged with ermine and embroidered with the arms of France and England. As soon as the company had taken position, hundreds of flambeaux and wax candles burst into flame, a cloud of incense rose from the altars, and the Archbishop of Reims, assisted by other bishops, began the Mass, which was chanted by the King's musicians to the accompaniment of Lully's violins. "I do not think there will be any better music in heaven," said Mme. de Sévigné.

At last Bossuet mounted the pulpit in his purple episcopal robes. He "preached with an eloquence something transported beyond his usual delicacy and sweetness," commenting on the irresistible charm, the rare gifts of mind, which had made this lady even greater than she was by birth; recalled her recent journey to England, and finally the night when the terrible news struck the Court — "Madame is dying — Madame is dead." At this point a great sob came from the whole assembly, and Bossuet himself stopped, tried to go on, and burst into tears. On the hand he put to his face a ring glittered, an emerald set with diamonds.

Vernon says, "The hearse was richly adorned. All the members of her family, with great silence and mourning, cast the badges of their employment into her grave, and as soon as her coffin was put in, there was a general weeping, a circumstance something unusual at these great ceremonies . . ."

"Never, since dying first came into fashion," remarked the flippant Lord Rochester, "was anyone so deeply lamented."

Henriette's death was the end of an era. With her, spontaneity and fun left the French Court, never to return with such an air. All the wild amusing children who had run with her through the green mazes of summer and helped her costume the ordinary with pleasant fantasy would soon be dead in the wars, shut away in religious orders, or tamed to the aging Louis's merciless routine. He himself, after that year, never danced again in a ballet.

The nymphs were all gone from the forest.

XV

TIDES OF LOVE AND WAR

YEARS LATER the Princesse Palatine was to ask Louise a delicate question. "I was curious to know why she remained so long
as a follower of Mme. de Montespan. God, she said, had touched
her heart and made her know her sin. She had thus thought it was
necessary to do and to endure that which was most agonizing for
her . . . to see herself disdained by the King. In the years after
she lost his love she suffered like the damned and offered to God
all her pain in expiation of her past guilt, for, since her fault had
been public, it necessary her penance too should be public . . .
Thus she remained with Mme. de Montespan."

Athénaïs herself was mystified by Louise's endurance. Her recovery at the last moment from a malady which would have killed
most people was strange enough, but her behavior ever since was
simply inexplicable. Was it lack of pride, or mere callousness, which
made her accept gently slights which would drive most women to
murder?

In a mood of experiment, Athénaïs had asked Louise one evening
to help her dress and to put the finishing brush to her coiffure —
to act the servant, in fact. And, ever since, Louise had done this as
a duty, enhancing the triumphant beauty that had been her own
ruin. There was something most amusing to the Marquise in this
spectacle of a duchess doing her bidding. Yet crazy, somehow. The
situation was beginning to make her a little nervous.

Perhaps La Vallière was actually mad. How else explain her
silent acceptance of such constant insults not only to herself but her

rank? Every night Louis dressed himself in her chambers and then left to spend his time with Montespan. Yes, that must be the answer — Louise's mind was giving way. Her passion for the King had never been natural.

And now this piety. It was said by the Duchesse's admirers — and, curiously, there were quite a few — that she was Bossuet's greatest convert since the death of Madame. Well, religion was harmless enough, and Louise's had the salutory effect of keeping her out of the way for at least part of every day.

Athénaïs herself greatly disliked Bossuet; he had no taste and little judgment. He was always making personal comments from the pulpit which, of course, one didn't dare to resent. Even though the Queen had accepted Montespan by now as her husband's mistress, Bossuet's preaching was disrespectful in the extreme. In two recent sermons he had barely left names unspoken. And in a third, addressed directly to the King, he told the whole episode of David and the heifer which was stolen from him and then later restored — and continued to that subsequent passage where David, now a king, carried off the wife of a servant and was deaf to the husband's outcry. Louis was greatly mortified on that occasion, and as a result suggested Athénaïs retire for a time to her house at Clagny.

It was a Jubilee year, when orators enjoyed special freedom and ordinary people had to be careful — a great papal absolution carrying free pardon of all past sins, excluding nobody, and thus causing ignorant orgies of joy in the streets. In return there was, naturally, a matter of certain prayers to be said, fasts observed, and pilgrimages to churches.

Clagny was a magnificent estate in that stretch of country skirting the forest of Villars d'Avrai beyond Versailles, quite suitable for Mme. de Montespan's purposes. She often held court there, receiving presents, entertaining foreign ambassadors, and introducing them to her children as if they were little princes of the blood.

Now she went there as the King asked, to escape embarrassment, and had scarcely arrived when a servant announced a visitor. It was Bossuet. He saluted her sternly, and without any introduction or apology gave his low opinion of her present position. For her own sake, he said, as well as that of the King and a public scandalized by her example, she must retire. Where? To the convent of Fontevrault. And when? Immediately. After a pause he added that good advisers had already cured the King of his guilty desires.

Bossuet now produced a letter written in Louis's own hand, stating that he had decided on a life of virtue. Athénaïs thought she was going to faint, but reread the letter. There seemed a certain ambiguity in the wording, quite unlike Louis's usual direct prose. It was highly suspicious. Bossuet stopped strolling around the room and asked for her decision. Smiling, she snuggled deeper into the cushions of the armchair. She'd see if she couldn't send this man's little foil flying with a quick twist.

Sweetly she said she was convinced of the sincerity of the holy men who waited on His Majesty — but wasn't it true that a shepherd owed something to his flock? She would give up the King when he, Bossuet, would do likewise with Mlle. de Malléon des Vieux. His perfect composure deflected the point of the sentence, and she saw that Court gossip had been wrong again. Disappointing! He bowed and left, saying that his errand was done and that he left her to her conscience — which, however, seemed so tranquil he should reproach himself for any further attempt to rouse it.

Athénaïs remained practicing tranquillity for several days longer before a second letter arrived from the King, this time brought appropriately by a lay messenger and inviting her to Versailles. Rumor had been busy as she expected, chipping away at the foundation of her pedestal, but this was quickly repaired. Her salon was crowded all day, as she loved to see it; all the most important people in France stood around watching the ritual of her boudoir, her enemies left their names at her door, and her armchair, praying stool, and cushions were replaced in the tribune of the chapel. But she was annoyed with Louis — very annoyed — and did not hesitate to let him know it.

The fame of Louis XIV had reached the world's remotest corners, even the African kingdom of Arda. Its black monarch had learned of the French conquest of Candia, and was anxious to gain a powerful friend. His envoys arrived at Court in heathen splendor to propose a political and commercial alliance, to ask Louis's support against English and Dutch settlers on his coasts, and to present marvelous, alarming gifts.

The King was given a tiger, a panther, and two superb lions, the Queen a golden pheasant which laughed in a human voice and a Moorish dwarf ten years old but only twenty-seven inches tall. Last, to Mme. de Montespan, with the same ceremony, addressing her as "the second wife of the King," they delivered in the name of their master a string of large pearls, two ornate bracelets, and an enormous sapphire. She, inquiring discreetly, learned that His Majesty of Arda had got the facts of Louis's home life from three traveling missionaries.

Maria Theresa was enchanted with her dwarf, Osman, ordered him a wardrobe of rich costumes, and treated him like a toy. Iridescent in peacock feathers, armored with jeweled embroidery, topheavy in satin turbans, he impishly carried her train through the apartments, sometimes stopping to bury his face in its folds and let himself be dragged over the polished parquet. Always with the Queen, on her knee, perched nearby on banister or mantelpiece, or rolling and kicking on the carpet, he irritated Louis. Maria Theresa, however, stubbornly refused to part with her pet. Thus it became necessary for all women of fashion to have Moorish dwarfs like Osman — a short caprice, but well recorded by Mignard and other portrait painters with an eye for contrasting skin tones, mahogany and gardenia.

His Majesty's aversion to blackamoors was soon to be dramatically vindicated. Maria Theresa, ready again to be brought to bed of a child, was the subject of prayers in all Paris churches. One day Osman jumped out suddenly from a corner, and startled her into a swoon. Within a few hours she gave birth — not to the promised prince, but a dreadful little caricature of a daughter, black from head to foot like something left too long in the oven. All in attendance were sworn to secrecy. The error was hastily baptized and then spirited away to Gisors. Eventually, if she lived, some convent would keep the unlucky princess sufficiently hidden. The *Gazette de France* reported that the royal infant had died a few minutes after baptism.

So ended little Osman's association with the Queen. He was from the devil.

Love had finally quenched the last flare of ambition in the Grande Mademoiselle. In other days there could have been no hesitating between Lauzun and Monsieur; one was an ordinary soldier with no fortune and no power except what he had in his terrible eye; the other was the second gentleman of the realm, commander of honors in any court of the world. But now Mademoiselle was forty, and her own fortune was big enough to support many luxuries. She would have one, this pepperpot Lauzun. The courtship began in earnest, she pursuing, dropping gaucheries like rocks into their conversations; he retreating, looking back to signal spurious indifference at her. On one occasion she, finding the ribbons of her sleeve undone, asked him to tie them. He demurred, saying he had no knack for such things. So Mme. de la Vallière performed the service, and Mademoiselle comforted herself with the thought that Lauzun had been unable to trust his passions, in such proximity to her bare arm. She continued to seek his advice on the subject of selecting a husband, and finally in December announced that her decision had been made. The bridegroom's name was written on a slip of paper, which he was conjured not to read until the following morning.

"It's you!" the paper said. With these words Lauzun was hoisted high up the pyramid of rank and power, unbelieving and somewhat frightened. Nobody else could believe it either. Courtiers met, drew each other aside, and discussed it with lifting eyebrows and shrugging shoulders.

Mme. de Sévigné wrote to her daughter.

> *I am going to tell you the most surprising, most marvelous, most miraculous, most triumphant, most astounding, most un-heard of, most singular, most extraordinary, most unbelievable, most unexpected . . . thing, which one can't believe in Paris . . . Well! It's necessary to tell you: M. de Lauzun will*

marry Sunday at the Louvre, guess who? I give you four guesses, I give you ten, I give you a hundred. That is very difficult to guess; it is Mme. de la Vallière. — Absolutely not, Madame. Then it's Mlle. de Retz? — Absolutely not, you're very provincial. Truly, we're great blockheads, you say, it's Mlle. Colbert. — Growing cold. — It's assuredly Mlle. de Créquy. — You don't have it. It's necessary finally to tell you: he marries, Sunday, at the Louvre, with the permission of the King, Mademoiselle, Mlle. de . . . Mlle. . . . guess the name: he marries Mademoiselle, my faith! by my faith! my sworn faith! Mademoiselle, the Grande Mademoiselle, Mademoiselle, daughter of late Monsieur; Mademoiselle, granddaughter of Henri IV; Mlle. d'Eu, Mlle. de Dombes, Mlle. de Montpensier, Mlle. d'Orléans, Mademoiselle, cousin germane of the King . . .

In a trance of happiness the bride prepared for her wedding. Besides the problem of what to wear, there were affairs of business and state to settle, the disposing of an impressive fraction of the property of France. To her darling she signed over the necessary titles, names, and ornaments to satisfy the marriage contract — four vast holdings including the Comté d'Eu and the duchies of Montpensier, Saint-Fargeau, and Châtellerault. It was specified that Lauzun should take the name Montpensier. Wonderful presents bearing his new crests and insignia were labored over through the nights by teams of goldsmiths and embroiderers.

But the worm was busy inside the apple. Lauzun, with such dazzling prospects, suddenly became a worthy enemy for several great men, Louvois among them. They saw their positions in the government menaced by "this little man" who would know how to use his assets so much more cunningly than harmless old Mademoiselle had ever done. Their separate jealousies rose and banded together like an army to march on the King.

On the Thursday before the wedding, therefore, at seven in the evening, His Majesty called the engaged couple to his room and told them that he had been convinced by wise heads that such a marriage as this would do discredit to his reputation. So, he said, he must regretfully withdraw consent after all.

"M. de Lauzun," said Mme. de Sévigné, "received this order with all the respect, all the submission, all the firmness, and the despair deserved by such a great fall. As for Mademoiselle, following her nature, she broke into sobbing, into cries, into violent grief, into excessive complaints; and all day she hasn't left her bed, and has swallowed only bouillons."

One of the afflicted woman's first visitors, the Duchesse de la Vallière, spoke out of her developing insight words more true than comforting. "I'm very sorry for you — a person in your position can only have taken these steps to no avail; this is worthy of pity. But there is no use in mourning for M. de Lauzun; the King will give him dignities and bounties. And it will be a happier thing for him not to marry."

Mademoiselle, naturally, found this statement tactless. But Louise, disenchanted at twenty-six, schooled by the frankness of Bossuet, was beginning to lose her sense of the importance of tact, to see things as they were, and to name them. Lauzun with his mercurial notions, his firework furies, was no man for a woman to pin her love and hopes on. Few were.

Winter ceremonies and pleasures unrolled like a long and richly patterned carpet. On the morning of February 7 a benediction was held for the Abbess of Fontevrault, Marie-Magdeleine-Gabrielle de Rochechouart. She was Montespan's sister, fully as clever and even more gorgeous to see. Louis enjoyed her company a great deal when she visited the Palais-Royal.

That same evening, the whole Court went to the Hôtel de Guise to witness by the light of two thousand fanciful lanterns the wedding of Henriette de Lorraine d'Harcourt, and to feast at midnight. Louise was there, very pretty and quite gay.

The following Monday, Their Majesties presented at the Tuileries, on the occasion of Monsieur's emerging from mourning, the ballet *Psyche,* and next evening ended the carnival season with a masquerade ball. A certain sensation resulted when, on the stroke of the hour, all masks were raised and it was discovered that neither of The Ladies was present. Everyone speculated on possible reasons. What could have happened in their common apartments?

Alone, earlier, Louise heard vagrant sounds of music as doors opened and closed. Except that she had no mask, a spy might have thought her costumed for the ball. She wore a coarse gray linen gown, no jewels, and her hair brushed down plain as a child's. She was writing a letter. It was short, because there was little to tell Louis — much less in the sentences than in the deep pauses between.

Eight years before, in this same month and palace, a sleepless girl had waited and hoped, and with morning had gone away to hide. How little experience of despair she had had — to weep because the man she loved spent a night alone. The woman who had inherited this girl's name and full-grown grief had both more and less to leave behind in the world. There were now a son and daughter. They did not know her very well, living as they did with the sufficient Mme. Colbert, so it was perhaps better that she leave without subjecting them to an emotional, puzzling goodbye.

Six in the morning, Shrove Tuesday, and it would soon be light. Louise put on a heavy cloak and went out of The Ladies' apartments without looking behind. Her carriage was waiting to take the road toward the convent of Sainte-Marie de Chaillot. Behind her the ball was still in progress, and nobody saw her leave but the guards.

It was Athénaïs who called her letter to the King's attention. He seemed thoughtful but not disturbed, and proceeded with the regular schedule as it had been planned. Nevertheless, when he got into his carriage for Versailles with Athénaïs on one side and Mademoiselle on the other, he suddenly surprised them by beginning to weep quietly. Montespan, who was upset for a variety of female reasons that day, also cried, and Mademoiselle joined them after a brief struggle for self-control. She had always been tearful at operas, weddings, and funerals, and was especially companionable in woe since losing Lauzun. During the day of political projects and correspondence, the King decided that Louise must not stay in her convent.

Lauzun was sent to reclaim the fugitive. Since he had recently become an implacable enemy of his longtime friend Montespan, he leapt away with alacrity to fetch her rival home. Louise refused to return, however, in spite of all his foxy blandishments, and the King after a little thought passed the assignment on to the Maréchal de Bellefonds, whom he knew to be her most trusted friend.

But to everybody's astonishment, Bellefonds had no better success. He brought Louis only a report of their conversation.

She would have left the Court sooner, after having lost the King's good graces, if she had been able to bear the thought of never seeing him again; this weakness has been so strong [she said, in her typical way] that even now she can scarcely make this sacrifice to God. She hopes above all that the passion she has for him will serve as her penitence, and thinks that, having given him her youth, it is not too much to give the rest of her life to the care of her soul.

Louis, very much moved, could scarcely hide his feelings. There was nothing left but the use of authority. He summoned Colbert and gave instructions. Colbert, who never failed a commission, brought Louise back that same evening into the royal presence. All witnesses were astonished at His Majesty's emotion, and utterly flabbergasted to see Mme. de Montespan, with eyes brimming and flooding becomingly, open her arms and embrace the prodigal.

There had been a wicked battle with the King over his determination to have La Vallière back, but since Montespan had lost she would carry off the scene like a great actress. Besides, there were other aspects to the case. The spectacle of Louise's soul in the process of salvation was surely not one Athénaïs could be expected to enjoy while her own continued in such disrepair. It was with some genuine resignation, then, that she welcomed Louise home from grace.

It was time for another of those military expeditions Louis enjoyed so much. They were beginning to seem a little tedious to the rest of the Court, especially the women, but all must follow.

Louise's casual enemies speculated on her chance of being invited. She was; and, consistent with that strange new dignity which overlay a sort of rueful humor, asked to be excused. Louis of course refused, and she obeyed. It was all like a ring game too often played before. She knew the truth. The King, master of all men, was still afraid of the Marquis de Montespan.

Recently a quarrel between a minor official of Perpignan and some men of the Marquis's company had been seized by Louvois as a pretext to do the King a service. "Try in one fashion or another," he wrote to the commander, "to implicate him, this captain . . . use any manner of breaking him with the appearance of justice . . . You can guess the reason well enough . . ."

The Marquis de Montespan, accordingly implicated, had been forced to leave his distant mountain retreat and escape to Spain. But now Louis was not certain it had been wise to drive the Marquis out; in France he could control the man's actions and even speech to some extent. Abroad, he might do as he liked. Louis and Athénaïs were thus more nervous than ever about the legal irregularity of their situation, and more anxious to save appearances. So Louise knew herself a prisoner.

The journey began. Louvois wrote to the Sieur Robert, intendant of Dunkirk, "Accommodate Mme. de Montespan in the chamber marked L and there make a second door communicating with the apartment of the King. Mme. la Duchesse de la Vallière will lodge in the chamber marked V, where it will be necessary to take the same precautions."

They were back by late summer. The Abbé Maucroix records approvingly among his observations of the returning courtiers, "Mme. de la Vallière appeared to me very pretty, with more roundness than was described to me." To others, also, her face, changed but not ravaged by melancholy, had a new look of serenity and sweetness. In secret she had begun to wear haircloth under her Court gowns, carefully cut to show no mark on the skin of arms and breasts.

At Fontainebleau, just at dusk when the light dissolves familiar things into sky colors, the Marquis de Saint-Maurice, out strolling with a friend along the canal, saw the King coming fast in a rich gilded and enameled *calèche* between the famous La Vallière and Montespan, both well coiffed, in déshabille, and behind them two other ladies. They were pulled by six white *isabelle* horses sumptuously harnessed, and attended, beside and behind, by four hundred cavaliers of high nobility, all on horseback, hat in hand.

All this equipage and this pomp came to us by the left side of the canal which is sixteen hundred steps long, fifty wide. The avenues at each side are twenty-five wide and bordered with great trees . . . The cascade at the head of the canal made an agreeable noise from its thousand jets and falls of water. Never had M. le Marquis Dagliani and I been so pleasantly surprised, nor have the makers of romances ever invented anything so charming . . .

The rich Abbey of Saint-Germain-des-Prés needed a new ghostly commander, and the King appointed Montespan's elder bastard, the Comte de Vexin, to the post.

To his surprise there were complaints from the Benedictine monks; some resented being put in charge of a child just out of the cradle. The mutinous talk could not be ignored, and Louis had to send the Grand Almoner to visit the good brothers and straighten out their philosophy. Let them not forget, he said, that previous abbots had been married princes and even soldiers. In any case, the Comte would be efficiently represented by his vicar-general until he was of fit age. The community was silenced but remained unresigned.

Mme. Scarron busied herself, and after a few days presented the new Abbot in full monastic costume to his enchanted parents. She had ordered the panels of his coach painted with the crozier, miter, and cross, and maneuvered one of her pious friends into the vicar-generalship. A most capable woman. Louis was beginning to like her very much; she gave his children more affection than Athénaïs did, who often announced how boring she considered them.

One day he asked Mme. Scarron whether sentiment would prevent her giving up her name. After a very brief hesitation she replied that her feelings for her late husband had never exceeded esteem and gratitude. Satisfied, Louis gave her a hundred thousand crowns for buying an estate he knew of with dependent marquisate, and from then on addressed her in public as Mme. de Maintenon.

Louise wrote,

> *I can scarcely describe Mme. Scarron — the word prude would be applicable to her, but that is a mere shade. She is at once a bigot and a* bel-esprit. *She is naturally very formal and strait-laced, but nevertheless has been seen acting the very humble servant of Mme. de Montespan, her reader, and her submissive friend. She is of a piety which appears all of a piece, alike stiff and inflexible; yet nonetheless, this piety has bent beneath the will of the King and has found its joints. Mme. Scarron is an admirable woman for whom a specific term should be invented . . . When she first appeared at Court, her robe of serge, her plain linen, and her black lace exhaled such an odor of pedantry that her very appearance gave the King the vapors. Suppleness and patience are, however, excellent qualities which operate wonderful conversions! She now has her horses, her* hôtel, *and a suite of servants; she is no longer the governess of the children of Mme. de Montespan, but those of the King, which her confessor declares to be quite another thing.*

To other observers, too, this rise of Mme. Scarron symbolized a climatic change at Court, the King's desire for personal respectability expressed in gift-giving to the respectable and devout. Mme. de Heudicourt, once Mlle. de Pons, Louise's old friend, was banished that season just for gossiping about His Majesty and Mme. de Montespan. Other free-talkers took warning.

This and the number of recent deaths in Louis's immediate circle were putting up walls of sobriety here and there. Mme. de Montausier was one of the most recent to go, having died that December after faltering on for three years. She had seen the specter of a woman one afternoon in a dark coign of the Tuileries, and had never been well since. And Louis's daughter, little Marie-Thérèse de France, died in her cradle in March, attended according to custom by many people of rank, including Louise and Athénaïs. Next day the old Madame, widow of Gaston d'Orléans, went as if swept up by death on his way out of the palace. All this was causing a revival of churchgoing, greatly to Louis's approval.

Disquieting news came that his old love, Marie Mancini, wife of the Constable of Colonna, was advancing on Paris. She and her sister Hortense, both wanton adventuresses, had fled from their husbands and landed in Provence with many jewels but no linen. Honest ladies on hearing the news cried out for their discipline, none louder than their own sisters, the Comtesse de Soissons and Mme. de Bouillon. "Those crazy fools!"

The Queen, experimenting for a time as regent, acted with unusual vigor and sent a *lettre de cachet* with orders to arrest Marie wherever she might be. Informed of this move, Louis said only, "Good," and refused to concern himself any further with the wrong-headed woman. She was soon arrested and locked up in a religious institution near Melun. In the old pagan days of his reign, Louis would have been more gallant.

In April the King, full of enthusiasm for cutting Holland to pieces, left to join the army at Charleroi. The Dutch deserved punishment; they were, unwisely, commercial competitors of France; the country was a nest of Protestants; some of the rich bourgeois had interfered in the Flemish campaign; and now some medals had been struck with flippant representations of the Sun, ridiculing Louis XIV. Admittedly, they were strong at sea, but had only twenty thousand soldiers, commanded by the Prince of Orange. He was one of Charles's and Henriette's nephews, only twenty-two and inexperienced in war. Any country so rich and so poorly defended as Holland was inviting invasion.

Suffering the consequences of a similar invitation to Louis, Mme. de Montespan, ready for another accouchement at any moment, was taken along and finally abandoned en route in the small dreary castle of Le Genitoy. Mme. Scarron and a crew of guards stayed with her. Condé marching by the Ardennes joined the King's forces, and almost before the local defenders could get out of bed and grasp sword and musket, four towns were seized. In Paris there was plenty of wine, and fireworks.

The campaign was proceeding not only with dispatch but with style. In preparation for this war Louis had completely reformed his Household; it now consisted of four companies of bodyguards, each made up of three hundred noblemen, two hundred gendarmes of the guard, two hundred light horse, five hundred musketeers — all men of birth selected for their youth and personal beauty — twelve companies of gendarmerie, and a hundred Swiss. These were special troops, armed with halberds, and charged with sentry duty over the house or tent occupied by His Majesty. In their blue Spanish coats laced with gold and silver they were objects of terror and admiration to the unsophisticated Dutch.

After this first whirlwind attack, young William of Orange realized his full danger and carried his defense line to the other side of the Rhine. The French held council, deciding to cross and cut communications between the Hague and Amsterdam. Louis suggested a bridge of boats, but learned from the peasants that the river was low and fordable at Toll Huys.

Condé asked for an officer to try this crossing and De Guiche plunged in at once. Since Henriette's death he had appeared absolutely indifferent to personal risk — even his admirers thought him something of a madman. He made the ford easily, and a cavalry regiment followed.

It was three o'clock in the morning of June 11, with the French forces on one bank and a few Dutch regiments on the other. In the crossing four horsemen were drowned, and Louis, about to enter the current, let himself be persuaded by Condé to take a boat instead. A few enemy shots flashed and clouded the darkness. The young Duc de Longueville was very drunk. Yelling "No mercy for these swine!" he fell on a group of Dutch soldiers asking quarter and killed their officer with a pistol, which brought a return fire on Louis's troops. A Dutch captain ran to Condé and put a pistol to his head; the Prince struck it aside but broke his wrist.

The Dutch were slaughtered.

Longueville's body was picked up later, all the fingers gone with their famous rings. In Paris it was subsequently found he had left his fortune to the small son of a woman of fashion — a circumstance her husband found embarrassing. However, he did not refuse the money.

The Dutch were noticeably disheartened by the Rhine crossing and gave up forty towns and villages in twenty-two days. Louis's advance guard was at the gates of Amsterdam, and the conquerors met only submission in the provinces of Gelderland, Averyssel, and Utrecht. But at Muyden there was a setback when the sluice gates were opened by suicidal patriots. The French should have secured these instantly, but Louvois's policy of slowness lost the play.

Now Jan de Witt sent his emissaries to the French camp to ask their terms. These were hard; Louis wanted cession of all the Dutch possessions in Flanders, Brabant, and Germany, abandonment of fortresses on the Rhine and Meuse, freedom of French commerce in all Dutch ports, forced acceptance of the Catholic religion by all provincials, and payment of a large indemnity. But in these conditions there was a tone of bravado. Louis had taken too many towns already and weakened his army by detaching garrisons, and at the same time he had released for very slight ransom twenty-eight thousand Dutch prisoners eager for revenge.

All the remaining power of the Low Countries lay in the hands of William of Orange. Desperate, he saved the country in the only way he could. Dikes were opened and the water poured in, washing towns away, destroying crops. Bloated bodies of cattle and men rotted in the treetops, but the French were halted.

Louis went back to Paris, leaving Turenne in command. At the Porte Saint-Denis happy citizens were building an Arc de Triomphe to celebrate the capture of three provinces and forty towns.

Irony, which can have various flavors, tasted like alum to the conqueror surveying the monument. There stood Saint-Denis to remind him every morning of death — now this, to recall defeat.

This war, he saw now, was no picnic in Flanders. What had he heard in the trenches, another day? "Sire, the wine is drawn and it must be drank."

XVI

THE FRIENDSHIP OF THE QUEEN

WITH THE King and Montespan away at war, Louise lived as
she liked. If it was not freedom, at least it was peace — at the very
least, quiet and time to think.

Sitting in her little *cabinet* she read the testimony of people who
had penetrated confusion to its core of knowing and become saints,
and her own words rose in response to theirs. She wrote, threw
away the paper, and rephrased what she had said to make the
meaning clear to her questioning self, until the candle wicks, un-
trimmed, drowned smoking in their sconces. *Réflexions sur la Miséricorde de Dieu* (*Reflections on the Mercy of God*) were meant for
no audience, but others would read them and be moved. In later
years she would attain celebrity among the serious-minded at Court.

When he was in Paris Bellefonds came almost every day to visit
Louise, either in her house near the Tuileries or at the impressive
Versailles *hôtel* where liveried servants stood guard as if for royalty.
He was concerned for the precarious health of her spirit, especially
after reading the *Réflexions,* which indicated to him the approach
of some crisis. Soon she must leave Court, he warned her, or be
prepared for destruction. Bossuet agreed with him. To live in sight
of the King and Athénaïs was to excite her worst feelings every
day, physical love and jealousy. What soul could survive intact
under such conditions? Nothing but complete retreat would do;
and, Bellefonds added, it must be to the holiest and most austere
of all convents, the Carmelites. But what if Louis would refuse

consent? And there were the children, growing up so handsome and intelligent. Their father loved them, it was true, but provision must be made for their protection, in case of his sudden death. Breaking out of the silk net of the world was not easy, even for a singleminded saint; and that Louise was far from being.

Bossuet's sermon on June 5 concerned the duty of the rich to the poor, a somewhat novel subject for the Court. A few days later M. Ribeyre, intendant at Tours, received a letter from Mme. de la Vallière stating her wish to "relieve the poor afflicted of the duchy," to diminish the tax, and to scatter charities throughout the parishes.

The same month a good Franciscan with a face like a walnut and the gaze of a child came questing for alms in Louise's neighborhood. She gave him a very large sum, and he said, surprised into speaking for heaven, "Madame, you are too charitable for God not to take pity on you. Hope in him. You will discover one day the effects of his compassion." How could he have guessed her need so truly? The words touched her with a sharp joy, and stayed afterward in her memory "like a happy presage."

Bellefonds's luck with the King had never been good. In 1668 he had lost the post of tutor to the Dauphin to M. Montausier, and later, having hoped to become governor of Paris, he saw the appointment go to Montespan's father, M. de Mortémart. Now he was ordered by Louvois as Minister of War to proceed to Créqui to serve under the command of Turenne. Humanly sensitive to questions of hierarchy, Bellefonds refused to obey a man of his own rank.

Louis, short-tempered those days, saw this refusal as mutiny and banished Bellefonds to Bourgueil. So Louise was left without her strongest friend's support. She wrote, worried, and waited.

But already another person was watching her with pity and admiration, almost ready to put out a hand — the Queen, Maria Theresa. She believed in charity, free and unsophisticated as the priests preached it, and for a long time she had been drawing near the discovery that Mme. de la Vallière was a worthy object. She had been happy, certainly, when it seemed the King no longer was infatuated with that girl, and slow to recognize that Mme. de

Montespan had replaced her. Then, crying in anger, humiliation, jealousy, loneliness, she had suddenly stopped, struck by a thought of penetrating satisfaction: somebody else was probably undergoing the same agonies that night.

It was a sort of bond between herself and Louise, whether she wished it or not, this common hurt. Impossible for a Christian to go on hating a fellow sufferer! And really, now that she remembered back through the years, La Vallière had been as nice as possible all the time, showing what consideration she could for a wife's feelings — utterly unlike this other one with her haughty manners, showing off her pregnancies and her jewels.

In addition to these considerations there was the Duchesse's remarkable repentance, as fine and bright to see as a bank of altar candles. Maria Theresa was a tireless seeker after edification; therefore she adopted it as a constant companion in the person of Louise. Soon they were almost inseparable. This was a combination fully as amazing to the Court as that of The Ladies had ever been. Where could the Queen have found an odder confidante? Together they made visits to the various convents of Paris, arriving one afternoon at the Grandes Carmelites of the Rue Saint-Jacques.

Yes, this was the place, Louise knew instantly, where she would come at last. When the doors first opened she stood still, redreaming something almost forgotten. The elevated tribune — the walls, the windows — the figures in white, and the small smoke of the lighted candles — she had seen all this before, long ago in a dream, when the world still seemed a fine inhabitable place. But it would not do to tell the Queen yet. They went in and knelt down side by side for their long devotions.

News of the passing of the Rhine arrived in Paris on June 14, and that same day the Queen was brought to bed of her sixth child, a boy, François. The ever present reporters said with marveling approval that the Duchesse de la Vallière attended Her Majesty with tireless care and affection and never left her bedside. Eight days later, Mme. de Montespan in her castle near the front also had a son, a hearty infant nothing like the big-eyed, blue-veined, frog-legged François, who seemed unlikely to live.

Louis was too busy at the time to pay much attention to either of these paternal accomplishments. His war was not going well. Eventually he was forced to recall Bellefonds to the siege of Maestricht, realizing that the Maréchal was too valuable a man to be wasted in exile.

One of Bellefonds's first acts, on return, was to open a stack of letters which had arrived ahead of him from the entranced Louise. "I remember very well our last conversations, and I have the vanity to tell you I have profited from them and am making marvels, it seems to me. I wish that you could judge this, for often one flatters himself without realizing it."

The year ended soberly for Louis. At times he almost wished he had never begun this ill-starred campaign.

Europe was alarmed by Holland's narrow escape, and William's envoys had been surprisingly successful in rousing several sleeping dragons against France. Their clanking scales could be heard by the troops of the Duc de Luxembourg, camped on the eerie ice landscape of the flooded country.

Frederick William, Elector of Brandenburg, had marched to Holland's aid but had been checked for the time being by Turenne. The Rhine princes were abandoning France, and Spain allying with Holland. Condé in Alsace was not certain of his ability to hold against the Germans.

Also, there were bitter interstaff battles. Louvois, jealous of Turenne's success, ordered him back to winter quarters. Turenne, raging to the King, got permission to chase the Elector of Brandenburg home instead. But new troubles always rose up behind every solution. Not even Molière could bring more than a rather tight-lipped smile from the King that year.

It was the winter Louis put on a wig for the first time, a monumentally constructed property hanging well below the shoulders. From its scrolls and waves his face looked out coldly, rather suspiciously, the eyes not so much studying as condemning, the flesh below the chin beginning to sag a little. Louise, seeing him as he would look for the rest of his life, thought for some reason of Versailles. Somewhere within the forbidding grandeur of its new walls

lay the Palace of Alcine, now almost hidden from sight, built in a
lighter mood and a freer time. Could it be possible that behind the
formal mask called Louis XIV, framed in its vast convention of
wig, anything remained of another man, young, remembered by
few, deeply loved? If so, he would never show himself again.

The King lost two sons that year — François, only a few months
old, and Montespan's young abbot, the Comte de Vexin. Athénaïs
had been too busy with social concerns to join Louis at their child's
deathbed. Keeping helpless watch, he remembered how often she
had remarked with sarcasm on his fatherly weakness — almost the
only weakness he had left — calling it "a bourgeois trait handed
down from Marie de Medici." But not all women were as hard as
she. Mme. Scarron, or, as he called her now, Maintenon, had been
stricken at losing her little charge so cruelly. After all, she had
been almost a mother to him. Leaving the house, red-eyed, Louis
said heavily, "Mme. de Maintenon knows how to love. There would
be great pleasure in being loved by her."

A bridge may stand intact after being fatally weakened by some
tide either of the river or human events. Thus it took Mme. de
Montespan a long time to notice the shakiness of her carefully laid
planks to the King's favor, and still longer to learn that something
had undermined the whole structure. Yet, psychically sensitive to
the behavior and even nonbehavior of other women, she began to
find fault with Mme. Scarron. Her way was to assert herself arrogantly with unreasonable demands, criticize sharply, and then,
when opposed, scimitar down all opposition.

One morning early in the new year, employer and servant were
caught by His Majesty in the middle of a furious quarrel. It had
reached the slapping point, almost the moment when Athénaïs
would shriek to her lackeys to lay hands on the miscreant. Both
women began talking to Louis, and he signaled Athénaïs to be
quiet. Then, insultingly, unforgivably, unbelievably, he took Mme.
Scarron's side. Nothing would ever be the same again.

Like an army which has suffered an ambush, Athénaïs withdrew
and regrouped her forces. She must think. Perhaps Louis had really

meant it when he said he was tired of her tantrums. She must try to control herself.

Years before, La Vallière had decided that henceforth, since Louis was tired of melancholy, she would be gay. Athénaïs had recognized this as sheer stupidity in Louise — to weary her lover and then to introduce her own successor. But, clever as Montespan was, she would not see the fatal parallel in her own career until too late.

Le Malade Imaginaire (*The Imaginary Invalid*), thought by his devotees to be Molière's funniest comedy, was scheduled for its fourth performance on February 17, 1673. Molière himself, holding the title role, was perhaps too much in character that day. He told Armande his chest pain was worse than usual, and she said he had better stay home in bed.

"What can I do? There are fifty workpeople living on the day's pay. What would they do if we call off the performance? I'd blame myself if I kept their bread from them for a day, if I'm actually able to go on stage." He sent for his actors, however, and told them everybody must be ready punctually at four. "Otherwise I shan't be there, and you may have to give back the money."

The candles were lighted and the performance began. Some of the audience noticed that as Molière pronounced the word "juro" in the Ceremony, he was stopped by a sort of momentary convulsion. He, aware of having caused a little stir, gave a forced smile afterward and went on, though with an effort.

La Grange, one of the troupe's diarists, wrote later,

> *This same day, after the play was over, about ten o'clock in the evening, M. de Molière died in his house in the Rue de Richelieu, having acted the role of the said Imaginary Invalid, very much troubled by a cold and inflammation of the lungs, which caused him to cough a great deal, so that in the strong efforts he made to spit he burst a vein in his body and did not live half an hour or three quarters of an hour . . .*

Now began a comedy too grim for popular taste, but one which would have appealed to the playwright's imagination. Two sisters of charity, to whom Molière had given hospitality, were with him as he died. Nevertheless, the Curé de Saint-Eustache refused to bury him. The dead man had been an actor, outside grace, and had not received the last sacrament.

Armande petitioned the Archbishop of Paris, Harlay de Champvalon, swearing that her husband had asked for the sacrament, that a valet and woman servant had run to two priests belonging to the church of Saint-Eustache, and been turned away. Then, she said, Molière's brother-in-law, Jean Aubry, had gone to fetch another priest — but by now the man in question was dead.

Permission for his burial in consecrated ground was finally given, perhaps as the result of secret intervention from the King. Five years earlier Louis would not have bothered with discretion. There were restrictions, however. No display or ceremony was allowed, and no solemn service might be said over this disreputable bier. But in spite of the Archbishop's warnings, a ceremony was held — reverently simple, as it should have been for an actor who had always, himself, refused to rant.

It was summer again, and campaign weather, with the ladies off in their new finery to the front. Maria Theresa and Louise installed themselves at Tournai in the house of the local bishop, Athénaïs and the sphinx Scarron in the citadel at the other end of town. Montespan was not sparkling very much. Trapped again by her marvelous fecundity, she gave birth to a girl on June 1 under conditions of the greatest inconvenience for everyone.

On the 24th, Louise was surprised by an unexpected visitor, Bellefonds, who had been sent at the head of four thousand cavaliers to defend the approaches of Tournai. The King was disquieted by certain enemy maneuvers, and it would indeed have been embarrassing to the French if a sudden attack had gained the Dutch two royal mistresses and a queen.

Bellefonds thought Louise's retreat from the world was overdue, and scolded her for delaying. A simple, loving man, he looked on her spirit as others may regard a bride ready for the wedding, touched at the sight of such hope, freshness, and fear. But, Louise reminded him, everything hung on the King's permission, and she must wait for the propitious moment. Until then the plan must be kept secret — if Louis were to learn by accident he would surely be enraged.

Soon a message came for the women to join His Majesty at Amiens. His military operations showed signs of being prolonged. On the road the Queen's party was passed by another returning to Paris, one of the King's *calèches* drawn by galloping horses that left them all in the dust. It was Mme. de Montespan taking her infant home. But she was back in their midst sooner than any would have thought possible, making all settings her stage, taking her place in Maria Theresa's carriage, having her lover accomplish little things.

He wrote at her dictation a letter to Colbert, urging haste with the remodeling of her Saint-Germain apartments; she wanted an aviary installed, the garden replanted. Her power, as far as anyone could see, was as great as ever. Few could get favors without her, none in spite of her. Somehow she had obtained full command of the Queen's maids of honor, and then used it to destroy the institution. The Girl Room, as it was called, was unnecessary and a bother — a pretty hydra which she decapitated with one slash. However, one thing nearly drove her mad: the fact that Louis would never be browbeaten into making her a duchess, as he had La Vallière. He was growing more cautious every year.

Six months passed, mortally long for Louise, before the Court returned to Paris through an autumn countryside of bronzing forests and vineyards. Too beautiful it was, the world, and a bird flying out of a bush could still shake a memory from the most carefully emptied mind, like a torn page from a desk drawer.

Louise knew ruefully that she was not proof yet against the world. Maybe she never would be. Soon she must speak to the King. But he was busy keeping a promise exacted by Montespan, the legitimizing of their offspring. Legally it was a very difficult matter. Because the mother's separation from her husband had never been pronounced, her name could not be mentioned; so Louis decided to disregard this requirement temporarily, and went on to the next formality, the baptism of his youngest daughter.

This took place December 18, 1673, in the church of Saint-Sulpice. The godfather was the child's own older brother, Louis-August, represented by the parish priest. The godmother was the Duchesse de la Vallière. She carried the baby to the baptismal font and endowed her with her own name, Louise-Françoise.

This was to have been a penance for Louise, but it failed its purpose — the baby was so pretty, and it had been a long time since her arms held one so little. The sister of her own children! She thought she saw a certain resemblance. So she was tricked into the loss of a penance again by her own stubborn nature — but couldn't keep from smiling just the same. It was only one more sign that her soul was ready for commission to greater severities than she herself could devise.

But she kept on talking sophistries to Bellefonds and Bossuet and herself. Regarding the necessary separation from her own children she thought as little as possible. The pain it caused belonged to the wrong side of her character, earth-rooted, guilty, just as their conception had been. Once more she visited the Grandes Carmelites of the Rue Saint-Jacques and felt she had not been mistaken; here was interior peace, a sense of freedom as sky seen through the striding order of arches, faces of profound innocence.

The rule of Carmel, she knew, was hard: rigorous exercises, continual mortification, fasting, the silence of death. But nothing easier would do. A thirst like hers could scarcely be quenched by a lifetime of steadily flowing self-denial. It was not certain she would be received, however; it was said the merely disappointed and capricious, no matter how important their names, were always refused the comfort of the Carmelites' austerity. Therefore she asked Bellefonds to intercede for her with his aunt, Mother Agnès de Jesus — once, in life, Judith de Bellefonds.

According to the rule, postulants must be of good faith and should have caused no scandal. Louise's request, therefore, was deliberated for a long time, but finally granted for charity's sake, on condition of her strict observance of the rule. The sisters, albeit holy, were not naïve. The Duchesse de la Vallière would certainly bring a large dowry to the convent, and it was said her penitence in the world for several years had been remarkable. She was a great sinner already on the way to salvation. They authorized the Maréchal de Bellefonds, accordingly, to promise her admission. But now with the door half open, Louise hesitated again, partly from fear of the King, partly because she was so tangled in Court life that the strands had to be cut one by one, and always secretly to prevent gossip.

Three men stood behind her decision, advising and encouraging — Bellefonds, Bossuet, in whose guidance she had placed herself completely, and a new friend, the Duc de Beauvilliers, a son of Saint-Aignan.

It was strange what turns life took; the father had lent his room for the ceremony of her deflowering, long ago; now the son prayed for her passage into Heaven.

The Comte de Guiche died in the dragging war that November at Kreutznach, and his corpse was brought home to lie in state in the convent church of the Capucines. Last of the great cavaliers, he had achieved in his person all the ideals of an old-fashioned chivalry. Not many people believed in them any longer, or would remember how handsomely he wore them, with what an air. He lay with his scarred sword hand over the other and the air through the opening church door bending the taper flames around him like standards.

XVII

WITHOUT REGRET

ATHÉNAÏS'S determination to see her children legitimized finally removed Louise's main difficulty. In 1671, all the King's power had failed to force the Marquis de Montespan to grant his wife a separation, and while he held firm he had kept the weapons of a fearful revenge. Conceivably, the Marquis might claim all her children as his own. What sacrilege to the royal blood! And how humiliating for Louis. But now the Marquis was in trouble. During his exile his fortune disappeared, the properties which had been his work and pride were sold, and his two sons brought to near-penury. He learned at last that his old mother was dying, and to buy the right to come home and see her he sold what he regarded as his honor and agreed to Louis's demands. The separation was accordingly pronounced, Athénaïs's bastards were legally acknowledged, and the Marquis was no longer a menace to the King's peace of mind.

There was no reason why Louis should wish to detain La Vallière, now that she had lost her importance as a decoy. But, she thought, he was so unpredictable. With one word he could defeat her years of penance, everything she hoped. How could she risk her soul on a single interview with Louis? Every day, at Bossuet's urging, she resolved again to speak to him, then let the chance go by, speechless with nervous fear.

Finally Bossuet came to her house one afternoon and said that gossip was beginning on the subject of her retreat. Further delay might prove disastrous.

Bellefonds wrote:

Mme. de la Vallière has great difficulty in speaking to the King and puts it off from day to day. She begged me to lay the matter before Mme. de Montespan. I said what I could. She doesn't care very much about the retreat, but it seems that the Carmelites cause concern. She covers this resolution with great ridicule. The King knows very well what is going on, but since he has said nothing to me, I wait in silence.

To Bossuet, arriving on the same errand, Athénaïs said merely that this idea of Louise's seemed terribly dangerous. Wouldn't it be setting a precedent for discarded mistresses? Annoying Bossuet with flippancies of this sort was obvious enjoyment for her. He answered with his usual calm, however, saying that no human power could oppose God once he had made his call heard so clearly.

Decidedly, Montespan wanted no part in this favor for La Vallière, whose choice of such a severe order seemed somehow a reproach, a reflection on others. The whole idea really made her quite impatient. Louise never had been responsible for her conduct, and somebody with sense should try to stop her from carrying out such a melodramatic plan. She called Mme. Scarron, who would be just the one, and sent her on the mission.

Mme. Scarron's tone was at once sympathetic and censorious. Had Mme. la Duchesse considered the perils of passing from a life of ease and refinement to that of the cloister? Wouldn't it be better to make a trial first, by entering some convent merely as a benefactress, until she felt strong enough and sure enough of herself to submit to such a stern rule? "In doing this," she concluded, "you would be serving God with no less piety."

"Would that be penitence?" Louise asked. "Such a life would be very pleasant. That is not what I am searching for."

"But have you considered that here you sit in cloth of gold, and in a few days you will be covered with homespun?"

Louise said, smiling, that for a long time she had slept on a hard mat and worn haircloth, and so was growing accustomed to such privations. Mme. Scarron gave up.

The Court had not been treated to such a subject for conversation since the Grande Mademoiselle's engagement; and Louise was besieged in her chambers by friends tearfully begging her to remain in the world and serve as an example. She laughed at this, but said soberly, "It would be horrible presumption to think myself fit to help anyone else." Some few of the visitors promised their prayers for her successful escape from Court; most were mere sightseers estimating her chances for sainthood. "The world is paying visits to Mme. de la Vallière," Bossuet wrote. "I hope . . . that we shall see her one day in a high degree of sanctity."

The King learned of all this from Athénaïs and others, but said nothing, and his face was unreadable to Louise. Now she asked Bossuet to present her request to His Majesty, but unaccountably, prince of the church though he was, he held back. It was a great responsibility; if he should handle the commission badly and get a refusal, Louise would be lost and he himself would have to share the weight of her damnation.

The Court waited for news, and still nothing happened.

Louis decided that the Carnival of 1674 must be particularly gay, to distract people's minds from the distressing military situation. Festivals began at Saint-Germain with comedies and operas every day, balls every week. To enliven them, he even forced himself to join the dancing, a diversion he had not enjoyed in recent years.

Capriciously, it appeared, the King decided that his daughter by Louise, Mlle. de Blois, now eight years old, should make her début in society. Some guessed he hoped to shake Louise's resolution by rousing her maternal pride. This could be no very difficult matter. The child was precocious, plainly destined to be a beauty, and had already devastated her dancing masters with her talent.

Louise, not entirely approving, but delighted in spite of herself, went to see Marie-Anne trying on her new grown-up gown at Mme. Colbert's, and rehearsing her dance steps.

Next day, January 12, the young princess entered the crowded ballroom with a slight air of ennui brought on by shyness, dressed in black velvet sewn with diamonds, and gripping the hand of a gentleman her own age, the Prince de la Roche-Aymon, a Conti. All observers were utterly enchanted as they watched this solemn couple begin to dance, calling them "the little fiancés."

> *Mlle. de Blois is* a chef-d'oeuvre [*Mme. de Sévigné wrote next day*]. *The King and everybody is ravished with her. She came in the middle of the ball to say to Mme. de Richelieu, "Madame, do you think the King is pleased with me?" She passed near Mme. de Montespan and said to her, "Madame, why don't you come to see your friends any more?" With all these little things coming from her pretty mouth, she enchanted all by her spirit.*

Louise, touched and disturbed, knew herself helpless to affect the future of this child so sweet, yet already so capable a diplomat. They were very formal with each other — "Mademoiselle" and "Good Mama" — and there could be nothing to say about the way Marie-Anne, languishing and sidling, admired the gorgeous Mme. de Montespan.

> *As for being moved — yes, I was* [*Louise wrote*]. *They had reason to say that Mlle. de Blois did it. I confess I had joy in seeing her, pretty as she is becoming, but at the same time I had misgivings, I avow. She will not keep me back for a moment. These are very opposed sentiments, I know, but I say them as I feel them.*

No, staying could satisfy neither her own need nor her children's, but she would leave them a souvenir. Mignard was commissioned to paint the three of them together, and since there was no time to lose, sittings began the same month. The result was a conventional group portrait of aristocratic people, and something more.

Seated, the Duchesse is shown looking outward, tranquil, a little distant, as if her thoughts are somewhere else. She wears a blue cloak falling over one shoulder and down to the floor, bodice and overskirt of rose silk with gold trimming; below, a falling fullness of cream-colored satin. Her lace is very fine, and a pear-shaped pearl hangs from her ear.

The six-year-old Comte de Vermandois sits on a cushion at her knee with black hair falling to the shoulders, as Louis wore his in early manhood, and playing at his role of Admiral of France with a pair of compasses and a big map. Beyond him, in a brocade gown looped stylishly up behind, stands Mlle. de Blois. She glances over her shoulder, arms reaching toward an urn of summer flowers on the table where she leans.

There are columns framing trees and sky, and a carved inscription: *Sic transit gloria mundi.* The Duchesse holds between uplifted fingers a rose; its petals are falling. Beside her on the table are two unopened books, *L'Imitation* and *La Règle de Sainte-Thérèse (The Rule of Sainte-Thérèse)*; behind on the floor a globe of the world, a mask, scattered playing cards, a jewel casket, coins spilling out of a purse. A guitar inlaid with ivory leans against a stool holding an open music book.

"Grace more beautiful than beauty," La Fontaine had said once. It was a phrase which might be read by the perceptive on more than one level, like Mignard's painting. Perhaps daughter or son would care enough to try, some day.

Mme. de Montespan looked at the finished painting with mixed feelings in which jealousy finally boiled to the top. There sat that noxious little Comte de Vermandois flaunting his Admiral's chart and compasses as if he were the most important of Louis's children. She remarked cuttingly to the King that another son of his, equally legitimate now, was still without any appointment and income. The bedeviled Louis obediently produced for her four-year-old Duc du Maine a commission as Colonel-General of the Swiss and Greys.

"Here is my whole difficulty," Louise wrote to Bellefonds. "Pray God to give me the necessary strength for this. To retire and become a religious costs me nothing; to speak to the King costs infinitely —"

In addition, some practical obstacles remained, among them the payment of her debts, amounting to a hundred and fifty thousand livres. Louise had never been a good business manager; money to her was like the water leaping from a fountain to run away, and her charities had opened new drains in the past few years. She appealed to Colbert, who was accustomed to dealing with the appalling financial entanglements of Mme. de Montespan. He sighed and considered the matter, ended by drawing up an act authorizing the Comte de Vermandois to give his mother the required sum; and submitted it for the King's signature.

Now Louise gathered all her jewels together and sent them to Louis, asking him to divide them between their son and daughter. After all her anguish, it could be as simple a gesture as this — a symbolic renunciation of the world's goods. Wouldn't he understand that she meant to save him a scene and wearying explanations?

Last, she submitted a list of liberalities which she hoped to see granted her family and servants. Louis signed without comment and returned it to Colbert — a pension of two thousand crowns for Mme. de Saint-Rémi, now a widow again; another of two thousand livres for Louise's stepsister, Mme. de Hautefeuille, who had many children and no money; a revenue of one hundred livres for each domestic of her house, and a dowry of six thousand livres to permit one of her devoted serving women to enter a convent. In addition a sum was left for the founding of a hospital in her duchy of Vaujours for the care of the sick and the rearing of the poor children of seven parishes.

At last I leave the world [she wrote on March 19]. It is without regret but not without difficulty. My weakness has kept me a long time without liking, or, to speak truly, with many chagrins . . . I find my feelings so resolved, so sweet, and at the same time so hard (all these seem contradictory, but I find all this inside) that the people to whom I show my-

self entirely admire more and more the extreme mercy of God in my regard.

Exultant at seeing victory so near, Bossuet wrote to Bellefonds:

I send you a letter of Mme. la Duchesse de la Vallière which will make you see that, by the grace of God, she is going to complete the design the Holy Spirit has put into her heart. She perseveres with admirable grace and devotion. The integrity of her soul carries all. In truth, these sentiments are something so divine that I cannot think on them without being in continual awareness of grace, and the mark of God's finger is the force and humility which accompany all her thoughts. She breathes only penitence: this ravishes and confounds me.

On April 10, 1674, Louise began her formal visits of farewell to friends and relatives, going first as ceremony required to the King. For those who lived at Court, April was the month of beginnings, a time for putting away old things and taking to the roads, and for this reason a time of memories. Even His Majesty was not quite immune.

Louise, cool and in perfect control of her emotions, said to him only what was expected in such a conventional interview, and wished him well.

He asked her whether she would consider putting this step off, reminding her of her recent dangerous illness and speaking of the absolutely irrevocable vows. At least, he said, she should choose an order less austere than the Carmelite, and let him make her Mother Superior, as befitted her rank and tender upbringing. She shook her head, thanking him. "When one is lost himself, is he able to give any help to others?"

Louis turned away as if the question had touched some waiting pain, and stood in silence for a moment; and Louise, perhaps uneasy for her own composure, curtsied and left the chamber.

That interview had used most of her reserve of courage. Afterward, in the Queen's presence and surrounded by her attendants, she knelt and asked pardon for the grief she had caused and the grave offenses of which she had so long been guilty. Halfway through, her voice broke and she had to pause.

Maria Theresa; even more unnerved, began crying openly, raised her up, and kissed her on the forehead, saying two or three times that pardon was granted with all her heart.

Sotto voce the Maréchal de la Motte remarked that the Duchesse certainly would not have needed to make her confession in front of the whole world. His words were repeated to Louise later. She remarked only that such a course had seemed appropriate to her in view of the fact that her sins had been committed with the same publicity.

It was common knowledge that Mme. de Montespan had been extremely upset when she heard of the King's emotional parting from La Vallière. To cover her anxiety she was very bright and vivacious all that day.

Louise ate her last supper at Court in Athénaïs's apartments, once those of The Ladies, and according to the Grande Mademoiselle, another guest, acquitted herself of this last duty with cheerful courtesy.

If Athénaïs occasionally fell into an abstracted manner it might have been that she felt a slight draft from the door so soon to open for herself — that waiting space of empty years in which she would stray like a deposed queen, hag-ridden by the fear of death, unable to find her way back to life. Then she would visit the woman known as Soeur Louise de la Miséricorde, to study her face in envy; but the secret of such repose would elude her forever in spite of her own hidden belt with its iron spikes, and her perpetual stitching of clothes for the poor. But on this night, says Mademoiselle, none but pleasant subjects were discussed.

On the morning of April 19 Louise dressed with splendid elegance and went to the King's Mass. Apparently His Majesty was deep in prayer the whole time, but as he left the chapel those nearest him observed that his eyes were red. "We have wept much," said Philippe to Louise, with a gallant little salute.

Had the King dreamed about a young man no longer at Court?

Or was he merely touched in the deeps beyond vanity by a compliment so delicate — that a woman should have loved him so greatly his only rival could be God? That day it was exactly thirteen years since "the little La Vallière" had left for Fontainebleau as a maid of honor. Then, too, she had moved through the assembled Court and been admired. But there had been no sober faces in that other crowd.

At twenty-nine Louise had come into her second age of beauty; the correspondents said she walked as if she were going to celebrate a triumph. Smiling, without pride or weakness, she joined her son and daughter in her carriage; the door closed and they rolled away followed by a few friends in other coaches, who would stay with her as long as they could.

In the streets the crowds were so thick that her equipage could hardly pass, but neither the noise nor the delay seemed to disturb her at all.

If there was a momentary sense of strangeness it came when the day, the sounds, her children, her finally deserted other self, were shut outside the heavy door; and inside the silence was louder than she remembered. Then she was walking toward the room where Mère Claire du Saint-Sacrement was waiting. On her knees she said, "My mother, I have always made such bad use of my will that I have come to place it in your hands forever."

There was to be a special favor for her, Mère Claire said, because she had already served five years of hard penitence in the world. She was to be allowed to put aside the usual noviitate period and cut her hair that same day.

Alone in her cell, bare as a sea cave, Soeur Louise de la Miséricorde took the shears in her hand, pulled down a long strand of that silver-gold stuff which had always caused so much talk in the world, and awkwardly, because there was no mirror, began snipping. The stone floor would need a stiff sweeping to catch all the wisps, she thought — even a breath could stir them, they were so light.

EPILOGUE

THE PRINCESSE DE CONTI left the convent of the Carmelites, and servants helped her into her sedan chair. Her face was a mask in the changing torchlight. She had just seen her mother die. It was two hours after midnight, June 7, 1710.

At twelve o'clock Soeur Louise de la Miséricorde had been given the last sacraments. The prior, seeing her in pain, had murmured, "God, you increase the suffering — increase also the patience." But the dying woman had more patience than she would need, now, after cultivating it for so many years. Not being able to speak, she merely smiled and moved a hand toward her daughter who stood stricken and sleep-disheveled at the foot of her pallet. After a while she shut her eyes and a difference fell on the watchers.

Thus ended thirty-five years of religious life. Louise, dead at sixty-five, left her community "as grievously afflicted by her loss as edified by her penitence."

It was the custom to present at the grilled gate of the convent the bodies of dead Carmelites, that family and friends might come decorously to look at those who had been so long veiled from the world's view. It had always been an orderly ritual, but now the nuns were astonished at the crowd shoving forward toward Soeur Louise's bier. None of them, in their innocence, had guessed the extent of her celebrity. They were forced to leave the doors open from dawn until five-thirty for several days, and four flurried sisters were kept busy receiving the reliquaries, medals, books, and images thrust on them from a never-ending line of aristocrats, bourgeois, and beggars. These objects were touched to the body and taken away heavy with sanctity.

Louise left behind her the same property she had been assigned on entering the order — a cell patterned on plans from Spain, having four bare walls, a door and window, a wooden bed in the shape of a coffin with straw mat and coarse cover, a chair, a crucifix, and one or two images. She was buried in her everyday robe of serge, veil and bandeau, and rope sandals.

Louis XIV said nothing when word was brought to him of this death; it was wondered whether he even heard. His wife, Mme. de Maintenon, however, fetched up a safe comment on the subject of virtue in general and then reworded it thoughtfully as if trimming it for later use. In old age she was more and more Heaven's handmaid, having caused Louis to revoke his grandfather's edict of religious toleration, with the consequent extermination of almost all Protestants infesting the kingdom. Her major good work at present was running a school for the daughters of poverty-stricken noble families.

Louis's reign, so gloriously begun, had petrified into the Old Régime — the Sun King himself into a rich old man tyrannizing his sullen impatient heirs.

Few others remained of the Court Louise had known. D'Artigny, Comtesse du Roure, and Mme. de Soissons were scarcely tolerated now among the respectable elite. The stigma of their reputation as poisoners preceded them everywhere, like foul breath. Montespan, still proud in misfortune, continued to receive visitors with the state of a reigning empress, but with Louise she lost her last friend.

In April 1676, two years after Louise became a nun, Athénaïs had come with the Queen to pay the convent a visit, and, full of energy, had organized a lottery for the sisters. While it was in progress she had drawn Soeur Louise aside, and enveloping her in reminiscent scents of ambergris, asked brightly, "Tell me, are you as happy in this place as everybody says?"

"No," Louise said, "I'm not happy here, but I'm content."

"Well, is there anything you'd like me to say to the King for you?"

"Whatever you like, Madame — whatever you like." The famous

blue eyes were untroubled, and Montespan withdrew with a slight shrug of her gauze scarves.

Soon after this meeting, the sorceress La Voisin was arrested with her accomplices in commercialized murder, and what she told during trial shocked all hearers. The King quickly suppressed certain parts of the evidence. He would not have the world know what crimes the mother of his children had committed against himself and society; but his door was closed to her forever after. At forty-four, a year after Maria Theresa's death, he married the widow Scarron and became for her what he had always promised the Queen — a faithful husband.

Athénaïs, in total disgrace, having been rejected in turn by her lover, the husband she had ruined, and the children she had brought up without love, came to the gate of the Carmelites and asked to see Louise. "What shall I do?" she cried, trembling with nervous exhaustion. Some advice was given.

She tried often in later years to follow it, but her nature was too fiery and restless to allow much self-discipline. She put on haircloth and took it off again, drank too much, and started projects for the poor. Her fear of death gradually became a mania; she made ladies-in-waiting sit up all night in her well-lighted bedroom in order that, waking from dreadful dreams, she might see them eating, sewing, or playing cards.

Meanwhile Louise worked on the narrow structure of her own life. It was as difficult as she had expected it to be, not because of the physical hardships, which she welcomed, but because of interference during those early years by well-meaning friends in the world. One day the Princesse Palatine arrived, leading by the hand a thin, intelligent little boy of eight — the Comte de Vermandois — Louise's son — of all four, the child most like herself. Then her resolve almost broke. But she kissed him and sent him away. When he died of a fever at sixteen, taking part in one of the King's campaigns, the nuns feared to bring her the news. They urged her to weep; but if she did it was in private, sparing their virginal sensibilities the spectacle of her grief, just as she had concealed from everyone the ravages of his birth.

About this time, a noble lady, probably the Queen, ordered the

publication of *Réflexions sur la Miséricorde de Dieu.* Louise was
not credited, but a preface made the author's identity obvious. The
book was a prompt success and numerous editions and translations
followed. In England it was openly printed under the name of the
Duchesse de Vaujours.

"The body has sinned, let the body be punished." She kept in
mind the words of the repentant Mme. de Longueville. Rising at
three in the morning, long before the rest of the community, she
spent the day in hard labor, scrubbing stone floors, trying through
prayer and fatigue to rid her mind of wrong thoughts, and retired
finally at eleven. She wore iron bracelets and belts until Mère
Agnès ordered her to stop this mortification, and lived on a diet of
bread, milk, and peas. Once, during a description of Christ's thirst
on the cross, her mind wandered back to a different scene. She
thought of the royal hunts at Fontainebleau, when, thirsty and hot,
she had taken the cup and drunk again and again from that delicious spring. For three years afterward she limited herself to half
a glass of water a day.

Still she remained strong and kept her characteristic spark of
gaiety, so that the other nuns had to be on guard against too great
enjoyment of her company. In middle age she asked to be sent to
a remote and impoverished order of the Carmelites, but was refused by the Mother Superior, who said, "Her example is too useful
to us and her person too dear for us to consent to this separation."

So Louise remained. As sacristine of the chapel, she was later
to take down with her own hands all its gold and silver ornaments,
which the nuns were sending to the royal treasury in the interests
of defending the country.

During the last years of her life she was increasingly unwell,
but refused to rest from her self-imposed schedule. "She let us
see only what she could not hide," said her prior afterward.

On the morning before her death she was found in a passage-
way between her cell and the chapel, unable to move or speak.
She had risen as usual two hours earlier than the other nuns. With
much outcry they carried her to the infirmary, since she could no
longer resist, and then tried to compose their faces to more cheerful

expressions. They felt it a duty to keep from the patient the knowledge of her danger, but she smiled and succeeded in saying a slow sentence: "Dying in pain is appropriate for a sinner."

The cemetery where Louise lay for most of the century below a small white stone bearing her religious name was dug up and obliterated during the Revolution. She is lost with her sisters, drifted with them away from the known places marked on the maps of antiquarians, into the chinks of supposition, into the parks and orangeries of Fontainebleau and Saint-Germain, Vincennes and Versailles.

Great Louis, too, was scattered in the indiscriminate war. Perhaps the idle wind has blown them together here and there.

BIBLIOGRAPHY

AND INDEX

BIBLIOGRAPHY

Bertrand, Louis. *Louis XIV* (Longmans, Green and Company, New York, 1928).

Bishop, Morris. *The Life and Adventures of La Rochefoucauld* (Cornell University Press, Ithaca, New York, 1951).

Bussy-Rabutin. *Histoire Amoureuse des Gaules* (Paris, 1665).

Capefigue, Jean-Baptiste. *Mlle. de la Vallière et les favorites des trois âges de Louis XIV* (Amyot, Paris, 1859).

Carré, Henri. *Mlle. de la Vallière: De la cour de Louis XIV aux grandes Carmélites 1644–1710* (Hachette, Paris, 1938).

Cartwright, Julia. *Madame: A 'Life of Henrietta,' Daughter of Charles I and Duchess of Orleans* (Seeley and Company, London, 1894).

Child, Theodore. *Wimples and Crisping Pins* (Harper and Brothers, New York, 1895).

Cousin, Victor. *The Youth of Mme. de Longueville* (D. Appleton and Company, New York, 1854).

Cuss, T. P. Camerer. *The Story of Watches* (Philosophical Library, New York, 1952).

Dangeau. *Mémoires ou Journal du Marquis de Dangeau* (Paris, 1817).

Dodd, Anna Bowman. *In and Out of Three Normandy Inns* (G. P. Putnam's, New York, 1929).

Eriau, Jean-Baptiste. *Louise de la Vallière de la Cour au Carmel* (Paris, 1931).

Fayette, Mme. de la. *The Secret History of Henrietta, Princess of England* (London, 1929).

263

Guillard, Comte de. *A Story of the Palais-Royal: or, the Loves of Louis XIV and Mlle. de la Vallière* (New York, 1874).

Haggard, Andrew C. P. *Remarkable Women of France* (S. Paul and Company, London, 1914).

Houssaye, Arsène. *Mlle. de la Vallière et Mme. de Montespan* (Paris, 1860).

Huddleston, Sisley. *Louis XIV in Love and War* (Harper and Brothers, New York, 1929).

Hugon, Cécile. *Social France in the XVII Century* (The Macmillan Company, New York, 1911).

Jackson, Lady Catherine Charlotte. *The Old Régime. Court, Salons, and Theatres* (G. Munro, New York, 1882).

Lacroix, Paul. *XVIIme Siècle Lettres, Sciences, et Arts* (Firmin-Didot, Paris, 1882).

Lair, Jules. *Louise de la Vallière et la jeunesse de Louis XIV* (Librairie Plon, Paris, 1881).

Lewis, Warren H. *The Splendid Century — Some Aspects of French Life in the Reign of Louis XIV* (William Sloane, New York, 1954).

Miltoun, Francis. *Castles and Châteaux of Old Touraine and the Loire Country* (L. C. Page and Company, Boston, 1909).

Montespan, Madame la Marquise de. *Mémoires* (Paris, 1829).

Pardoe, Julia. *Louis XIV and the Court of France* (Harper and Brothers, New York, 1855).

Poëte, Marcel. *La Promenade à Paris au XVIIe Siècle* (A. Colin, Paris, 1913).

Sandars, Mary F. *Lauzun: Courtier and Adventurer. The Life of a Friend of Louis XIV* (Hutchinson and Company, London, 1908).

Sedgwick, Henry D. *The House of Guise* (Bobbs-Merrill, Indianapolis, 1938).

Sévigné, Mme. de. *Letters of Madame de Sévigné* (Ginn and Company, Boston, 1899).

Silin, Charles I. *Benserade and his Ballets de Cour* (Johns Hopkins Press, Baltimore, 1940).

Trollope, Henry M. *The Life of Molière* (E. P. Dutton and Company, New York, 1905).

Vallière, Louise de la. *Lettres de Mme. La Duchesse de la Vallière, Morte Religeuse Carmélite, Avec un Abrège de Sa Vie Pénitente.*

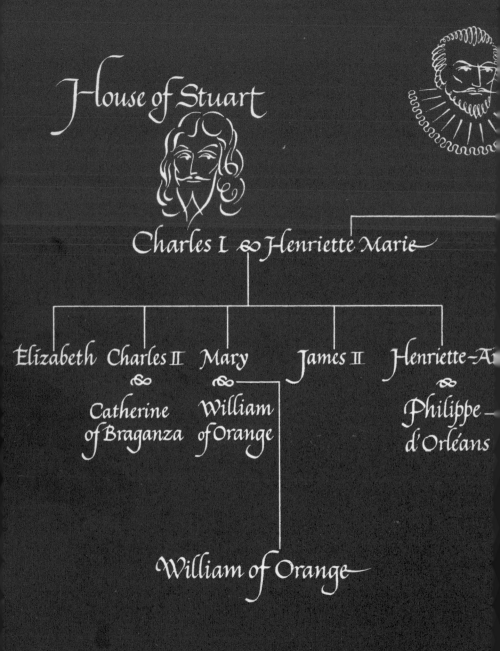

House of Stuart

Charles I ∞ Henriette Marie

Elizabeth   Charles II   Mary   James II   Henriette-A
∞   ∞   ∞
Catherine   William   Philippe –
of Braganza of Orange   d'Orléans

William of Orange